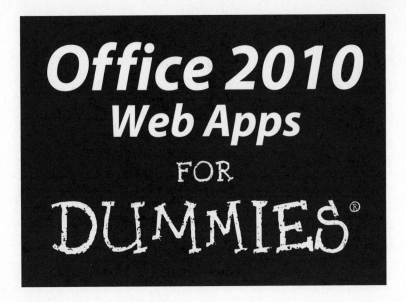

Office 2010
Web Apps
FOR
DUMMIES®

by Peter Weverka

WILEY

Wiley Publishing, Inc.

Office 2010 Web Apps For Dummies®

Published by

Wiley Publishing, Inc.

111 River Street

Hoboken, NJ 07030-5774

www.wiley.com

Copyright © 2011 by Wiley Publishing, Inc., Indianapolis, Indiana

Published by Wiley Publishing, Inc., Indianapolis, Indiana

Published simultaneously in Canada

For general information on our other products and services, please contact our Customer Care Department within the U.S. at 877-762-2974, outside the U.S. at 317-572-3993, or fax 317-572-4002.

For technical support, please visit www.wiley.com/techsupport.

Wiley also publishes its books in a variety of electronic formats. Some content that appears in print may not be available in electronic books.

Library of Congress Control Number: 2010937059

ISBN: 978-0-470-63167-6

Manufactured in the United States of America

10 9 8 7 6 5 4 3 2 1

WILEY

About the Author

Peter Weverka is the bestselling author of many *For Dummies* books, including *Office 2010 All-in-One Desk Reference For Dummies,* as well as 35 other computer books about various topics. Peter's humorous articles and stories — none related to computers, thankfully — have appeared in *Harper's, SPY,* and other magazines for grown-ups.

Dedication

For Emma Rouault.

Author's Acknowledgments

This book owes a lot to many hard-working people at the offices of Wiley Publishing in Indiana. I would especially like to thank Mary Bednarek for considering me for this book and Katie Mohr for pushing it along. For the umpteenth time, I also want to thank Susan Christophersen for being such a good editor.

Technical editor Nick Simons made sure that all the instructions in this book are indeed accurate, and I would like to thank him for his diligence. I would also like to thank Rich Tennant for the witty cartoons you will find on the pages of this book and Broccoli Information Mgt. for writing the index.

Finally, I want to thank Sofia (in Vermont), Henry (in Hawaii), and Addie (in San Francisco) for a great summer.

Publisher's Acknowledgments

We're proud of this book; please send us your comments at http://dummies.custhelp.com. For other comments, please contact our Customer Care Department within the U.S. at 877-762-2974, outside the U.S. at 317-572-3993, or fax 317-572-4002.

Some of the people who helped bring this book to market include the following:

Acquisitions and Editorial

Project and Copy Editor:
Susan Christophersen

Executive Editor: Steve Hayes

Technical Editor: Nick Simons

Editorial Manager: Jodi Jensen

Editorial Assistant: Amanda Graham

Sr. Editorial Assistant: Cherie Case

Cartoons: Rich Tennant
(www.the5thwave.com)

Composition Services

Project Coordinator: Patrick Redmond

Layout and Graphics: Carl Byers, Joyce Haughey, Lavonne Roberts

Proofreaders: Melissa Cossell, Evelyn C. Wellborn

Indexer: Broccoli Information Mgt.

Publishing and Editorial for Technology Dummies

    Richard Swadley, Vice President and Executive Group Publisher

    Andy Cummings, Vice President and Publisher

    Mary Bednarek, Executive Acquisitions Director

    Mary C. Corder, Editorial Director

Publishing for Consumer Dummies

    Diane Graves Steele, Vice President and Publisher

Composition Services

    Debbie Stailey, Director of Composition Services

Contents at a Glance

Table of Contents

Introduction

● ●

*T*his book is for users of the Office Web Apps, the online versions of Word, Excel, PowerPoint, and OneNote. Respectively, these applications are called Word Web App, Excel Web App, PowerPoint Web App, and OneNote Web App.

Anyone can use the Office Web Apps. You don't have to pay a fee or even install Office 2010 software on your computer. All you need is an Internet connection and an account with Windows Live. Moreover, users of the Office Web Apps can collaborate online with one another to create Word documents, Excel worksheets, PowerPoint presentations, and OneNote notebooks. As long as both of you are connected to the Internet, you and a colleague can work together even if one of you is in Maine and the other is in Arizona.

I show you everything you need to make the most of the Office Web Apps in this book. On the way, you have a laugh or two. No matter how much or how little skill you bring to the table, this book will make you a better, more proficient, more confident user of the Office Web Apps.

What's in This Book, Anyway?

This book is your guide to making the most of the Office Web Apps. It's jam-packed with how-to's, advice, shortcuts, and tips. Here's a bare outline of the seven parts of this book:

- ✔ **Part I: Getting Acquainted with the Office Web Apps:** Introduces the Office Web Apps, explains how to sign up to use them, and shows how to create files with them. You also discover how to make your browser work with the Office Web Apps, do tasks that are common to all four Office Web Apps, and create and use diagrams, clip art, and pictures.

- ✔ **Part II: Sharing Files and Collaborating with Others:** Explains how to store Office files on Windows Live, an online service that Microsoft provides for storing files, and how to store files with SharePoint Services, a Microsoft software program. You also find out how to share files with colleagues and work simultaneously with others in an Office Web App, as well as how to open a file in Office 2010 starting from an Office Web App.

✔ **Part III: Word Web App:** Explores the online word processor, including how to format text, assign styles to text, create tables and lists, and spell-check your work.

✔ **Part IV: Excel Web App:** Demonstrates how to crunch numbers with the online spreadsheet program. You discover how to enter data, use formulas, use functions in formulas, and sort and filter data.

✔ **Part V: PowerPoint Web App:** Shows how to design and create presentations with the online version of PowerPoint. You find out how to create slides, format text, create lists, and give a presentation.

✔ **Part VI: OneNote Web App:** Describes how to take and organize notes with the online version of OneNote.

✔ **Part VII: The Part of Tens:** Each chapter in Part VII offers ten tidbits of information — general information about the Office Web Apps themselves, file sharing, and configuring a browser to run the Office Web Apps.

What Makes This Book Different

You are holding in your hands a computer book designed to make mastering the Office Web Apps as easy and comfortable as possible. Besides the fact that this book is easy to read, it's different from other books about the Office Web Apps. Read on to see why.

Easy-to-look-up information

This book is a reference, and that means that readers have to be able to find instructions quickly. To that end, I have taken great pains to make sure that the material in this book is well organized and easy to find. The descriptive headings help you find information quickly. The bulleted and numbered lists make following instructions simpler. The tables make options easier to understand and compare.

I want you to be able to look down the page and see in a heading or list the name of the topic that concerns you. I want you to be able to find instructions quickly. Compare the table of contents in this book to the book next to it on the bookstore shelf. The table of contents in this book is put together better and presents topics so that you can find them in a hurry.

A task-oriented approach

Most computer books describe what the software is, but this book explains how to complete tasks with the software. I assume that you came to this book because you want to know how to *do* something — crunch some numbers or create a PowerPoint presentation with a colleague. You came to the right place. This book describes how to get tasks done.

Meaningful screen shots

The screen shots in this book show only the part of the screen that illustrates what is being explained in the text. When instructions refer to one part of the screen, only that part of the screen is shown. I took great care to make sure that the screen shots in this book serve to help you understand the Office Web Apps and how they work. Compare this book to the next one on the bookstore shelf. Do you see how clean the screen shots in this book are?

Foolish Assumptions

Please forgive me, but I made one or two foolish assumptions about you, the reader of this book. I assumed that:

- ✔ Your computer is connected to the Internet. To use the Office Web Apps, you must have an Internet connection.
- ✔ You are kind to foreign visitors and small animals.

Conventions Used in This Book

I want you to understand all the instructions in this book, and in that spirit, I've adopted a few conventions.

To show you how to step through command sequences, I use the ➪ symbol. For example, in the Firefox Web browser, you can open the View menu and choose Toolbars➪Menu Bar to hide or display the menu bar. The ➪ symbol is just a shorthand method of saying, "After you open the File menu, choose Toolbars on the menu, and then choose Menu Bar on the submenu.

To give some commands, you can press combinations of keys. For example, pressing Ctrl+B boldfaces text. In other words, you can hold down the Ctrl key and press the B key to apply boldfacing to text. Where you see Ctrl+, Alt+, or Shift+ and a key name or key names, press the keys simultaneously.

Another way to give a command is to click a button. When I tell you to click a button, you see a small illustration of the button in the margin of this book (unless the button is too large to fit in the margin). The button shown here is the Paste button, the one you can click to paste data into a file.

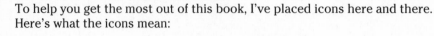
Icons Used in This Book

To help you get the most out of this book, I've placed icons here and there. Here's what the icons mean:

Next to the Tip icon, you can find shortcuts and tricks of the trade to make your adventures in the Office Web Apps more enjoyable.

Where you see the Warning icon, tread softly and carefully. It means that you are about to do something you may regret later.

When I explain a juicy little fact that bears remembering, I mark it with a Remember icon. When you see this icon, prick up your ears. You will discover something that you need to remember.

When I am forced to describe high-tech stuff, a Technical Stuff icon appears in the margin. You don't have to read what's beside the Technical Stuff icons if you don't want to, although these technical descriptions often help you understand how a feature works.

Part I

Getting Acquainted with the Office Web Apps

The 5th Wave

By Rich Tennant

"The odd thing is he always insists on using the latest version of Office."

In this part . . .

Hello, this is your captain speaking. Thank you for flying with the Office Web Apps. In the next five chapters, you take off, soar above the clouds, and discover the basics of using Word Web App, Excel Web App, PowerPoint Web App, and OneNote Web App.

Please observe the "Fasten your seat belt" sign. And if I ask you to hold your breath and flap your arms to help the plane stay aloft, please do so promptly.

Chapter 1

Introducing Office Web Apps

In This Chapter

▶ Understanding what Web applications are

▶ Storing and sharing files on the Internet

▶ Using the Office Web Apps to collaborate with others

▶ Examining how the Office Web Apps work with Office 2010 software

▶ Looking at how to get up and running with the Office Web Apps

▶ Resisting the urge to right-click and press shortcut keys

*T*he Office Web Apps are online versions of four popular Microsoft Office applications: Word, Excel, PowerPoint, and OneNote. Respectively, the Office Web Apps are called *Word Web App, Excel Web App, PowerPoint Web App,* and *OneNote Web App.*

This chapter looks into what a Web application is and how Web applications such as the Office Web Apps are different from other applications. It shows how you can use the Office Web Apps to share files with others and collaborate with others on Word, Excel, PowerPoint, and OneNote files. You also see how to use the Office Web Apps in conjunction with Office 2010 programs and what you need to know before setting up your computer to use the Office Web Apps. Finally, this chapter looks into a few peculiarities of using online Web applications.

What Are the Office Web Apps, Anyway?

In my opinion, Microsoft could've chosen a better name than "Office Web Apps." Say *Office Web Apps* three times and you soon discover that the name is a tongue twister. What does the name mean, and what are the Office Web Apps?

Introducing Web applications

The "Web App" portion of the name "Office Web Apps" stands for *Web application.* A Web application is a software program that runs from a Web site on the Internet. Web applications are sometimes called *online applications* because the software to run them isn't stored on individuals' computers, but rather on a Web server on the Internet.

To run a Web application, you start from your computer and open Internet Explorer, Firefox, or another Web browser. Then, using your browser, you go to a Web site where you can run the Web application. From there, you start the Web application, open a file, and get to work. Files you work on, like the Web application itself, are stored on the Internet, not on your computer.

Figure 1-1 shows a Web application in action, in this case Excel Web App. Notice the browser window and how Excel Web App appears inside the browser window. Wherever you go and whatever you do with an Office Web App, you do it inside a browser window. When you give commands to run an Office Web App, the commands are transmitted by your browser over the Internet to the Office Web App.

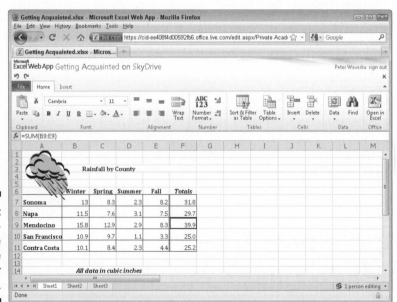

Figure 1-1:
Web applications are run inside a browser window.

Web applications present an important advantage over applications stored on a personal computer. You never have to install, uninstall, re-install, or upgrade Web applications because technicians do it for you on the Web server where the Web application is maintained. All the work of maintaining the application and keeping it up-to-date is done for you.

Meeting the Office Web Apps

The "Office" portion of the name "Office Web Apps" refers to Microsoft's famous Office software. The Office Web Apps are online versions of Excel, PowerPoint, Word, and OneNote. Using the Office Web Apps doesn't cost anything. Microsoft provides the Office Web Apps for free.

Figure 1-2 shows three of the four Office Web Apps (the fourth, Excel Web App, appears in Figure 1-1). Meet the Office Web Apps:

- **Word Web App:** For creating letters, reports, and other documents. Part III (Chapters 9 and 10) describes Word Web App.

- **Excel Web App:** For crunching numbers in worksheets. Part IV (Chapters 11 and 12) explains Excel Web App.

- **PowerPoint Web App:** For creating slide presentations to show to an audience. Part IV (Chapters 13 and 14) looks into PowerPoint Web App.

- **OneNote Web App:** For storing and organizing notes. Part VI (Chapters 15 and 17) explains the OneNote Web App.

The first thing you notice when you run an Office Web App is how measly it is compared to its Office counterpart. The Office Web Apps are abridged versions of Office programs. PowerPoint Web App, for example, doesn't offer nearly as many commands and features as PowerPoint 2010. Still, that needn't concern you if Office 2010 is installed on your computer. As I explain later in this chapter, you can, merely by clicking a button, take the Word, Excel, PowerPoint, or OneNote file that you're working on with an Office Web App and open it in Word 2010, Excel 2010, PowerPoint 2010, or OneNote 2010. And after you open the file in an Office 2010 program, you can take advantage of all the commands that the program offers.

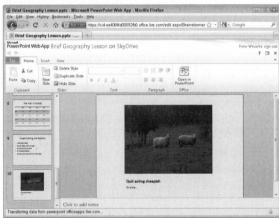

Figure 1-2:
From top
to bottom:
Word,
PowerPoint,
and
OneNote
Web App.
(Excel Web
App is
shown in
Figure 1-1.)

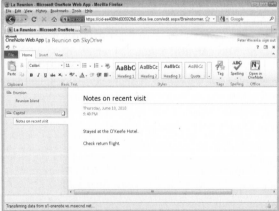

Storing Files on the Internet

Here's something else that is unique about computing with Web applications like the Office Web Apps: The files you work on aren't stored on your computer, but rather on Web servers on the Internet.

Does keeping your files on the Internet rather than your computer's hard drive seem odd to you? If it does, consider whether you already store files on the Internet. Web-based e-mail services such as Gmail and Yahoo! Mail store users' e-mail — their files — on Web servers, not on users' hard drives. If you send and receive e-mail with Gmail or Yahoo! Mail, you already store and edit files online.

Storing files on the Internet makes it possible to work on files wherever you have an Internet connection. You don't have to be in your office or your home or even carry your laptop with you. From a hotel room or friend's house, you can open a Web browser, connect to the Web site where your files are stored, open a file in an Office Web App, and get to work. And because your files are kept in one place, not on one or more computers, you don't have to copy files between computers or wonder whether you're working on the most up-to-date copy of a file.

Storing files on the Internet also frees you from having to back up files. Technicians back up files on the Web server, and if a file is corrupted and needs restoring, they can restore the file. Most people are not very good about backing up their files. Giving this wearisome task to a technician is very nice indeed.

Sharing Files on the Internet

Storing files on the Internet makes it possible to share files on the Internet, too. The files aren't kept on one person's computer. They're kept on the Internet, on a Web server, where everyone with an Internet connection and permission to edit the files can edit them.

Using an Office Web App, two people can work on the same file. For that matter, a dozen or a hundred people can work on the same file using an Office Web App. One person in Timbuktu and another in Vladivostok can collaborate with one another.

This ability to share files is one of the great advantages of the Office Web Apps. In fact, being able to share files is the greatest advantage. By themselves, the Office Web Apps aren't anything to crow about, but the users' ability to share files, and to work on a shared file in an Office Web App or an Office 2010 program, is what makes the Office Web Apps special.

The Office Web Apps and Office 2010

As I mention earlier in this chapter, the Office Web Apps leave a lot to be desired when you compare them to Office 2010 software. For comparison purposes, Figure 1-3 shows Word Web App and Word 2010. Just by glancing at the figure, you can see that Word Web App falls far short of Word 2010 in the number of features and commands it offers. Word Web App, Excel Web App, PowerPoint Web App, and OneNote Web App are stripped-down versions of Word, Excel, PowerPoint, and OneNote. The Office Web Apps don't have nearly as many features or amenities as their Office 2010 counterparts.

Click the Open In button to open a file in an Office 2010 program

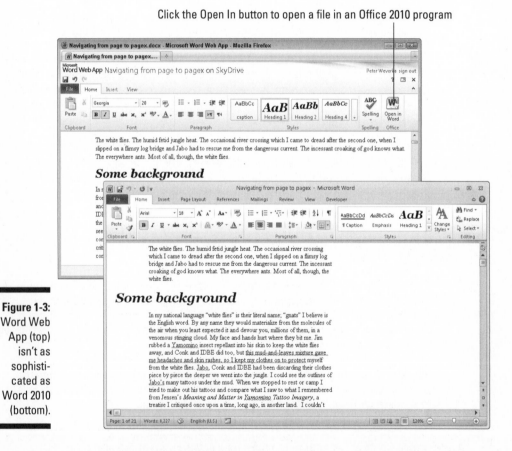

Figure 1-3: Word Web App (top) isn't as sophisticated as Word 2010 (bottom).

Microsoft designed the Office Web Apps as companion software to Office 2010. Each Office Web App has a button called Open In that you can click to open a file in an Office 2010 program. As shown in Figure 1-3, for example, you can click the Open In Word button in Word Web App to open the Word document you're working on in Word 2010. After the file opens in the Office 2010 program, you can call on all the Office 2010 commands. Having Office 2010 software on your computer makes it possible, by clicking the Open In button, to share files with others and draw upon the many commands in Word 2010, Excel 2010, PowerPoint 2010, and OneNote 2010.

If you think you can use the Office Web Apps by themselves for your computing needs, you aren't entirely wrong. People with modest computing needs can get by without having to run Office 2010 programs along with the Office Web Apps. But realistically, the Office Web Apps don't have enough *oomph* to suit most people, and unless Office 2010 software is installed on your computer and you can call on Office 2010 programs when you need them, you may get frustrated with the Office Web Apps.

By the way, there's a hitch where sharing files online with Office 2010 programs is concerned. When people share files on the Internet and one person opens a file in an Office 2010 program, others can't edit the file in the Office Web App until the person who opened it in the Office 2010 program closes it. Opening a file in Word 2010, Excel 2010, or PowerPoint 2010 effectively blocks others from opening and editing the file with an Office Web App except in the case of OneNote.

Office Web Apps: The Big Picture

The good news is you can get up and running with the Office Web Apps in a matter of minutes if you have an Internet connection. Testing the waters doesn't require any special software or high-tech gadgetry on your part.

To use the Office Web Apps, start by setting up an account with Windows Live, or if your computer is connected to a network, start by talking to your network administrator about using the Office Web Apps with SharePoint 2010. Setting up your computer to work with Windows Live and SharePoint is a subject of Chapter 2.

Windows Live is a Microsoft Web site that offers Web-based applications and services. One of these services is called SkyDrive. Use SkyDrive to create files with the Office Web Apps, store files, and share files. Chapters 6 and 7 explain how to run the Office Web Apps on SkyDrive.

SharePoint is software that Microsoft provides for sharing files on a local network. Using SharePoint, you can run the Office Web Apps from and store your files on a server that is owned and operated by the company you work for. Chapter 8 explains how to store and share files with SharePoint.

Safeguarding your privacy

You should know right away that privacy matters more than usual when you're using the Office Web Apps. Because files are kept on a Web server, not your computer, they are easier for strangers to open and see. Folders in which you store files can be set as private, and you can decide who can and can't open the files in a folder. As nice as these safeguards are, however, the fact remains that your files are still on a Web server, where prying eyes are more likely to find them.

When you create files with the Office Web Apps and decide how to store them online, give a moment's thought to your privacy and to the privacy of the people whose files you work on. Do all you can to make sure files don't fall into the wrong hands.

After you get set up with Windows Live or SharePoint, you can create your first Office Web App file. Chapter 2 explains how to create, open, and close files, as well as how to open them in an Office 2010 program. (Click the Open In button, as I mention earlier.)

In case you haven't noticed already, you steer and operate Office Web Apps through a Web browser. Microsoft recommends using these browsers with the Office Web Apps: Firefox, Internet Explorer, Safari, or Chrome. Chapter 3 explains how to download and install these browsers, as well as how to handle problems that may arise with cookies and JavaScript, the computer programming language that the Office Web Apps are written in.

Going without Right-Clicks and Shortcut Keys

The Office Web Apps take some getting used to when it comes to right-clicking and pressing shortcut keys.

In an Office program, right-clicking gets you a shortcut menu with useful commands and buttons. But right-clicking in an Office Web App usually doesn't help you very much. Opportunities to right-click and choose commands are few and far between. If you're the kind of person who right-clicks often, you have to cure yourself of this habit if you want to use the Office Web Apps.

You also soon discover that shortcut keys are scarce in the Office Web Apps. Ctrl+B (for boldfacing text), Ctrl+I (for italicizing text), and a few other shortcut key combinations are available, but the Office Web Apps don't offer nearly the number of shortcut keys as the Office 2010 software.

Chapter 2

Getting Started with the Office Web Apps

In This Chapter

▶ Using the right Web browser

▶ Installing the Silverlight add-on

▶ Getting signed up to use the Office Web Apps

▶ Creating, opening, and closing files with an Office Web App

▶ Looking at Office Web App oddities

▶ Getting acquainted with the Office Web Apps interface

▶ Finding more room to work on-screen

*C*hapter 1 explains what the Office Web Apps are. This chapter tells you how to set up your computer to run the Office Web Apps and how to do basic tasks such as creating new files, opening files, and closing files. You also find out which browser to use with the Office Web Apps, how to install the Silverlight add-on, what the Office Web Apps interface is all about, and how to get more room to work on-screen in an Office Web App. Full speed ahead!

Making Sure You Have the Right Browser

A *browser,* also known as a *Web browser,* is a computer program that displays Web pages on the Internet. Browsers come with commands for going from Web page to Web page, bookmarking Web pages, and doing any number of things to make your adventures on the Internet more rewarding.

To use the Office Web Apps, Microsoft says you should have one of these browsers:

- ✔ Firefox version 3.0 or later
- ✔ Internet Explorer version 7.0 or later
- ✔ Safari version 4.0 or later
- ✔ Chrome 5.0 or later

Chapter 3 explains how to download, install, and update these browsers, as well as how to find out which version of Firefox, Internet Explorer, Safari, or Chrome is on your computer.

Installing Microsoft Silverlight

Microsoft strongly recommends installing Silverlight on your computer if you intend to run the Office Web Apps. Silverlight is an *add-on program.* An add-on, also known as a *plug-in,* is an auxiliary program that gives other programs more functionality. Silverlight is designed to make videos, animations, and games run faster and more smoothly on Web browsers.

These pages explain how to tell whether Silverlight is installed on your computer, how to download and install Silverlight, and how to make sure that the Silverlight add-on on your computer is up-to-date.

Finding out whether Silverlight is installed

Silverlight may already be installed on your computer. You never know. Follow these steps to find out whether the add-on is installed and spare yourself the trouble of installing it:

- ✔ **Firefox:** Choose Tools ➪Add-ons. The Plugins tab of the Add-Ons dialog box opens, as shown in Figure 2-1. You see an alphabetical list of add-ons installed on your computer. Look for Silverlight Plug-In to see whether it is installed.

- ✔ **Internet Explorer:** Choose Tools➪Manage Add-Ons. The Manage Add-Ons dialog box appears, as shown in Figure 2-1. Under Add-On Types, make sure Tools and Extensions is selected. If necessary, open the Show drop-down list and choose All Add-Ons. Then, under "Microsoft Corporation" in the list, look for Microsoft Silverlight.

✔ **Safari:** Choose Help⇨Installed Plug-Ins. The Installed Plug-Ins window appears, as shown in Figure 2-1. Scroll in the window and look for Silverlight Plug-In.

✔ **Chrome:** Click the Tools button and choose Extensions on the drop-down list. A list of extensions appears. See whether Silverlight is on the list. Later in this chapter, "Getting an up-to-date version of Silverlight" explains how to update to the most recent version of Silverlight.

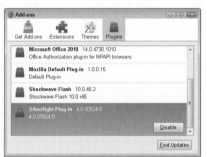

Figure 2-1:
Seeing whether Silverlight is installed in Firefox (upper left), Internet Explorer (middle), and Safari (upper right).

Downloading and installing Silverlight

To download and install Silverlight, start by opening your browser and going to the Silverlight Web site at this address:

```
www.silverlight.net
```

On the Get Started page at the Web site are instructions for downloading and installing Silverlight. Downloading and installing the software takes only a couple of minutes.

Getting an up-to-date version of Silverlight

Just because Silverlight is installed on your computer doesn't mean you have the latest version of the add-on. Follow these instructions in the three Web browsers Microsoft recommends using to get an up-to-date version of Silverlight (only the Firefox browser offers a convenient way to find out whether your version of Silverlight is up-to-date):

- ✔ **Firefox:** Choose Tools⇨Add-Ons to open the Plugins tab of the Add-Ons dialog box (refer to Figure 2-1). Then click the Find Updates button. Your browser opens a window at its Plugin Check Web site (`www.mozilla.com/en-US/plugincheck`) that tells you which add-ons are installed on your computer and whether they are up-to-date. If Silverlight needs updating, click the Update button.

- ✔ **Internet Explorer, Safari, and Chrome:** Go to the Plugin Check Web site at this address:

  ```
  www.mozilla.com/en-US/plugincheck
  ```

  After a minute or two, with a little luck, the Web site tells you whether Silverlight needs updating. Click the Update button if it needs updating.

Not keeping add-ons up-to-date exposes your computer to the risk of attacks by viruses and malware.

Signing Up with Windows Live

Everyone with an Internet connection can use the Office Web Apps by signing up with Windows Live. Windows Live is an online service that Microsoft offers for sharing files and sending e-mail, among other services. (You can also use the Office Web Apps if you have access to a SharePoint Web site, as the next topic in this chapter explains).

Signing up with Windows Live doesn't cost anything. After you sign up with Windows Live, you can create Word documents, Excel worksheets, PowerPoint presentations, and OneNote notebooks with the Office Web Apps. You can also upload files from your computer to Windows Live, open the files, and edit them with Word Web App, Excel Web App, PowerPoint Web App, and OneNote Web App.

To sign up with Windows Live, go to this Web site and click the Sign Up button (not the Sign In button):

```
http://home.live.com
```

You come to the Create Your Windows Live ID window, as shown in Figure 2-2. Fill in this screen and click the I Accept button.

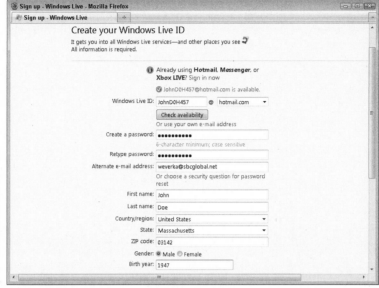

Figure 2-2:
Signing
up to use
Windows
Live (and
the Office
Web Apps).

If you intend to share files on Windows Live, be sure to create a Hotmail account when you sign up with Windows Live. To create a Hotmail account, choose Hotmail.com, not Live.com, on the drop-down list next to the text box where you enter your Windows Live ID, and don't click the Or Use Your Own E-Mail Address link. You need a Hotmail account to send e-mail invitations to the people with whom you will share files.

After you sign up, you land in the Home window. Chapters 6 and 7 explain how to get from place to place, create folders, share files, and do all else in Windows Live. Store your files on SkyDrive, the portion of Windows Live that is devoted to file sharing.

Signing Up with SharePoint

Your company may exchange files and collaborate through SharePoint 2010, a Microsoft software package designed to help coworkers share files. People who share files with SharePoint 2010 do so through SharePoint Web sites similar to the one shown in Figure 2-3. These Web sites are maintained on a company intranet or on the Internet. Besides sharing files, people with access to a SharePoint 2010 Web site can run the Office Web Apps from the site.

Figure 2-3:
The Home page of a SharePoint Web site.

You must have permission from a network administrator to access a SharePoint Web site. The administrator gives the URL of the SharePoint site, a username, and a password. Chapter 8 looks into running the Office Web Apps from a SharePoint Web site.

Creating a New File

Because files you create with the Office Web Apps are not stored on your computer, creating a file with an Office Web App is a bit different from creating a conventional file. Rather than create the file and give it a name when you save it for the first time, you name the file before you create it. And you choose where to store the file before you create it, not when you save it the first time.

Follow these steps to create a file with an Office Web App:

1. Open the folder where you want to store the file.

Your choice of folders determines where the file will be stored.

2. **Click the New button to open its drop-down list.**

   Figure 2-4 shows the New button and its drop-down list in Windows Live.

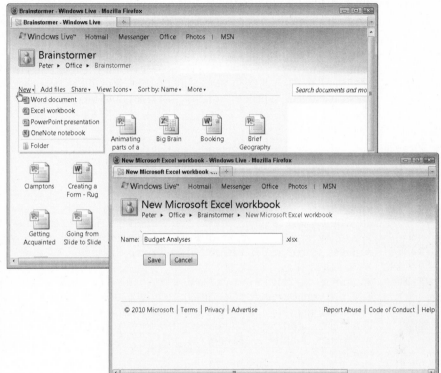

3. **Choose an option on the drop-down list.**

   Choose what kind of file you want to create:

   - *Word Document:* Create a letter, report, or other document. Part III (Chapters 9 and 10) describes the Word Web App.

   - *Excel Workbook:* Create a worksheet for crunching numbers. Part IV (Chapters 11 and 12) explains the Excel Web App.

   - *PowerPoint Presentation:* Create a presentation for showing slides to an audience. Part V (Chapters 13 and 14) looks into the PowerPoint Web App.

   - *OneNote Notebook:* Create a notebook for storing and organizing notes. Part VI (Chapters 15 and 16) explains the OneNote Web App.

The New window opens, as shown on the right side of Figure 2-4.

4. **In the Name text box, enter a name for your document, workbook, presentation, or notebook.**

5. **Click the Save button.**

Your new Office file opens in an Office Web App.

You can also upload Word, Excel, PowerPoint and OneNote files from your computer to Windows Live or a SharePoint Web site and open the files you uploaded in an Office Web App. Chapter 6 explains how to upload files to Windows Live; Chapter 8 explains how to upload files to a SharePoint Web site.

Opening and Closing Files

To get to work on a file, you have to open it first. And, of course, you close a file when you're finished working on it and want to stop and smell the roses. The following pages explain opening and closing files stored in Windows Live and files stored in a SharePoint Web site.

Sometimes you try to open a file and you can't do it because someone opened it before you. Except for OneNote notebooks, two people can't always open the same file in an Office Web App or Office 2010 program. The peculiarities of file sharing in the different Office Web Apps are examined in Chapter 10 (Word), Chapter 12 (Excel), Chapter 14 (PowerPoint), and Chapter 16 (OneNote).

Opening a file stored in Windows Live

How you open a file that you store in Windows Live depends on whether you want to open it in an Office Web App or an Office 2010 program. To start, open the folder where the file is stored. From the Folder window, as shown in Figure 2-5, use these techniques to open a file:

✔ **Open the file right away in an Office Web App:** Switch to Details view (if you aren't already there) and click the Edit in Browser link, as shown in the topmost screen in Figure 2-5. When you use this technique, the file opens right away in an Office Web App. The bottommost screen in Figure 2-5 shows a file in an Office Web App. To switch to Details view in the Folder window, click the View link and choose Details on the drop-down list.

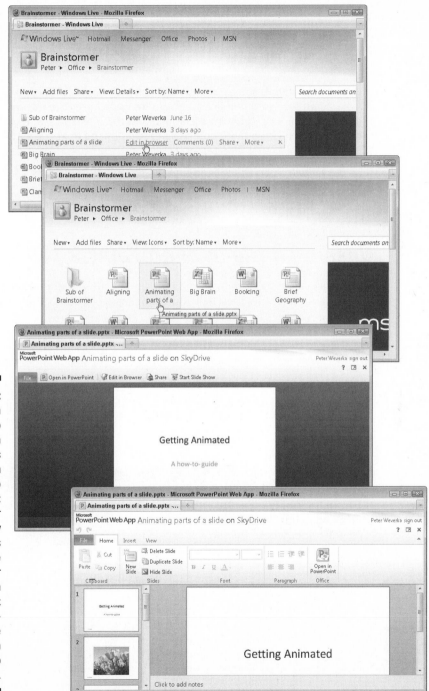

Figure 2-5:
Opening an Office Web App file in Windows Live (from top to bottom): The folder window in Details view; the Folder window in Icons view; the File window; the file open in an Office Web App.

✔ **Open the file from the File window (examine the file before opening it):**
Click the name of the file you want to open, as shown in the second screen in Figure 2-5. The File window opens, as shown in the third screen in Figure 2-5. You can scroll in the File window to examine the file without opening it. To open the file from the File window:

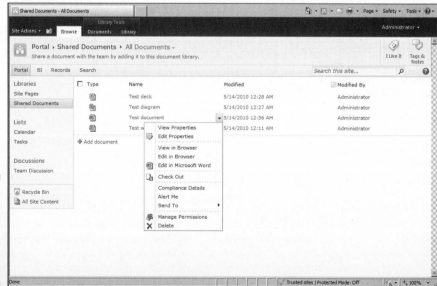

• *Open in an Office 2010 program:* Click the Open In button. This button is named after the kind of file you're dealing with. For example, if a PowerPoint file appears in the File window, the button is called Open in PowerPoint. The file opens in an Office 2010 program so that you can edit it.

• *Open in an Office Web App:* Click the Edit in Browser button. The file opens in an Office Web App, as shown by the bottommost screen in Figure 2-5.

Opening a file in SharePoint 2010

To open an Office file from a SharePoint site, locate the document in the Document Library and open its drop-down list, as shown in Figure 2-6. Then choose one of these options:

✔ **View in Browser:** Opens the file in an Office Web App. You can view the file but not edit it (unless you click the Open In or Edit in Browser button).

✔ **Edit in Browser:** Opens the file in an Office Web App so that you can edit it.

✔ **Edit in Microsoft Word, Excel, PowerPoint, or OneNote:** Opens the file in Word 2010, Excel 2010, PowerPoint 2010, or OneNote 2010.

Figure 2-6:
Opening
an Office
file at a
SharePoint
Web site.

Opening a file in Office 2010

The Office Web Apps offer a special command called Open In that you can click to open a file in an Office 2010 program. When you're working along in an Office Web App and you want to take advantage of a command found in the Office 2010 version of Office Web App, choose the Open In command:

✔ Go to the Home tab and click the Open In button.

✔ On the File tab, choose Open In.

For example, in PowerPoint Web App, click the Open in PowerPoint button or go to the File tab and choose Open in PowerPoint. Your file opens in an Office Web App program.

Although the file you open in an Office 2010 program looks as though it is located on your computer, the file is located on a Web server. Editorial changes you make are saved to the file on the Web server, not to a file located on your computer's hard drive.

Closing a file

Closing a file is considerably easier than opening one. Use one of these techniques to close a file in an Office Web App:

✔ Click the Close button. This button is located in the upper-right corner of the screen.

✔ Go to the File tab and choose Close.

A Tour of Office Web App Oddities

The moment you open an Office Web App for the first time, you notice a few oddities. For example, where is the Save button? The Office Web Apps aren't like other programs:

✔ **Save button:** Except in Word Web App, you won't find a Save button. You don't need one. Your work is saved automatically in Excel Web App, PowerPoint Web App, and OneNote Web App. You have only to click the Save button to save your work in Word Web App.

✔ **Save/Refresh button:** By clicking the Open In button in Word, Excel, PowerPoint, or OneNote Web App, you can open a file you store online in Word, Excel, PowerPoint, or OneNote 2010. And after you open the file in Word, Excel, PowerPoint, or OneNote 2010, the Save button looks a little different. It looks different to remind you that the editorial changes you make are saved not to a file on your hard disk, but rather to a file kept online on a Web server.

- ✔ **Sharing files in Office Web Apps and Office 2010:** More than one person can work on the same file with an Office Web App, but not if one of them has already opened the file in an Office 2010 program. For example, if one person opens an Excel file in Excel 2010 and someone else comes along and wants to open it in Excel Web App, he or she is out of luck. Except in the case of OneNote, you can't share a file if one person has opened it in an Office 2010 program.

- ✔ **The OneNote exception:** OneNote isn't particular about sharing a file when some people open the file in OneNote Web App and others open it in OneNote 2010. All OneNote users can successfully open the file and edit it at the same time.

- ✔ **Password-protected files:** If you'd like to upload a password-protected file to Windows Live or a SharePoint Web site and share it with others, think again. You can't open the file in an Office Web App. Office Web Apps can't open password-protected files.

Knowing Your Way around the Office Web Apps Interface

The *interface,* also called the *user interface,* is a computer term that describes how a software program presents itself to the people who use it (and you probably thought "interface" meant two people kissing). These pages give you a quick tour of the Office Web Apps interface.

The File tab

In the upper-left corner of all Office Web Apps is the File tab, as shown in Figure 2-7. On the File tab, you find commands for doing various things, including opening a file in an Office 2010 program and closing a file.

The Quick Access toolbar

As you edit a file in an Office Web App, you see the *Quick Access toolbar* in the upper-left corner of the screen above the File tab (refer to Figure 2-7). This toolbar offers two trusty buttons:

✔ Click the Undo button if you regret making an editorial change and want to reverse it.

✔ Click the Redo button if you regret clicking Undo. It reverses what the Undo button did.

Word Web App offers a third button on the Quick Access toolbar — the Save button. Click it to save your work.

File tab

Quick Access toolbar

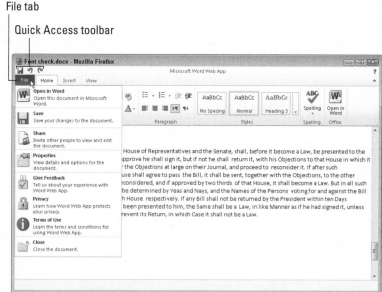

Figure 2-7:
The File tab
and Quick
Access
toolbar are
always
available.

The Ribbon and its tabs

Across the top of the screen is the *Ribbon,* an assortment of different *tabs;* click a tab to undertake a task. For example, click the Home tab to take advantage of the commands in the Font group for changing the appearance of text. Practically speaking, your first step when you start a new task is to click a tab on the Ribbon.

To make the Ribbon disappear and get more room on-screen, click the Minimize the Ribbon button. This button is located on the right side of the Ribbon. While the Ribbon is minimized, you can click a tab name to display a tab. Click the button a second time to see the Ribbon again.

Context-sensitive tabs

Sorry for dropping the term *context sensitive* on you. I usually steer clear of these horrid computer terms, but I can't help it this time because Microsoft calls some tabs "context sensitive," and I have to call them that, too.

To keep the Ribbon from getting too crowded with tabs, some tabs appear only in context; that is, they appear on the Ribbon after you insert or click something in the file you are working on. Figure 2-8 shows, for example, that after I clicked a picture, an additional tab, the (Picture Tools) Format tab, appeared on-screen. This tab offers commands for formatting pictures. The idea behind context-sensitive tabs is to direct you to the commands you need and exclude all other commands.

Figure 2-8:
After you insert or select an item, context-sensitive tabs may appear on the Ribbon.

If you're looking for a tab on the Ribbon but can't find it, you probably can't find it because the tab is context sensitive. You have to insert or select an item on-screen to make some tabs appear.

The anatomy of a tab

All tabs are different in terms of the commands they offer, but all are the same insofar as how they present commands. On every tab, you will find groups and buttons. Some tabs also offer galleries. Groups, buttons, galleries — what's up with that?

Groups

Commands on each tab are organized into *groups.* For example, the Home tab in Word Web App is organized into six groups: Clipboard, Font, Paragraph, Styles, Spelling, and Office. Group names appear below the buttons and galleries on tabs.

Groups tell you what the buttons and galleries above their names are for. For example, the buttons on the Font group are for formatting text. Examine group names to help find the command you need.

Buttons

Go to any tab and you will find buttons of all shapes and sizes. Square buttons and rectangular buttons. Big and small buttons. Buttons with labels and buttons without labels. Is there any rhyme or reason to these button shapes and sizes? No, there isn't.

What matters is not a button's shape or size but whether a downward-pointing arrow appears on its face:

- ✔ **A button with an arrow:** Click a button *with* an arrow and you get a drop-down list with options you can choose.

- ✔ **A button without an arrow:** Click a button *without* an arrow and you complete an action or open a dialog box.

- ✔ **A hybrid button with an arrow:** Some buttons serve a dual purpose as a button and drop-down list. By clicking the symbol on the top half of the button, you complete an action; by clicking the arrow on the bottom half of the button, you open a drop-down list.

You can find out a button's name by moving the pointer over it. You see a pop-up box with the button's name in it.

Galleries

Built into some tabs are galleries like the one shown in Figure 2-9. The gallery in the figure pertains to SmartArt diagrams. A *gallery* presents you with visual options. To open a gallery, click its More button, the button to its right. Click a gallery choice to apply it to your document, worksheet, presentation, or notebook.

Click the More button to open the gallery in a drop-down list

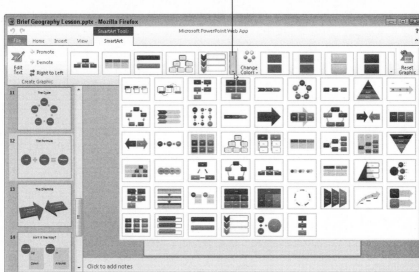

Figure 2-9:
Galleries
present you
with visual
choices.

Getting More Room in Office Web App Screens

The Office Web Apps can seem kind of claustrophobic. You don't have much room to work on-screen. You can, however, do one or two things to capture extra space in the window for focusing on your work:

 ✔ **"Pop out" the screen:** In Word, PowerPoint, and OneNote Web App, click the Pop-Out button to open a second, larger window to work in. This button is located in the upper-right corner of the screen, beside the Close button, as shown in Figure 2-10. To enlarge the screen, the name of the program and the filename are removed. (After you click the Pop-Out button, the Close button and Pop-Out button disappear. To close your file, go to the File tab and choose Close.)

 ✔ **Remove the Ribbon:** Click the Minimize the Ribbon button. This button is located on the right side of the Ribbon, as shown in Figure 2-10. You can click a tab name to redisplay a tab on the Ribbon. Click the Maximize the Ribbon button (as it is now called) a second time to see the Ribbon again.

As Figure 2-10 demonstrates, you acquire much more room on-screen by popping the screen out, removing the Ribbon, and removing extraneous menu bars and toolbars from the browser window. Chapter 3 explains how to make more room in your browser window for the Office Web Apps.

Minimize the Ribbon button

Pop-Out button

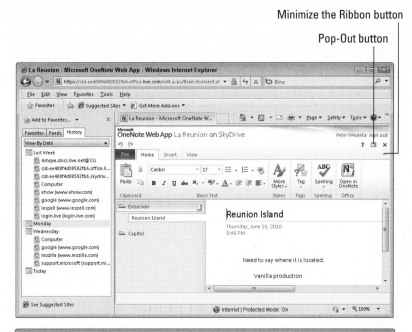

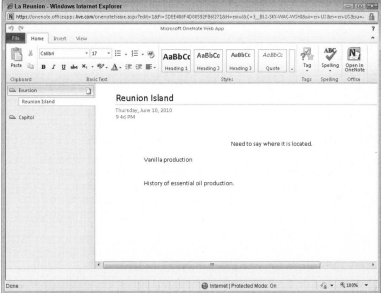

Figure 2-10:
OneNote
Web App
over-
burdened
(top) and
OneNote
Web App
stripped of
all things
extraneous
(bottom).

Chapter 3

Making Your Browser Work Better with the Office Web Apps

In This Chapter

▶ Installing and updating Firefox, Internet Explorer, and Safari

▶ Allowing and blocking first- and third-party cookies

▶ Enabling JavaScript

▶ Getting more room on-screen for the Office Web Apps

▶ Bookmarking your folders and files

*T*he fundamental difference between the Office Web Apps and the Office software is that you run an Office Web App through a browser window. For that reason, when you run Excel, PowerPoint, Word, or OneNote Web App, you are at the mercy of your browser. Unless your browser is configured properly, you can't use the Office Web Apps. And unless you make room in your browser window for the Office Web Apps, you can catch claustrophobia. You can get crowded out by your browser and not have very much room to work.

This chapter explains how to configure your browser for the Office Web Apps. It also shows you a few tricks to make working in your browser with an Office Web App a little easier. (For a quick rundown of Office Web App browser issues, see Chapter 20.)

Installing the Right Browser

A *browser*, also called a *Web browser*, is a computer program that connects to and displays Web pages on the Internet. Microsoft is kind of coy about which browser to use with the Office Web Apps. Microsoft says you can use any browser but recommends these three:

✔ Firefox version 3.0 or later

✔ Internet Explorer version 7.0 or later

✔ Safari version 4.0 or later

✔ Chrome 5.0 or later

I take this recommendation to mean you should use Firefox, Internet Explorer, Safari, or Chrome to run the Office Web Apps. Figure 3-1 shows three of the four browsers in action. The pages that follow explain how to find out which version of Firefox, Internet Explorer, Safari, or Chrome you have; install the browsers; and update your browser software.

Finding out which browser version you have

Maybe you don't need to install browser software because the right version of Firefox, Internet Explorer, Safari, or Chrome is already installed on your computer. Follow these instructions to find out which browser version is installed:

✔ **Firefox:** Choose Help⇨About Mozilla Firefox. A message box tells you which version of the software you have. If you don't see the menu bar and you can't choose Help, right-click the Navigation toolbar and choose Menu Bar. (If you can't do that because the Navigation toolbar isn't displayed, press and release the Alt key to momentarily display the menu bar; then choose View⇨Toolbars⇨Menu Bar.)

✔ **Internet Explorer:** Choose Help⇨About Internet Explorer. A message box lists which version of the software you have. If the menu bar isn't displayed, choose View⇨Toolbars⇨Menu Bar. (If you can't open the View menu because the menu bar isn't displayed, press the Alt key.)

✔ **Safari:** Choose Help⇨About Safari. A message window tells you which version of the software you have. If you can't open the Help menu because the menu bar isn't displayed, press the Alt key to display the menu bar (and choose View⇨Show Menu Bar to permanently display it).

✔ **Chrome:** Click the Tools button (in the upper-right corner of the screen) and choose About Google Chrome on the drop-down list. The About Google Chrome dialog box appears. It tells you which version of Chrome you have and whether your version of it is up-to-date.

Later in this chapter, "Updating Firefox, Internet Explorer, Safari, and Chrome" explains how to install the latest version of these Web browsers if your version is outdated.

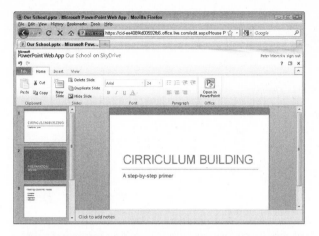

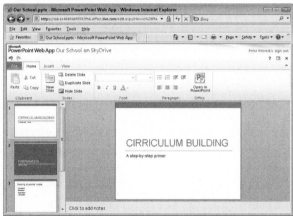

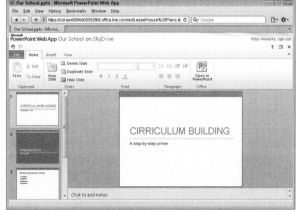

Figure 3-1:
PowerPoint
Web App
in (top to
bottom)
the Firefox,
Internet
Explorer,
and Safari
browser.

Why Firefox is the best browser

Microsoft makes Internet Explorer and the Office Web Apps, and because both are made by the same party, you might conclude that Internet Explorer is the best browser for running the Office Web Apps. But you'd be wrong if you came to that conclusion.

Firefox is far and away the best browser, even for running the Office Web Apps. It works faster, it isn't as susceptible to viruses and malware, and it's easier to get the hang of. What's

more, Firefox comes with a spell checker that is especially useful with Excel Web App and PowerPoint Web App, which don't have built-in spell checkers.

More people use Internet Explorer than Firefox because Internet Explorer is installed automatically on every Windows computer. But you owe it to yourself to download and get to know Firefox. It really is a superior browser.

Downloading and installing Firefox, Internet Explorer, Safari, and Chrome

Using Firefox, Internet Explorer, Safari, and Chrome doesn't cost a farthing. You can download these browsers for free. If your computer runs the Windows operating system, Internet Explorer is already installed on your computer (Internet Explorer, like Windows, is a Microsoft product).

Go to these Web sites to download and install one of the three browsers that Microsoft recommends using with the Office Web Apps:

- ✔ **Firefox:** www.mozilla.com
- ✔ **Internet Explorer:** www.microsoft.com/windows/internet-explorer
- ✔ **Safari:** www.apple.com/safari/download
- ✔ **Chrome:** www.google.com/chrome

The Safari browser was designed originally for use on Macintosh computers. Although Apple makes a version of Safari for Windows, in my experience, it is unwieldy and hard to operate on a Windows computer.

Updating Firefox, Internet Explorer, Safari, and Chrome

Firefox, Internet Explorer, Safari, and Chrome, the four browsers that belong to the exclusive club of browsers that work with the Office Web Apps, all offer update options and options for deciding when and how to update. These options are described forthwith.

Updating Firefox

Unless you changed the default settings, Firefox checks for updates automatically. When an update is available, you see the Software Update dialog box, and you can click OK in this dialog box to upgrade Firefox. Here is the skinny on updating the Firefox browser:

✔ **Checking for updates:** Choose Help➪Check for Updates. If an update is available, you see a dialog box with a button you can click to upgrade to the latest version of Firefox.

✔ **Choosing update options:** Choose Tools➪Options and go to the Advanced category in the Options dialog box. From there, visit the Update tab, as shown in Figure 3-2. You find options for updating automatically and telling Firefox how to manage updates.

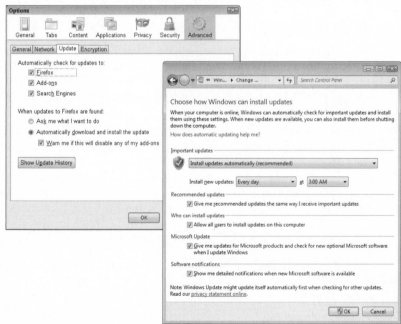

Figure 3-2: Choosing how to handle updates in Firefox (left) and Internet Explorer (right).

Updating Internet Explorer

Internet Explorer is part of the Windows operating system. For that reason, the only way to update Internet Explorer is to update the Windows operating system on your computer. Follow these instructions to update Windows and, at the same time, update Internet Explorer:

- ✔ **Checking for updates:** Choose Tools⇨Windows Update. The Windows Update window opens. If an update to Internet Explorer is available, select it in the window and click OK.

- ✔ **Choosing update options:** Choose Tools⇨Windows Update, and in the Windows Update window, click the Change Settings link. The Choose How Windows Can Install Updates window opens (refer to Figure 3-2). Change update settings and click OK.

If you don't see the Command bar in Internet Explorer, choose View⇨Toolbars⇨ Command Bar (or right-click a toolbar and choose Command Bar).

Updating Safari

To check for updates of Safari, open the Apple menu and choose Software Updates on the drop-down list. You see a list of available updates. If Safari is on the list, select it and click the Install button.

Updating Chrome

To check for Chrome updates, click the Tools button (in the upper-right corner of the screen) and choose About Google Chrome on the drop-down list. If an update is available, you see the Update button in the About Google Chrome dialog box. Click this button to update your copy of Chrome.

Considering the Cookie Question

To run the Office Web Apps, cookies must be allowed on your computer. If you attempt to open a folder where you store Office files and your browser blocks cookies, you see a screen like the one in Figure 3-3. "Cookies must be allowed," it tells you.

Figure 3-3: To run the Office Web Apps, your browser must accept cookies.

What to do? These pages explain what a cookie is and how you can block nefarious third-party cookies but still allow innocent first-party cookies on your computer.

What is a cookie?

When you visit most Web sites, they attempt to place a *cookie* on your computer. A cookie is a small encoded text file that marks you as a visitor to a Web site and stores information about you.

In the beginning, the cookie was designed for the convenience of Web site visitors. Cookies work like this: The second time you come to a Web site, the Web site reads the cookie it deposited earlier on your computer, and the Web site accordingly does something to make your second visit easier than your first. If you've ever had the experience of going to a Web site and seeing your name already entered in a login screen, you know what a cookie is. The cookie recorded your login name. When you returned to the Web site, the cookie entered your login name for you so that you wouldn't have to enter it yourself.

As well as helping returning visitors to Web sites, cookies are a means of monitoring traffic on a Web site. Cookies transmit information about visitors to Web site developers, who use the information to track visitors and examine what visitors do at Web sites and how long they do it.

Problems with third-party cookies

Cookies also have another, darker, more sinister use from that described in the previous section. Some Web sites contract with ad networks that deposit cookies on visitors' computers. This list of ad network names will give you an idea what ad networks do: DoubleClick.com, FastClick.com, Shopnow, and Valueclick. The cookies that ad networks place on computers track visitors' behavior across many Web sites on the Internet with the goal of targeting advertisements at people.

A cookie that an ad network places on a computer is called a *third-party cookie.* The other, innocent cookie, the one that Web sites you visit place on your computer, is called a *first-party cookie.* In the interest of protecting our privacy, browsers give you the opportunity to block third-party cookies but allow first-party cookies.

Firefox (choose Tools⇨Start Private Browsing), Internet Explorer (choose Tools⇨InPrivate Browsing), Safari (choose Edit⇨Private Browsing), and Chrome (click the Tools button and choose New Incognito Window) give you the opportunity to browse in private. Browsing in private means visiting Web sites on the Internet without your browser's recording which pages you visit or accepting cookies from Web sites. Cookies are blocked when you browse in private, and for that reason, you can't use the Office Web Apps in private browsing mode.

Handling cookies in Firefox, Internet Explorer, Safari, and Chrome

By themselves, cookies can't harm a computer. Cookie code is text-based, not executable, which means that a cookie can't act like a virus or malware program to hijack your computer or destroy data. But many people believe that third-party cookies are a violation of privacy and should be blocked.

To use the Office Web Apps, your browser must allow cookies — or at least first-party cookies. Read on to discover how to change the cookie settings in Firefox, Internet Explorer, and Safari, the four browsers that Microsoft recommends using with the Office Web Apps.

Handling cookies in Firefox

Follow these steps to tell the Firefox browser how to handle cookies:

1. **Choose Tools⇨Options.**

   The Options dialog box opens.

2. **Go to the Privacy tab.**

   Figure 3-4 shows the Privacy tab.

3. **Open the Firefox Will drop-down list and choose Use Custom Settings For History.**

4. **Choose cookie settings.**

   Tell Firefox your preferences for managing cookies:

   - *Allow all cookies:* Select the Accept Cookies from Sites and Accept Third Party Cookies check boxes.

   - *Block third-party cookies:* Deselect the Accept Third-Party Cookies check box.

5. **Click OK.**

Handling cookies in Internet Explorer

Follow these steps in Internet Explorer to state your cookies preferences:

1. **Choose Tools⇨Internet Options.**

   The Internet Options dialog box appears.

2. **Go to the Privacy tab.**

   Figure 3-4 shows the Privacy tab.

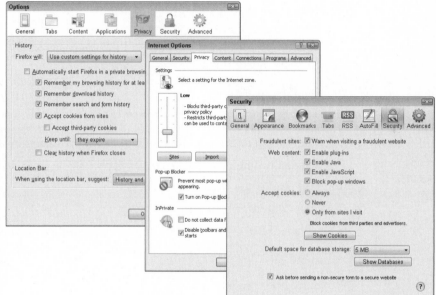

Figure 3-4:
Changing
cookie
settings in
Firefox (left),
Internet
Explorer
(middle),
and Safari
(right).

3. **Drag the Settings slider to change cookie settings.**

   Choose how you want to handle cookies:

   - *Allow all cookies:* Drag the slider all the way to the bottom, to the Accept All Cookies setting.

   - *Block third-party cookies:* Drag the slider to the Low setting.

4. **Click OK.**

Handling cookies in Safari

Follow these steps in Safari to tell the browser how to handle cookies:

1. **Choose Safari⇨Preferences (or choose Edit⇨Preferences on a Windows machine).**

   The General dialog box opens.

2. **Go to the Security tab.**

    Figure 3-4 shows the Security tab.

3. **Under Accept Cookies, select an option button.**

    Tell Safari your cookies preferences:

    - *Allow all cookies:* Select the Always option button.
    - *Block third-party cookies:* Select the Only from Sites I Visit option button.

    You're done. The Safari browser doesn't believe in clicking the OK button in dialog boxes.

Handling cookies in Chrome

Follow these steps in Chrome to tell the browser how to handle cookies:

1. **Click the Tools button and choose Options on the drop-down list.**

    The Google Chrome Options dialog box appears.

2. **Go to the Under the Hood tab.**

3. **Click the Content Settings button.**

    In the Content Settings dialog box, tell Chrome how to handle cookies:

    - *Allow all cookies:* Don't select any check boxes.
    - *Block third-party cookies:* Select the Block All Third-Party Cookies Without Exception check box.

4. **Click Close in the Content Settings dialog box and Close in the Google Chrome Options dialog box.**

Getting Right with JavaScript

The Office Web Apps run by the good graces of a computer language called JavaScript. Chances are JavaScript is enabled on your computer and you never have to think about JavaScript when you run the Office Web Apps, but if you try to run them and JavaScript is disabled, you see the window shown in Figure 3-5. It tells you in no uncertain terms that JavaScript must be enabled in your browser to run the Office Web Apps.

Figure 3-5:
Whoops!
Somebody
disabled
JavaScript.

Follow these instructions in Firefox, Internet Explorer, Safari, and Chrome to enable JavaScript:

✔ **Firefox:** Choose Tools➪Options. The General tab of the Options dialog box opens. Go to the Content tab, select the Enable JavaScript check box, and click OK.

✔ **Internet Explorer:** Choose Tools➪Internet Options, and go to the Security tab in the Internet Options dialog box. Then click the Custom Level button to open the Security Settings – Internet Zone dialog box. In the Scripting section, under Active Scripting, select the Enable option button. Finally, click OK twice.

✔ **Safari:** Choose Safari➪Preferences (or Edit➪Preferences on a Windows machine). The General dialog box opens. Go to the Security tab and select the Enable JavaScript check box.

✔ **Chrome:** Click the Tools button, choose Options on the drop-down list, and go to the Under the Hood tab in the Google Chrome Options dialog box. Then click the Content Settings button, and in the Content Settings dialog box, go to the JavaScript tab and select the Allow All Sites to Run JavaScript option button.

Getting More Room to Work In

Not to mention any names, but some browsers are better than others at keeping toolbars, menu bars, command bars, and the status bar from crowding the screen. To prevent claustrophobia, you need to clear this stuff aside when you work in an Office Web App. You need the extra room so that you can work in your Office Web App without bruising your elbows.

Figure 3-6 shows the Firefox browser with and without all its cumbersome toolbars and other accoutrements. Notice how much extra room you get when you strip all the clutter away.

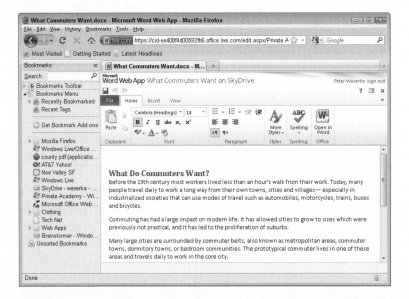

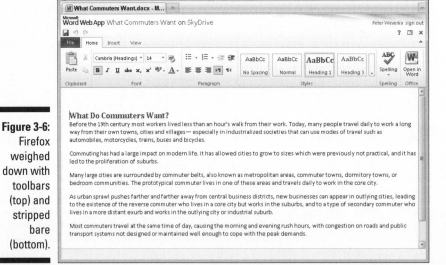

Figure 3-6:
Firefox weighed down with toolbars (top) and stripped bare (bottom).

In Firefox, Internet Explorer, and Safari, use these basic techniques to hide and display toolbars, command bars and the status bar:

- **View menu:** Open the View menu and choose options there.

- **Right-click a menu bar or toolbar:** Right-clicking opens a drop-down list with hide and display commands.

Chrome prides itself on having a sleek, uncrowded browser window. All you can do in Chrome to get more room on-screen is hide the Bookmarks bar by pressing Ctrl+B.

 Press F11 (or choose View➪Full Screen) in Firefox, Internet Explorer, or Chrome to strip away all but the Web page you're viewing. Pressing F11 is a great way to get a good look at an Office Web App. When you want to see the toolbars and whatnots again, press F11 a second time.

Bookmarking Files and Folders

In Internet terminology, to *bookmark* means to save a Web address so that you can return to it later. Browsers offer special bookmarking commands for saving Web addresses. After you have bookmarked a Web page, you need only choose its name on the Bookmarks or Favorites menu to revisit it.

One way to get around the problem of navigating to folders and files is to bookmark folders and files. Rather than click here and there to get to a folder or file, you can simply choose a bookmark. These pages explain how to bookmark files and folders and how to select a bookmark to get to a file or folder in a hurry.

Bookmarking a folder or file

Each folder and Office Web App file in SkyDrive and SharePoint has a Web address, albeit a slightly different type of address from the ones you're used to seeing. You can enter that address in an address bar on your browser to go straight to a folder or file on SkyDrive or SharePoint. You can save the file or folder as a bookmark and go straight to it as well.

Open a folder or file and follow these instructions to bookmark it:

- **Firefox:** Choose Bookmarks➪Bookmark This Page (or press Ctrl+D). You see the Page Bookmarked dialog box, as shown in Figure 3-7. Enter a name for the folder or file, choose a folder to store it in (if you want), and click Done.

✔ **Internet Explorer:** Choose Favorites⇨Add to Favorites. You see the Add Favorite dialog box, as shown in Figure 3-7. Select a folder for the Web page (click the New Folder button, if necessary, to create a new folder); then click the OK button.

✔ **Safari:** Choose Bookmarks⇨Add Bookmark (or press Ctrl+D). In the dialog box that appears, as shown in Figure 3-7, enter a name for the bookmark and click the Add button.

✔ **Chrome:** Click the Bookmark button (the star next to the Reload This Page button). The Bookmark dialog box appears. On the Folder drop-down list, choose a folder for storing the bookmark. Then enter a bookmark name and click Done.

Figure 3-7: Bookmarking a folder or file in Firefox (top), Internet Explorer (middle), and Safari (bottom).

Going to a folder or file you bookmarked

After you bookmark a folder or file in SkyDrive or SharePoint, visiting it is simply a matter of clicking once or twice. Everything should be this easy.

Following are instructions for going to a bookmarked page in Firefox, Internet Explorer, and Safari.

- ✔ **Firefox:** Open the Bookmarks menu and choose a bookmark.

- ✔ **Internet Explorer:** Open the Favorites menu and choose a bookmark.

- ✔ **Safari:** Choose Bookmarks⇨Bookmarks Bar and choose a bookmark on the submenu.

- ✔ **Chrome:** Click the bookmark's name on the Bookmarks bar. (If the Bookmarks bar isn't displayed, click the Tools button and choose Always Show Bookmarks Bar on the drop-down list.)

Chapter 4

Doing Common Tasks

Spend a few moments with the Office Web Apps and you soon see that they have many features and commands in common. For example, the Home tab in all four Office Web Apps offers commands for changing the appearance of text. I am happy to report that many commands work the same way in Word Web App, Excel Web App, PowerPoint Web App, and OneNote Web App.

This chapter explains a handful of tasks that are done the same way in all or most of the Office Web Apps. Master the tasks described in this chapter and you are well on your way to being an Office Web App wizard.

Changing Views

How's the view from here? Chances are it could be better, and you can change views by visiting the View tab. This tab is found in Word, PowerPoint, and OneNote Web App. Go to the View tab when you want to get a better look at your work or see it from a different point of view. For example, click the Editing View button to see the Ribbon; click the Reading View button to see what your file looks like on the printed page or the big screen. Sometimes it's necessary to switch to Reading View to see pictures and clip art images in files.

Figure 4-1 shows a Word document in Editing view (top) and Reading view (bottom). After you switch to Reading view, you have to click the Edit in Browser button to return to the view you started in.

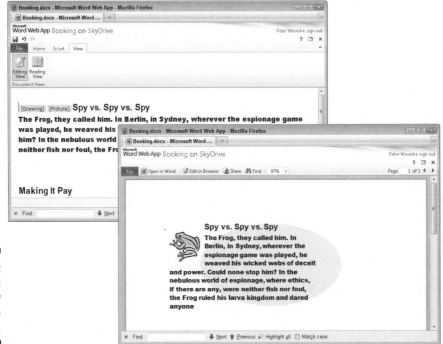

Figure 4-1:
Change
views by
going to the
View tab.

On the subject of views, the Office Web Apps don't offer the Zoom commands found in their Office 2010 counterparts. That's a shame, because being able to zoom in and out prevents eyestrain. Still, you can zoom in and out by using the Zoom commands in your browser. Choose View⇨Zoom or press Ctrl+plus sign (to zoom in) or Ctrl+minus sign (to zoom out).

Undoing and redoing

If I were to choose a command for the Hall of Fame, it would be the Undo command. This command allows you to reverse an action you regret doing. I wish real life were like that.

The Undo command "remembers" your previous editorial or formatting change. As long as you catch your error in time, you can undo your previous action by clicking the Undo button on the Quick Access toolbar.

And if you regret clicking the Undo button? Click the Redo button. It redoes what you just undid (or something like that). The Redo button is located next to the Undo button on the Quick Access toolbar.

Selecting Text

Before you can do anything to text — move it, copy it, boldface it, delete it — you have to select it. Here are speed techniques for selecting text:

To Select	Do This
A word or number	Double-click the word or number.
A few words or numbers	Drag over the words or numbers.
A block of text	Click the start of the text, hold down the Shift key, and click the end of the text.
All text	Press Ctrl+A.

Cutting, Copying, and Pasting Text

In the course of human events, it often becomes necessary to move or copy text from place to place. On the Home tab, the Office Web Apps offer buttons for moving and copying text or data, and you can press shortcut keys as well:

- ✔ **Cutting text:** Cut text to move it from one place to another. Click the Cut button or press Ctrl+X. Text you cut is placed on the Clipboard (a temporary storage area) so that you can paste it elsewhere.

- ✔ **Copying text:** Copy text to copy it from one place to another. Click the Copy button or press Ctrl+C. Text you copy lands on the Clipboard.

- ✔ **Pasting text:** Paste text after you cut or copy it to the Clipboard and you're ready to move or copy it elsewhere. Click where you want to paste the text and click the Paste button or press Ctrl+V.

Some browsers don't allow you to use the Clipboard by clicking buttons. If you click the Cut or Copy button and your browser shows you a "Cannot Access Clipboard" message, use shortcut keys to copy and move text and data.

Changing the Appearance of Text

What text looks like is determined by its font, the size of the letters, the color of the letters, and whether font styles such as italics or boldface have been applied to the text. And what text looks like sets the tone for your file. A party invitation requires large, bold, colorful letters, but a Dear John letter calls for something more subdued.

A *font* is a collection of letters, numbers, and symbols in a particular typeface, including all italicized and boldfaced variations of the letters, numbers, and symbols. *Font styles* include boldface, italics, and underline. By convention, headings are boldfaced. Italics are used for emphasis and to mark foreign words in text.

To change the appearance of text, select the text, go to the Home tab, and choose commands in the Font group, as shown in Figure 4-2. (In OneNote Web App, choose commands in the Basic Text group.) The following pages look at the various and sundry ways to change the font, font size, and color of text, as well as how to assign font styles to text.

Font group

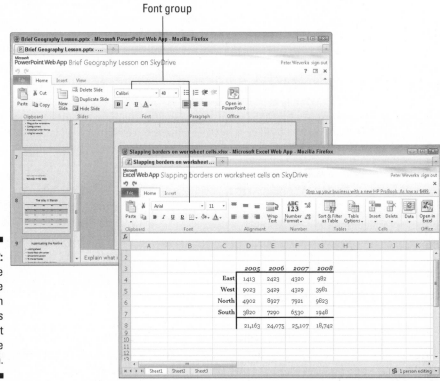

Figure 4-2: Change the appearance of text with commands in the Font group on the Ribbon.

Choosing fonts for text

If you aren't happy with a font choice, follow these steps to change fonts:

1. **Select the words or letters that need a new font.**

   Earlier in this chapter, "Selecting Text" describes all the ways to select text.

2. **On the Home tab, open the Font drop-down list.**

3. **Choose a font.**

Avoid using too many different fonts in a file, because a file with too many fonts looks like alphabet soup. The object is to choose a font that helps set the tone. An aggressive sales pitch calls for a strong, bold font; a technical presentation calls for a font that is clean and unobtrusive. Make sure that the fonts you select help to communicate your message.

Changing the font size of text

Font size is measured in *points;* a point is $\frac{1}{72}$ of an inch. The larger the point size, the larger the letters. Follow these steps to change the font size of text:

1. **Select the words or letters that need resizing.**

   Earlier in this chapter, "Selecting Text" explains various ways to select text.

2. **On the Home tab, open the Font Size drop-down list and choose a point size.**

Applying font styles to text

Select text, and on the Home tab, click the Bold, Italic, Underline, Double Underline, Strikethrough, Subscript, or Superscript button to apply a font style to text. Not all the Office Web Apps offer these buttons, but here they are in case you get the opportunity to click them:

✔ **Bold:** Boldface text calls attention to itself.

✔ *Italic:* Italics are used for emphasis, when introducing a new term, and to mark foreign words such as *voilà, gung hay fat choy,* and *magnifico!* You can also italicize slide titles to make titles a little more elegant.

✔ <u>Underline:</u> Underline text to call attention to it, but use underlining sparingly.

✔ **Double Underline:** Double-underline text to *really* call attention to it.

✔ **Strikethrough:** By convention, ~~strikethrough~~ is used to show where passages are struck from a contract or other important document.

✔ **Subscript:** A *subscripted* letter is lowered in the text. In this chemical formula, the 2 is lowered to show that two atoms of hydrogen are needed along with one atom of oxygen to form a molecule of water: H_2O.

✔ **Superscript:** A *superscripted* letter or number is one that is raised in the text. Superscript is used in mathematical and scientific formulas, in ordinal numbers (1st, 2nd, 3rd), and to mark footnotes. In the theory of relativity, the 2 is superscripted: $E = mc^2$.

To remove a font style, select the text and click the font style button a second time. For example, to remove boldface from text, select it and click the Bold button.

Changing the color of text

The Home tab offers two buttons for changing the color of text, one that changes the letters' color and one that highlights text. Select the text and use these techniques to splash color on text:

- ✔ **Changing text color:** Click the Font Color button and choose a color on the drop-down list.
- ✔ **Highlighting text:** Click the Text Highlight Color button and choose a color on the drop-down list. To remove highlighting, choose No Color on the list.

Aligning Text

As shown in Figure 4-3, where text appears in a text frame, page, slide, or notebook page is governed by how it is aligned. The slide in Figure 4-3 includes left-aligned, centered, and right-aligned text. Use the Align buttons on the Home tab to realign text.

Most Common Girls' and Boys' Names - 2006

Emily	Jacob
Emma	Michael
Madison	Joshua
Isabella	Ethan
Ava	Matthew
Abigail	Daniel
Olivia	Christopher
Hannah	Andrew
Sophia	Anthony
Samantha	William

Figure 4-3: Left-aligned, centered, and right-aligned text.

Click in the text you want to realign and then click one of these buttons on the Home tab to realign text (in OneNote, click the Paragraph Alignment button and choose an option on the drop-down list):

✔ **Align Left:** Lines up text along the left side of the slide, note, page, or spreadsheet cell. Typically, paragraphs and list items are left-aligned. Click the Align Left button or press Ctrl+L.

✔ **Center:** Centers text, leaving an equal amount of space on both slides. Titles are often centered. Click the Center button or press Ctrl+E.

✔ **Align Right:** Lines up text along the right side of a box or frame (or area). Right-aligned text is uncommon but can be used artfully in titles. Click the Align Right button or press Ctrl+R.

Excel Web App offers buttons — Top Align, Middle Align, and Bottom Align — for aligning data vertically as well as horizontally in cells.

Lists, Lists, and More Lists

Everybody is fond of lists, and the Office Web Apps give you the opportunity to create three types of list: bulleted, numbered, and nested, as shown in Figure 4-4. A bulleted list is an unranked list with each item marked with a solid, hollow, or square bullet. Numbered lists show rank or step-by-step procedures. A *nested list,* also called a *sublist,* is a list inside another list.

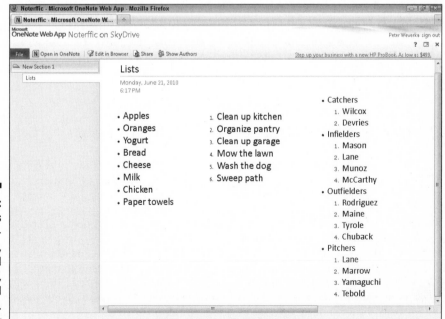

Figure 4-4: Three types of list: bulleted (left), numbered (middle), and nested (right).

Word Web App, PowerPoint Web App, and OneNote Web App offer the Bullets and Numbering buttons on the Home tab to create bulleted and numbered lists. Creating a nested list is a matter of indenting the subordinate parts of the list. Follow these instructions to create lists:

 ✔ **Bulleted list:** Click the Bullets button and write the list, pressing Enter as you complete each item; or, if you already entered items for the list, select the list and click the Bullets button. You can open the drop-down list on the Bullets button and choose a different style of bullet.

 ✔ **Numbered list:** Click the Numbering button and enter items for the list. As you press enter, the list is numbered. You can also select an unnumbered list and click the Numbering button to enter numbers all at one time. To choose a different numbering scheme, open the drop-down list on the Numbering button and choose a numbering option.

 ✔ **Nested list:** Create a numbered or bulleted list, select the part of the list that belongs in a sublist, and click the Increase Indent button. If the Office Web App applies bullets or numbers to the list and that isn't what you want, click the Bullets or Numbering button while the sublist is still selected.

You can open the drop-down list on the Bullets or Numbering button and choose an option to help set the sublist apart from the rest of the list. Click the Decrease List Level button if you want to return a sublist to the parent list.

To remove bullets or numbers from a list, select the list and click the Bullets or Numbering button. Here's a little trick: To convert a numbered to a bulleted list (or vice versa), drag over the list to select it, go to the Home tab, and then click the Bullets or Numbering button.

Spell-Checking Your Work

For those of us who can't spell, Word Wep App and OneNote Web App provide a spell-checker, but not a very good one. The only way to spell-check words in Word Web App and OneNote Web App is to check them one at a time, as shown in Figure 4-5. If you're the cosmopolitan sort who writes in more than one language, you can mark text as foreign-language text and spell-check it.

 Don't trust the smell-checker to be accurate all the time. It doesn't really locate misspelled words — it locates words that aren't in its dictionary. For example, if you write "Nero diddled while Rome burned," the spell checker doesn't catch the error. Nero *fiddled* while Rome burned, but because *diddle* is a legitimate word in the spelling dictionary, the spell-checker overlooks the error. The moral: Proofread your files carefully and don't rely on the spell-checker to catch all your smelling errors.

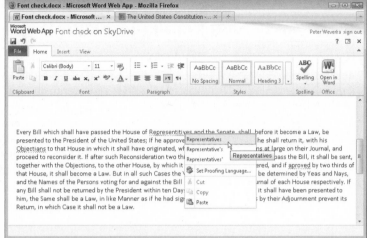

Figure 4-5:
Correcting
a misspell-
ing in Word
Web App.

Spell-checking one word at a time

Spelling errors are underlined in red in Word documents and OneNote note-books. To correct these errors, right-click a redlined word and choose an alternative spelling on the drop-down list, as shown in Figure 4-5, or click in the word and correct the misspelling yourself. To search for misspellings, go to the Home tab and click the Spelling button.

Spell-checking foreign-language text

Follow these steps to mark text as foreign-language text and be able to spell-check it:

1. **Select the text.**

2. **Open the drop-down list on the Spelling button and choose Set Proofing Language.**

   You see the Language dialog box.

3. **Select a language and click OK.**

   Next time you click the Spelling button to run a spell-check, the Office Web App will check the text you selected in Step 1 against a dictionary of the language you chose in Step 3.

Spell-checking in Firefox

Firefox is unique among browsers in that it comes with a spell-checking mechanism. This ability to check for misspellings is yet another reason to choose Firefox over other browsers. If you run Firefox, you can spell-check in Excel Web App and PowerPoint Web App as well as Word Web App and OneNote Web App.

Writing more than one line of text in the Firefox browser activates the browser's spell-checker.

Words that Firefox thinks are misspelled are underlined in red. To fix a misspelling, click in the redlined word and edit it.

If Firefox isn't detecting misspelled words, choose Tools➪Options, visit the Advanced area in the Options dialog box, and go to the General tab. Then select the Check My Spelling As I Type check box.

All about Hyperlinks

A *hyperlink* is an electronic shortcut from one place to another. If you've spent any time on the Internet, you know what a hyperlink is. Clicking hyperlinks on the Internet takes you to different Web pages or different places on the same Web page. In the Office Web Apps, you can hyperlink a word such that clicking the word takes viewers to a Web page. These pages explain how to create and edit hyperlinks.

Creating a hyperlink

To create a hyperlink in an Office Web App, you must know the Web address of the Web page you want to link to and type this address in a dialog box. It's easy to make a mistake when typing an unwieldy Web address in dialog box, but you can get around this problem by going to the Web page you want to link to and copying its address. Click in the Address bar to select the Web address, right-click the address, and choose Copy on the shortcut menu to copy the address to the Clipboard. Later, you can paste the address into the Link dialog box.

Follow these steps to hyperlink a word or phrase to a Web page on the Internet:

1. **Select the text that will form the hyperlink (in Excel Web App, click a worksheet cell).**

   After you create the hyperlink, the text you select will appear in blue to indicate that it is a hyperlink. Anyone who moves the pointer over the hyperlink will see the pointer change to a hand and know that clicking the text activates a hyperlink.

2. **On the Insert tab, click the Link button (or press Ctrl+K).**

   In Excel Web App, this button is called Hyperlink. You see the Link dialog box, as shown in Figure 4-6.

Pop-up hyperlink description

Hyperlink Web address   Hyperlink

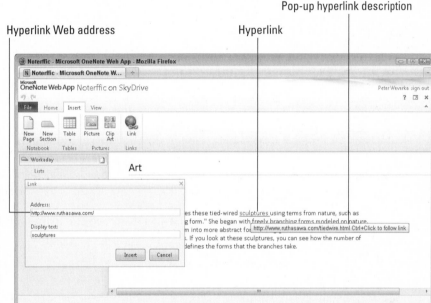

Figure 4-6: Enter the target of the hyperlink in the Link dialog box.

3. **In the Address text box, enter the address of the Web page you want to link to.**

   You can type the address or paste it into the Address text box by copying the address, right-clicking in the Address text box, and choosing Paste on the shortcut menu that appears (or pressing Ctrl+V).

   The Display Text box lists the word or phrase you selected in Step 1. Don't alter the text in this text box; doing so changes the text in your file.

4. **Click the Insert button.**

   I would test the hyperlink if I were you to make sure it takes viewers to the right Web page. To test a hyperlink, Ctrl+click it or right-click it and choose Open Link on the shortcut menu.

Editing hyperlinks

Right+clicking a hyperlink opens a drop-down list with commands for editing, selecting, opening, and copying the link.

To correct a hyperlink that goes to the wrong destination, right-click it and choose Edit Link on the shortcut menu. You see the Link dialog box (refer to Figure 4-6). Enter the correct Web address of the hyperlink in the Address text box and click OK.

Printing Your Work

Predictions to the contrary, the paperless office is not yet upon us. You often have to print Word documents, Excel worksheets, PowerPoint presentations, and OneNote notebooks to proofread them or distribute them to colleagues.

Follow these steps to print your work:

1. **Go to the File tab.**

2. **Choose Print (or press Ctrl+P if you don't see the Print command).**

   The Print dialog box appears.

3. **Choose what to print, how many copies to print, and other print settings.**

4. **Click the OK button.**

   Hark! I hear the sound of paper being squeezed through the printer as your file is printed.

Chapter 5

Handling Artwork and Diagrams

A picture, so they say, is worth a thousand words. Whether it's worth a thousand words or merely 950 is debatable. What is certain is that a carefully chosen picture or clip-art image helps others understand you better. The image reinforces the ideas or information that you're trying to put across.

This chapter explains how you can use Word, PowerPoint, and OneNote Web App to make pictures — photographs, graphics, and clip-art images — part of your Word documents, PowerPoint presentations, and OneNote notebooks. It also looks into graphic file formats, other issues pertaining to graphics, and how to place a SmartArt diagram in a PowerPoint presentation.

All about Picture File Formats

Graphics and photographs come in many different file formats, and some are better than others, depending on your purposes. These pages explain what you need to know about graphic files to use them wisely, the difference between bitmap and vector graphics, and what resolution is. You also hear a word or two about copyright issues.

Bitmap and vector graphics

All graphic images fall into the bitmap or vector category:

- ✔ A *bitmap graphic* is composed of thousands upon thousands of tiny dots called *pixels* that, taken together, form an image (the term "pixel" comes from "picture element").

- ✔ A *vector graphic* is drawn with the aid of computer instructions that describe the shape and dimension of each line, curve, circle, and so on. You can't see vector graphics in the Office Web Apps except by switching to Reading view. The Office Web Apps don't offer commands for editing vector graphics.

The difference between the two formats is that vector graphics do not distort when you enlarge or shrink them, whereas bitmap graphics lose resolution when their size is changed. Furthermore, vector images do not require nearly as much disk space as bitmap graphics. Drop a few bitmap graphics in your file and soon you're dealing with a file that is close to 750K in size.

Table 5-1 describes popular bitmap graphic formats; Table 5-2 lists popular vector graphic formats.

Table 5-1	Bitmap Graphic File Formats
Extension	*File Type*
BMP, BMZ, DIB	Microsoft Windows Bitmap
GFA, GIF	Graphics Interchange Format
JPEG, JPG, JFIF, JPE	JPEG File Interchange Format
PICT	Macintosh PICT
PNG	Portable Network Graphics
RLE	Bitmap File in RLE Compression Scheme
TIF, TIFF	Tagged Image File Format

Table 5-2	Vector Graphic File Formats
Extension	*File Type*
CDR	CorelDRAW
CGM	Computer Graphics Metafile
EMF	Enhanced Windows Metafile
EMZ	Windows Enhanced Metafile

Extension	File Type
EPS	Encapsulated PostScript
PCT	Macintosh PICT
WMF	Windows Metafile
WPG	WordPerfect Graphics

Resolution

Resolution refers to how many pixels comprise a bitmap image. The higher the resolution, the clearer the image. Resolution is measured in *dots per inch* (dpi), sometimes called *pixels per inch* (ppi). Images with more dots — or pixels — per inch are clearer and display more fineness of detail.

High-resolution images look better but require more disk space than low-resolution images. Figure 5-1 illustrates the difference between a high-resolution and low-resolution photograph.

Figure 5-1:
A high-resolution photo (left) and the same photo at low resolution (right).

Choosing file formats for graphics

One of the challenges of using graphics and photographs is finding a balance between high-quality, high-resolution graphics and the need to keep file sizes to a minimum. Here are some tips for choosing graphic file formats:

✔ Consider sticking with vector graphics if you're including graphics in your file strictly for decoration purposes. Vector images are easy to come by, don't require very much disk space, and can be resized successfully in Word, PowerPoint, and OneNote Web App.

The all-important copyright issue

To save any image on the Internet to your computer, all you have to do is right-click it and choose Save Picture As. By starting from Google Image Search (www.images.google.com), you can scour the Internet for any image you need. Never before has it been easier to obtain images for your own use.

Still, obtaining images and using them legally are two different matters. Would it surprise you to know that the vast majority of graphics can't be used without the owner's permission? The copyright laws have a "fair use" provision for borrowing written words. You can quote others' words as long as you cite the author and work and you don't quote passages longer than 250 to a thousand words (the "fair use" provision is vague on this point). The copyright law regard-

ing graphics is quite straightforward. Unless you have the owner's permission, you can't legally use a graphic.

Sometimes it's hard to tell who owns a graphic. The artist or photographer (or his or her estate) doesn't necessarily own the copyright because artists sometimes relinquish their copyrights when they create works for hire. The only way to get permission to use a graphic is to ask. Contact the owner of the Web site with the image you want, the publisher if the image is in a book, or the museum if the work is owned by a museum. You will be asked to write a letter describing precisely how you intend to use the image, reproduce it, and distribute it. Your letter should also say how long you intend to use it and at what size you intend to reproduce it.

✔ For photographs, make JPEG your first choice. JPEG images have a fairly high resolution. If the file you're working on is meant to be displayed on the Internet, you can't go wrong with JPEGs; they are the de facto photograph standard on the Internet.

✔ If you're dealing with black-and-white photos or resolution doesn't matter, use GIF files. These files eat up the least amount of disk space.

Inserting a Picture on a Page, Slide, or Note

After you've weighed the merits of different kinds of pictures and decided which one is best for your presentation, you can insert it on a page, slide, or note. Word Web App, PowerPoint Web App, and OneNote Web App offer the Picture command for inserting pictures from your computer or network.

Follow these steps to insert a picture on a page, slide, or note:

1. **Click where you want the picture to go.**

2. **On the Insert tab, click the Picture button.**

   As shown on the left side of Figure 5-2, you see the Insert Picture dialog box. In PowerPoint Web App, you can also open this dialog box by clicking the Picture icon in a slide's content placeholder frame.

Figure 5-2: Click the Picture button to insert a picture on your computer.

3. **Click the Browse button in the Insert Picture dialog box.**

   You see the File Upload dialog box, as shown in Figure 5-2. In Windows Vista, you can open the drop-down list on the Views button and choose an option to get a better look at the files and filenames. In Windows 7, click the Change Your View icon near the right side of the toolbar.

4. **Locate the picture file you want, select it, and click the Open button.**

   Here are a couple of tricks for discovering more about a picture you want to insert:

   • Move the pointer over a picture in the File Upload dialog box to get information about its file type, dimensions, and size.

   • Right-click the picture and choose Properties on the shortcut menu that appears. The Properties dialog box opens. On the Details tab, you find the file's dimensions, resolution, and other useful information.

5. In the Insert Picture dialog box, click the Insert button.

Go to the (Picture Tools) Format tab to see how you can change the size of your picture. Later in this chapter, "Changing the Size of a Graphic" describes how to resize your picture.

To delete a picture, click to select it and then press the Delete key.

Decorating Files with Clip-Art Images

Word Web App and OneNote Web App give you the opportunity to use clip-art images in your work. Read on to find out what clip art is and how to place clip-art images in Word documents and OneNote pages with Word Web App an OneNote Web App.

What is clip art?

In the old days, long before the invention of computers, people would buy clip-art books. They would literally cut, or clip, images from these books and paste them into posters, letters, and advertisements. Today's clip art is the digital equivalent of the clip art in those old books. Using Word Web App or OneNote Web App, you can go online to a Microsoft Web site, find a clip-art image you like, and paste into a Word document or OneNote page. Clip art you get from Microsoft isn't encumbered by licensing restrictions; it's in the public domain, and you can use it as you wish. Microsoft offers literally thousands of clip-art images.

Figure 5-3 shows examples of some clip-art images that come from Microsoft. Use images like these to decorate your Word documents and OneNote pages. Use them to help illustrate an idea or simply to add a little liveliness to the page. In my experience, the hardest task where clip art is concerned is finding the right image. You can choose from so many images that finding the right one is a chore.

Figure 5-3:
Examples
of clip-art
images.

Finding and inserting a clip-art image

Follow these steps to insert a clip-art image on a Word document page or OneNote page:

1. **Click where you want the image to go.**

2. **On the Insert tab, click the Clip Art button.**

   You see the Insert Clip Art dialog box, as shown in Figure 5-4.

Enter a search term

Select an image

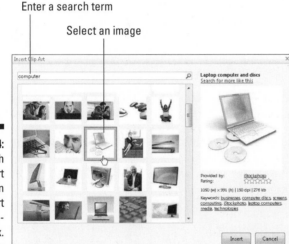

Figure 5-4: Search for clip-art images in the Insert Clip Art dialog box.

3. **In the Search text box, enter a keyword that describes the clip art image you need; then press Enter or click the Search button (it's on the right side of the text box).**

   Depending on the search term you enter, you see few or many clip-art images. Scroll to find one that excites you. Images may include photographs as well as clip art. The right slide of the dialog box tells you the image's size in pixels, its resolution (its dpi setting; see the "Resolution" section, earlier in this chapter, for more details), and its size in kilobytes.

   TIP

   To discover more about an image, right-click it and choose View Image Info on the shortcut menu that appears. The Page Info dialog box opens and you can see the clip art's file type and other information.

4. **Select a clip-art image.**

5. **Click the Insert button.**

   The clip-art image lands in your Word document or OneNote page. To delete a clip-art image, select it and click the Delete button.

The next topic in this chapter, "Changing the Size of a Graphic," explains how to change an image's size on the (Picture Tools) Format tab.

Changing the Size of a Graphic

Select a picture or clip-art image and visit the (Picture Tools) Format tab to change its size. To see the tab, you must first click a picture or image. As shown in Figure 5-5, the (Picture Tools) Format tab offers commands for enlarging and shrinking images:

✔ Click the Grow or Shrink button to enlarge or shrink the image by increments.

✔ Enter a measurement in the Scale text box to enlarge or shrink the image with respect to its original size.

The (Picture Tools) Format tab also offers the Alt-Text button, which you can click to enter alternative text in the Alternative Text dialog box (see Figure 5-5). *Alternative text* is what visitors to a Web page see while the image is loading on a page, or in the unlikely event of a visitor turning off the display of images on Web sites, what the visitor sees instead of the image. Enter alternative text to describe images so that visitors know what's there before images actually appear onscreen.

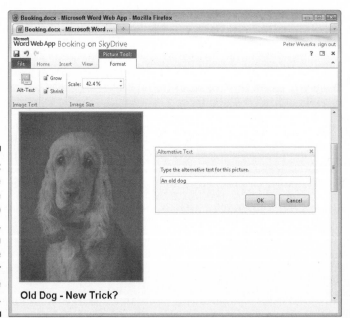

Figure 5-5:
On the (Picture Tools) Format tab, change an image's size and enter alternative text.

Making a SmartArt Diagram

Along with charts and tables, diagrams are the best way to present your ideas. Diagrams clearly show, for example, employees' relationships with one another, product cycles, workflow processes, and spheres of influence. A diagram is an excellent marriage of images and words. Diagrams allow an audience to literally visualize a concept, idea, or relationship.

The remainder of this chapter explains how to construct diagrams in PowerPoint Web App. It shows how to customize a diagram by changing its appearance, shape, and direction. (If you need help with PowerPoint basics, go to Part V, Chapter 13.)

The basics: Creating a diagram

In PowerPoint Web App, diagrams are made from *SmartArt graphics.* These diagram graphics are "interactive" in the sense that you can move, alter, and write text on them. You can alter these diagrams to your liking.

The first step in creating a diagram is to select a layout in the SmartArt drop-down list shown in Figure 5-6. After you select a diagram, the next step is to make the diagram your own by doing some or all of these tasks:

- **Enter the text:** Enter text on each shape, or component, of the diagram. See "Handling the text on diagram shapes," later in this chapter.

- **Add and remove shapes:** Enter more shapes on or remove shapes from the diagram. See "Adding and removing diagram shapes."

- **Changing a diagram's overall appearance:** Choose a different color scheme or 3-D variation for your diagram. See "Choosing a look for your diagram."

- **Promote and demote shapes:** Select part of a diagram and raise or lower it in the diagram hierarchy. See "Promoting and demoting diagram shapes."

- **Changing direction:** You can flip horizontally oriented diagrams around so that they point the opposite direction. See "Changing a diagram's direction."

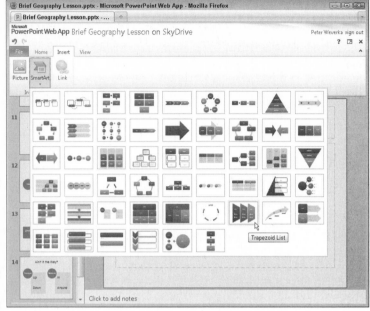

Figure 5-6:
Start from
an initial
diagram
on the
SmartArt
menu.

Creating the initial diagram

Choose carefully when you create your initial diagram. If the diagram you chose initially doesn't do the job, you can swap it for a different diagram. How successful the swap is depends on how far along you are in creating your diagram and whether your diagram is complex. Better to choose well at the beginning.

Follow these steps to create a SmartArt diagram:

1. **Go to or insert the slide where you want to show the diagram.**

   To place a diagram on a slide, the slide must show the SmartArt icon. In other words, you must choose the Title and Content, Two Content, Comparison, or Content With Caption slide layout to create a slide if you want to place a diagram on it.

2. **Open the SmartArt drop-down list.**

   Figure 5-6 (shown earlier in this chapter) shows this menu. You can open it two ways:

- On the Insert tab, click the SmartArt button.

- Click the SmartArt icon in a content placeholder frame. Going this route opens the (SmartArt Tools) SmartArt tab. Open the Layouts menu to see the diagram choices.

3. **Click to select a diagram.**

There are 51 diagrams in all. Move the pointer over a diagram to read its name. The diagram appears on your slide after you click its name.

If you change your mind about the diagram you chose, go to the (SmartArt Tools) SmartArt tab, open the Layouts menu, and choose a different diagram.

To edit a diagram, click to select it. The (SmartArt Tools) SmartArt tab appears on the Ribbon. Visit that tab to see commands for editing your diagram.

To delete a diagram, click to select it and then click the Delete key.

Handling the text on diagram shapes

Follow these steps to enter or edit text on a diagram:

1. **Click the diagram to select it.**

You have to select a diagram to make the (SmartArt Tools) SmartArt tab appear.

2. **On the (SmartArt Tools) SmartArt tab, click the Edit Text button (or double-click the diagram).**

Where diagram shapes used to be, you see a bulleted list like the ones shown in Figure 5-7. Each bulleted item in the list corresponds to one diagram shape.

3. **Enter or edit the items on the bulleted list.**

4. **Click outside the diagram.**

The diagram shapes reappear.

Adding and removing diagram shapes

PowerPoint Web App doesn't make it easy to add and remove shapes. In my experience, you often have to resort to the Undo button as you experiment with adding shapes to and removing shapes from a diagram.

To add or remove shapes, visit the (SmartArt Tools) SmartArt tab and click the Edit Text button (or double-click the diagram). Your diagram is transformed into a bulleted list. Add bulleted items to the list to add shapes; remove bulleted items to remove shapes from the diagram. After you click outside the diagram and diagram shapes reappear, you see whether your experiment failed or succeeded. If your experiment in adding or removing shapes failed, click the Undo button and try, try, try again.

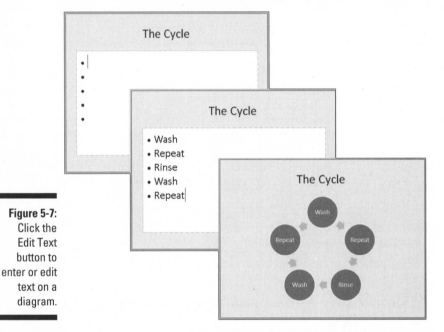

Figure 5-7: Click the Edit Text button to enter or edit text on a diagram.

Changing a diagram's overall appearance

The (SmartArt Tools) SmartArt tab offers a couple of handy commands for changing the overall appearance of a diagram. You are encouraged to test these commands to see whether you can make your diagram look a little more spiffy:

✔ **Changing colors:** Click the Change Colors button and choose a color scheme on the drop-down list.

✔ **Choosing SmartArt styles:** Open the SmartArt Styles gallery and choose a style. Some of the 3-D styles are very interesting and can turn a drab diagram into something a little more meaningful, as shown in Figure 5-8.

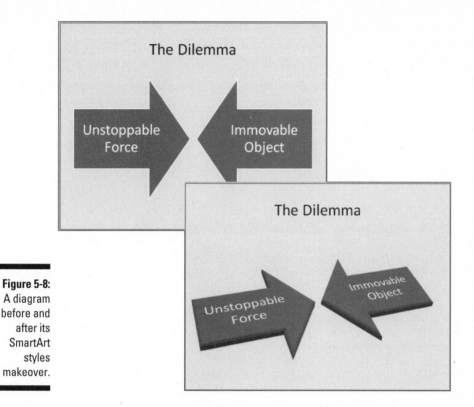

Figure 5-8:
A diagram
before and
after its
SmartArt
styles
makeover.

Promoting and demoting shapes in a diagram's hierarchy

Shapes in hierarchy diagrams are ranked by level. You might find that a shape is on the wrong level in the hierarchy. In an organizational chart, for example, it would be a catastrophe if the vice president were ranked higher in the chart than the president, and in cases like those, it is necessary to promote or demote shapes.

You can move a diagram's place in the hierarchy higher or lower by following these steps:

1. **Select the diagram and go to the (SmartArt Tools) SmartArt tab.**

2. **Double-click the diagram (or click the Edit Text button).**

   The diagram appears in the form of a bulleted list with sublist entries. The further an item is indented in the list, the lower it is in the hierarchy.

3a. **Select a list item and click the Promote button to raise it in the hierarchy.**

3b. **Select a list item and click the Demote button to lower it.**

4. **Repeat Step 3 until all items have been promoted or demoted as suits you.**

5. **Click outside your diagram.**

   Not a very elegant way to promote and demote shapes, is it? If you're anything close to average, you have to try several times before your diagram looks just right.

Changing a diagram's direction

As long as your diagram is horizontally oriented, you can change its direction. You can flip it over such that the rightmost shape in your diagram becomes the leftmost shape, and what was the leftmost shape becomes the rightmost shape. If arrows are in your diagram, the arrows point the opposite direction after you flip the diagram. You can't flip vertically oriented diagrams this way. Sorry, but diagrams that run north to south, not west to east, can't be rolled over.

Figure 5-9 shows an example of a horizontally oriented diagram chart that was flipped over. Notice how the shapes are in opposite order and the arrow points in a different direction. Change the direction of a diagram to illustrate a concept in better terms or to contrast separate processes that operate in different directions.

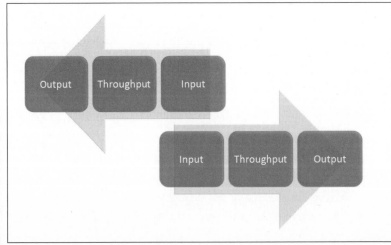

Figure 5-9:
You can flip horizontal diagrams so that they run the opposite direction.

Follow these steps to flip a horizontally oriented diagram:

1. **Select the diagram.**

 2. **On the (SmartArt Tools) SmartArt tab, click the Right to Left button.**

   If you don't like what you see, click the button again or click the Undo button.

Part II
Sharing Files and Collaborating with Others

The 5th Wave   By Rich Tennant

"You ever notice how much more streaming media
there is than there used to be?"

In this part . . .

"**S**haring is caring," as the saying goes, and in Part
II, you see how to show how much you care as
you discover how to share files with others using the
Office Web Apps and their counterparts in Office 2010.

Chapters 6 and 7 look at sharing files with SkyDrive, a service in Windows Live designed for sharing folders and
files with other people. Chapter 8 looks into sharing files
at a SharePoint Web site. SharePoint Web sites are private
and are operated by companies for their employees.

Chapter 6

All about SkyDrive

In This Chapter

▶ Understanding what SkyDrive is and how it works

▶ Logging in to Windows Live

▶ Choosing how private you want to be

▶ Finding your SkyDrive folders in Windows Live

▶ Creating, navigating, renaming, and deleting folders

▶ Creating a new file with an Office Web App

▶ Opening and editing files with an Office Web App or Office 2010 program

▶ Uploading and downloading files

SkyDrive is part of Windows Live, a collection of free online services and software products offered by Microsoft. SkyDrive was designed to store files online, but you can use the service as well to create, edit, and share Word, Excel, PowerPoint, and OneNote files.

This chapter introduces SkyDrive. It shows you how to sign up with Windows Live and create folders in SkyDrive for storing your files. You also discover how, after you create a folder, to create Word, Excel, PowerPoint, and OneNote files and store them in SkyDrive. You find out how to manage, upload, and download files, as well as how to edit Office files you keep at SkyDrive.

By the way, this chapter covers running the Office Web Apps in Windows Live SkyDrive, but you can also run Office Web Apps without keeping your files at Windows Live. Using a software product called SharePoint 2010, you can run the Office Web Apps from a server on a local network. For example, you can run the Office Web Apps from and store your files on a server that is owned and operated by the company you work for. If this topic interests you, turn to Chapter 8.

The Big Picture: Storing, Creating, and Editing Files at SkyDrive

On the theory that it's better to look before you leap, following is a brief description of everything you need to know to create and store Word, Excel, PowerPoint, and OneNote files at SkyDrive.

Doing the set-up dance

To use the Office Web Apps and share files online, start by setting up an account with Windows Live, the Microsoft Web site that offers Web-based applications and services. As Chapter 2 explains in detail, you can set up a Windows Live account by going to this Web address: `http://home.live.com`. When you set up the account, Windows Live gives you a SkyDrive folder for storing files.

The Office Web Apps work with four browsers: Internet Explorer, Firefox, Safari, and Chrome. Chapter 3 explains how to download and install these browsers on your computer.

Microsoft recommends installing Silverlight on your computer if you want to use the Office Web Apps. Silverlight is a Microsoft application designed to deliver media over the Internet. You can download and install Silverlight starting at this Web address: `www.silverlight.net`.

Working with folders and files in SkyDrive

After you get your Windows Live account, you can begin storing files on SkyDrive. Figure 6-1 shows the SkyDrive window in Windows Live. To store and organize your files, you create folders and subfolders in SkyDrive. (See "Creating a folder," later in this chapter.)

It almost goes without saying, but folders sometimes need deleting, moving, and renaming. SkyDrive offers commands for doing these folder-management tasks. (See "Deleting, moving, and renaming folders," later in this chapter.

To get from place to place at Windows Live, and to open the SkyDrive folder or a folder you created, use the Windows Live navigation bar, the SkyDrive navigation bar, and the Back and Forward buttons in your browser. (See "Navigating to the SkyDrive window" and "Going from folder to folder in SkyDrive," later in this chapter.)

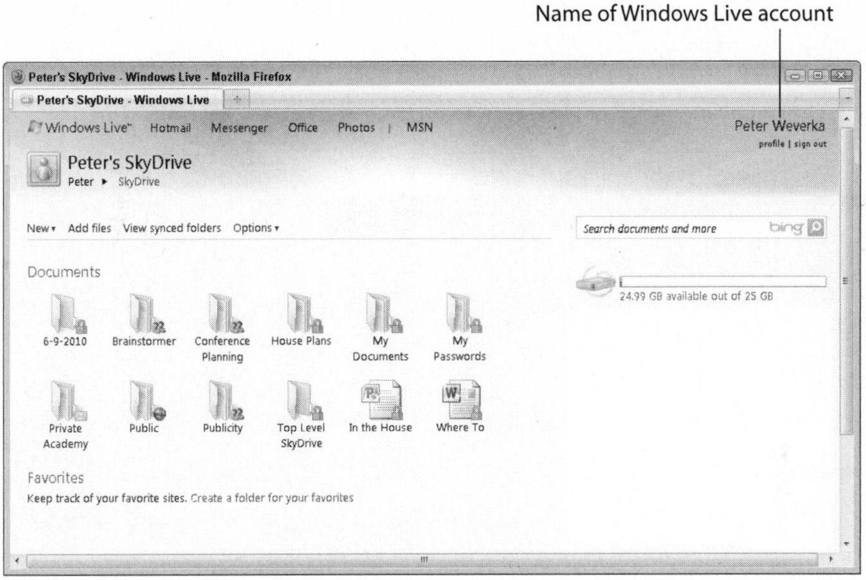

Name of Windows Live account

Figure 6-1:
Windows
Live show-
ing the
SkyDrive
window.

To create a document, worksheet, presentation, or notebook with an Office
Web App, go to the folder where you want to store your new file and choose
the New command. (For details, see "Opening and Editing Office Files Stores
on SkyDrive," later in this chapter.)

If Word 2010, Excel 2010, PowerPoint 2010, and OneNote 2010 are installed on
your computer, you can work on Office 2010 files on a SkyDrive folder with
an Office 2010 program. (See "Opening and editing a SkyDrive file in an Office
2010 program.")

The next chapter in this book explains how to share and coauthor Office files
with other people in SkyDrive.

Signing In to Windows Live

After you create an account with Windows Live (see Chapter 2), you can
begin creating Office files and storing your files in SkyDrive at Windows Live.

As shown in Figure 6-2, sign in to Windows Live by going to the address listed
here, entering your ID and password, and clicking the Sign In button:

```
http://home.live.com
```

Figure 6-2:
Enter your
Windows
Live ID and
password
to sign in to
Windows
Live.

After you sign in, your Home page at Windows Live opens. After you start receiving e-mail, your most recent e-mail messages appear on the Home page. Later in this chapter, "Navigating to the SkyDrive Window" explains how to get to the SkyDrive window, which is where you store your files.

Windows Live asks you to change your password every 72 days for security purposes. To change your password at any time, click your username (located in the upper-right corner of the screen) and choose Account on the drop-down list. Then, in the Account Overview window, click the Change link beside the word "Password." You come to the Change Your Password window, where you can change your password.

Click the Sign Out link when your visit to Windows Live is finished. This link is located in the upper-right corner of the window below your username.

Choosing Privacy Options

Windows Live aspires to be a social network similar to Facebook and MySpace. This book doesn't cover the social network aspects of Windows Live, but besides using it to store and share files with the Office Web Apps, you can use it to present yourself on the Internet, share photos, and, of course, build a circle of online friends.

Whether or not you intend to use Windows Live as a social network, you owe it to yourself to visit the Profile page and choose a privacy option. Privacy options determine whether people can find you at Windows Live and what access they have to files you store in SkyDrive.

Follow these steps to choose a privacy option:

1. **Click the Profile link.**

   This link is located in the upper-right corner of the screen below your Windows Live name. Clicking it takes you to the Profile page (if you haven't chosen privacy options yet, you go straight to the Privacy Options page).

2. **Click the Privacy Settings link, if necessary, to get to the Privacy Options page.**

   The Privacy Options page describes the privacy settings — Public, Limited, and Private. (If you want, click the Advanced link to read a detailed description of the three settings.)

3. **Choose a privacy option.**

   From the point of view of someone who wants to store and perhaps share files on SkyDrive, here is what the three options mean:

   - *Public:* Other people in Windows Live can see all your files unless you store them in shared or private folders. (Chapter 7 explains what shared and private folders are.) I *do not* recommend choosing this option if you value whatever it is you keep in your files and you don't want others to see it.

   - *Limited:* Friends on Windows Live as well as people you invite to view the contents of your folders can open a folder if you share it. As I explain in Chapter 7, you can declare that others on Windows Live are your friends, and you can give these friends privileges in regard to what they can do inside your folders. Moreover, as Chapter 7 explains, you can declare that a folder is shared but that only certain people can open it. Choose this option if you want to share files on SkyDrive with your Windows Live friends.

   - *Private:* Nobody, friend or otherwise, can see your folders unless you share them and invite them to come in for a look. Choose this option if you use SkyDrive only to store files, not share them, or you want to share files but not with friends on Windows Live.

4. **Click the Save button.**

   You can return to the Privacy Options page at any time by clicking the Profile link and then clicking the Privacy Settings link on the Profile page.

Navigating to the SkyDrive Window

After you sign in to Windows Live, you land in the Home window, which is fine and dandy, but to use the Office Web Apps and store files on SkyDrive, you need to start at the SkyDrive window. The SkyDrive window is the place where you keep the folders that store your files.

As shown in Figure 6-3, follow these steps to go to the SkyDrive window:

1. **Move the pointer over the Windows Live link on the Windows Live taskbar.**

   The Windows Live taskbar is located along the top of the screen. It includes the Windows Live, Hotmail, Messenger, Office, and Photos links.

2. **On the drop-down list that appears, choose SkyDrive.**

   You land in the SkyDrive window. It lists top-level folders you created. If you just started using SkyDrive, you see one folder in the window — My Documents. Windows Live creates this folder for you. You can create folders of your own here, as "Creating a folder" explains later in this chapter.

Windows Live taskbar

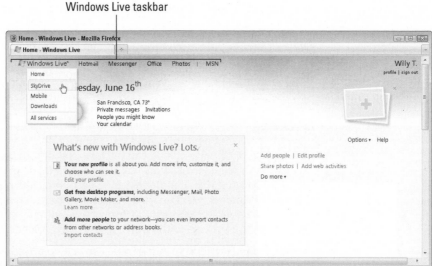

Figure 6-3:
Going to the
SkyDrive
window at
Windows
Live.

Managing Your Folders

All folders you create for storing files are kept in SkyDrive. SkyDrive can store up to 25GB of files. The measurement bar on the right side of the SkyDrive window tells you how many gigabytes (GB) remain available for storing files.

To begin with, SkyDrive gives you one folder called My Documents for storing files. These pages explain how to create folders of your own, get from folder to folder in SkyDrive, and do folder-management tasks such as renaming, deleting, and moving folders.

A word about organizing your folders

Before you create a folder in SkyDrive, give a moment's thought to how to organize the folders you will create. Handling and managing folders in SkyDrive is considerably more difficult than handling and managing folders in an application such as Windows Explorer, where you can expand the folder tree and see how folders branch out from one another. In the SkyDrive window, you can see the contents of only one folder at a time.

Unless you come up with a scheme for organizing folders, you may have a hard time finding them. Plan ahead and organize your folders by project, by date, or by some other method. This way, when you need to open, delete, copy, or move a folder, you'll know where to find it.

Creating a folder

How you create a folder depends on whether you create a top-level folder or a subfolder of another folder. When you create a top-level folder, you are asked about folder permissions and given the opportunity to upload files to the folder. These pages explain how to create top-level folders and subfolders.

Creating a top-level folder

Follow these steps to create a top-level folder for storing files:

1. **Go to the SkyDrive window.**

   The previous section in this chapter explains how to open this window. (In brief: Click Windows Live on the Windows Live taskbar and choose SkyDrive.)

2. **Click the New button and choose Folder on the drop-down list, as shown in Figure 6-4.**

   The Create a Folder window opens.

3. **In the Name box, enter a descriptive name for the folder.**

4. **Click the Change link.**

   Options for sharing the folder and inviting others to visit it appear, as shown in Figure 6-4.

5. **Using the Share With slider, choose an option to make the folder public, shared, or private.**

   The Share With options matter if you intend to share and coauthor files in your new folder with other people. Chapter 7 explains the Share With settings in detail and how to change a folder's Share With settings.

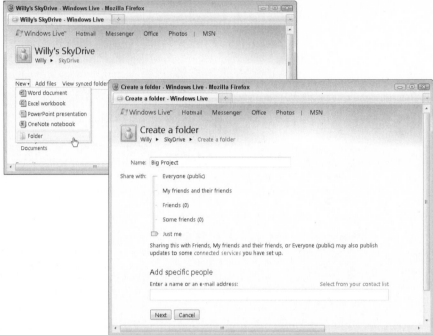

Figure 6-4:
Creating a
new top-
level folder.

For now, choose Just Me, the default setting, to create a private folder that only you can open. You can change Share With settings later (as Chapter 7 explains in minute detail).

6. Click the Next button.

The Add Documents window appears in case you want to upload files from your computer to the new folder. See "Uploading files to a folder on SkyDrive," later in this chapter, if you want to upload files.

7. Return to the SkyDrive window (click Windows Live and choose SkyDrive on the drop-down list).

Your new folder appears in the SkyDrive window. Congratulations, you just created a new top-level folder.

Creating a subfolder inside another folder

A *subfolder* is a folder inside another folder. Create a subfolder by starting inside a folder you already created or by starting inside the default My Documents that SkyDrive created for you. A subfolder inherits Share With permissions from its parent folder. This is why, when you create a subfolder, you aren't asked to choose a Share With setting for sharing files in the folder with others.

Follow these steps to create a subfolder:

1. **Open the folder that your new folder will go inside.**

   To open a folder, click its name. The next topic in this chapter describes how to navigate from folder to folder.

2. **Click the New button and choose Folder on the drop-down list.**

   You see the Create a New Folder window.

3. **In the Name box, enter a name for the folder.**

4. **Click the Create Folder button.**

   If you want to upload files from your computer to the subfolder you created, see "Uploading files to a folder on SkyDrive," later in this chapter.

Going from folder to folder in SkyDrive

After you accumulate a few folders on SkyDrive, getting to the folder you want to open can be an arduous, interminable journey. To help you on your way, SkyDrive offers different techniques for going to a folder:

✔ **The drill-down method:** Starting in the SkyDrive window (move the pointer over the Windows Live link and choose SkyDrive), click a top-level folder to display its subfolders. If necessary, keep drilling down this way until you reach the folder you want to open.

✔ **The Office link method:** On the Windows Live taskbar, move the pointer over the Office link and choose Recent Documents or Your Documents on the drop-down list, as shown in Figure 6-5. The Office window opens. This window is a convenient entré into the folders on SkyDrive:

   • *Recent Documents:* Lists documents you recently opened as well as, on the left side of the window, your top-level folders organized under the headings "Personal" and "Shared." Click the name of a folder to display its files and subfolders.

   • *Your Documents:* Lists all top-level folders under the headings "Personal" and "Shared." Click the name of a folder to display its files and subfolders.

✔ **The SkyDrive navigation bar method:** The *SkyDrive navigation bar* — located below the folder name — lists the path to the folder that is currently open. To backtrack, click the name of a folder on the path, as shown in Figure 6-6.

✔ **The browser button method:** Click the Back or Forward button in your browser to open a folder you previously opened.

Choose an Office menu option

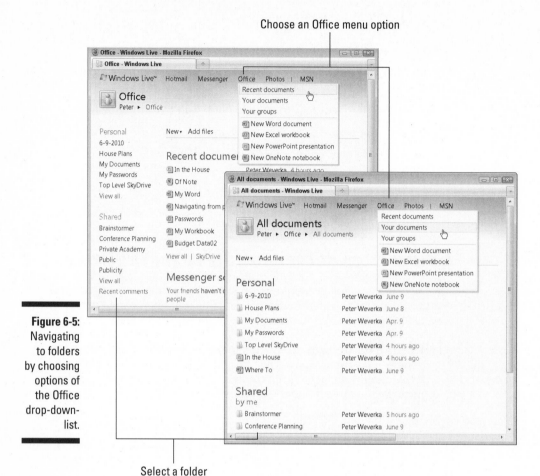

Figure 6-5:
Navigating
to folders
by choosing
options of
the Office
drop-down-
list.

Select a folder

SkyDrive navigation bar

Figure 6-6:
Click a
folder name
on the
SkyDrive
navigation
bar to open
a folder.

By bookmarking a folder in your browser, you can go straight to a folder without having to navigate to it in Windows Live. After you choose the bookmark (and enter your Windows Live ID and password if you haven't yet signed in to Windows Live), the folder opens. Chapter 3 explains how to bookmark folders and files in the Firefox, Internet Explorer, and Safari browsers.

Examining a folder's contents

To get a better look at what's inside a folder, take advantage of the View and Sort By options in the Folder window:

- **View:** Click the View link and choose Icons, Details, or Thumbnails on the drop-down list. In Details view, you can see who edited files, when files were last edited, and whether comments were written about the file.

- **Sort By:** Click the Sort By link and choose Name, Date, Size, or Type to arrange folders and files in different ways in the Folder window.

Deleting, moving, and renaming folders

To delete, move, or rename a folder, start by opening it. Then, in the Folder window, use these techniques:

- **Moving a folder:** Click the More link and choose Move on the drop-down list. You see a list of your folders on SkyDrive. Select a folder and then choose Move This Folder Into command. You can move only subfolders, not top-level folders.

- **Deleting a folder:** Click the More link and choose Delete on the drop-down list. Then click OK in the confirmation dialog box to delete the folder and all its contents.

- **Renaming a folder:** Click the More link and choose Rename on the drop-down list. Then enter a name in the New Name text box and click the Save button. You can't rename the My Documents folder.

You can't rename or delete a folder if it belongs to someone else and you don't have the right permissions. For more information about permissions, see Chapter 7.

Think twice about renaming, moving, and deleting folders that you share with coworkers. A coworker who tries to open a shared folder that was renamed, moved, or deleted sees the "missing item" message shown in Figure 6-7. After you rename or move a folder you share with others, you likely have to reissue an invitation to your coworkers to share it. Chapter 7 explains how to share folders with others and send out invitations to share folders.

Linking Windows Live IDs

People with multiple personalities who have more than one Windows Live ID can access their different IDs without having to log in to each one. By *linking* Windows Live IDs, you can log in once and switch back and forth between different IDs without entering an ID name and password each time.

Follow these steps to link Windows Live IDs:

1. **Click your username (located in the upper-right corner of the screen) and Options on the drop-down list.**

2. **In the Options window, click the Linked IDs link.**

   The Manage Linked IDs window opens. If your ID is linked to other IDs, they are listed here.

3. **Click the Add Linked ID link.**

4. **Enter the password of the ID you are currently in, enter your other Windows Live ID, enter your other ID's password, and click the Link button.**

To log in with a second ID, click your username in the upper-right corner of the screen and choose the other ID's name on the drop-down list.

To "unlink" an ID, return to the Manage Linked IDs window and click the Unlink link beside the name of the ID that you no longer want your current ID to be linked to.

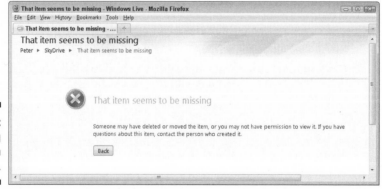

Figure 6-7:
The missing
item
message.

Creating an Office File in SkyDrive

I'm happy to report that creating an Office file — a Word, Excel, PowerPoint, or OneNote file — in SkyDrive is quite easy. Follow these steps to create an Office file with an Office Web App:

1. **Open the folder where you want to store the file.**

   Earlier in this chapter, "Going from folder to folder in SkyDrive" explains how to open folders and subfolders.

   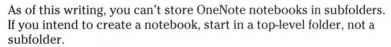

   As of this writing, you can't store OneNote notebooks in subfolders. If you intend to create a notebook, start in a top-level folder, not a subfolder.

2. **Click the New button or move the pointer over the Office link on the Windows Live taskbar.**

3. **Choose an option on the drop-down list, as shown in Figure 6-8.**

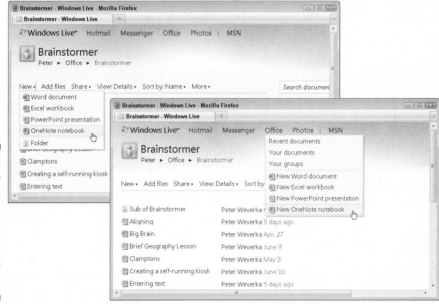

Figure 6-8: Click New or Office to create a document, workbook, presentation, or notebook.

Choose among these options:

- *Word Document:* Create a letter, report, or other document. Part II (Chapters 9 and 10) describes the Word Web App.

- *Excel Workbook:* Create a worksheet for crunching numbers. Part III (Chapters 11 and 12) explains the Excel Web App.

- *PowerPoint Presentation:* Create a presentation for showing slides to an audience. Part IV (Chapters 13 and 14) looks into the PowerPoint Web App.

- *OneNote Notebook:* Create a notebook for storing and organizing notes. Part V (Chapters 15 and 16) explains the OneNote Web App.

The File window opens.

4. **In the Name text box, enter a name for your document, workbook, presentation, or notebook.**

5. **Click the Save button.**

Your new Office file opens.

Opening and Editing Office Files Stored on SkyDrive

Opening a Word, Excel, PowerPoint, or OneNote file that you store on SkyDrive is a tad different from opening an Office file stored on a computer. You have the choice of viewing a file before you open it, opening it in your browser, or opening it in an Office 2010 program. These pages explain how to open an Office file and what's what in the File window, the window you can open to preview your file.

Opening and editing a file in an Office Web App

Follow these steps to open and edit a Word, Excel, PowerPoint, or OneNote file in an Office Web App:

1. **In SkyDrive, open the folder where the file is stored.**

   Earlier in this chapter, "Going from folder to folder in SkyDrive" explains how to open folders and subfolders.

   If you recently edited the file you want to open, you can get to it quickly by moving the pointer over Office on the Windows Live taskbar and choosing Recent Documents on the drop-down list (refer to Figure 6-5). You see, in Detail view, a list of files you recently edited. Move the pointer over a filename and choose the Edit in Browser link to open the file right away in an Office Web App.

2. **Click the name of the file you want to open and edit.**

    As shown in Figure 6-9, the file opens in a preview window if you clicked a Word, Excel, or PowerPoint file. (OneNote files open right away without appearing first in the preview window.)

    You can't edit the file this way, but you can scroll through it to see what it's all about. If this isn't the file you want to edit, click the Close button (the *X* on the right side of the window) or go to the File tab and choose Close.

    You can bypass the preview window and open a file right away in an Office Web App by switching to Details view in the folder window and selecting the Edit in Browser link beside a file's name.

3. **Click the Edit in Browser button to open the file in an Office Web App and begin editing.**

    Elsewhere in this book, I describe how to edit Word Web App files (Part III), Excel Web App files (Part IV), PowerPoint Web App files (Part V), and OneNote Web App files (Part VI).

    Whether you can edit a file that is kept in a folder that you share with others depends on whether you are the owner of the file and the permissions you have been given for opening the file. Chapter 7 explains how to handle shared files.

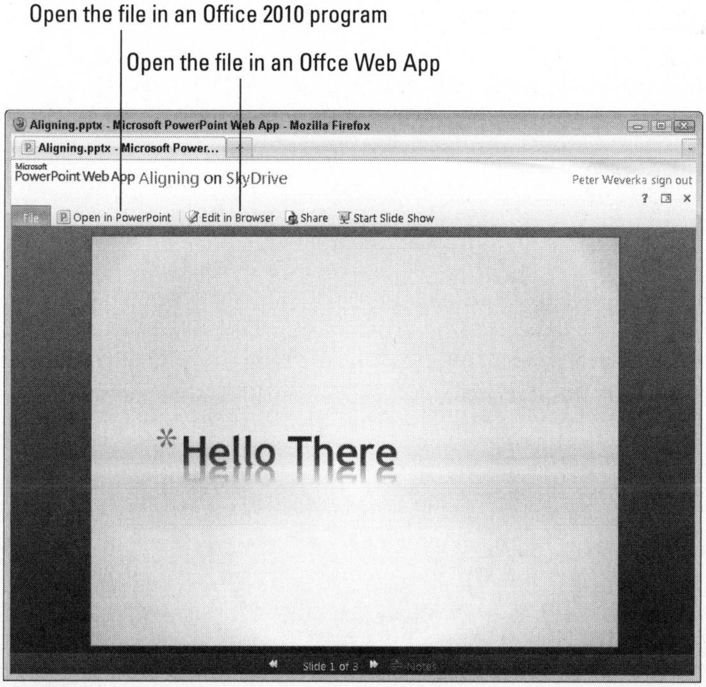

Open the file in an Office 2010 program

Open the file in an Offce Web App

Figure 6-9:
You can examine the file in a preview window before opening it.

Retrieving an earlier version of a file

For your convenience and to rescue you when you overwork a file, SkyDrive keeps copies of earlier versions of files and gives you the opportunity to revisit an earlier version and restore it as the official version if you so desire. Each time you close a file, a new version is created and kept on hand.

To examine older versions of a file, click the file's icon to open it in the preview window, and then go to the File tab and choose Properties.

You land in the Properties window. From there, click the Version History link. The preview window opens the latest version of the file and lists older versions.

To examine an older version of a file, click its date and time designation on the left side of the window. The older version appears in the preview window. To restore an older version and make it once again the official version of the file, click the Restore link.

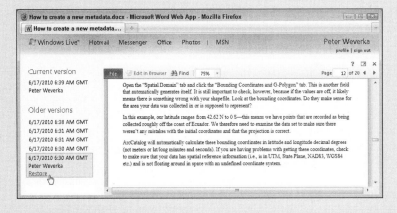

When you finish editing a file, click the Close button (the *X* on the right side of the window) or visit the File tab and choose Close.

To open more than one file at the same time, rather than click a file's icon, right-click it and choose Open Link in New Window or Open Link in New Tab. A new window or tab opens. (In Internet Explorer, the commands are called Open in New Window and Open in New tab.)

Opening and editing a SkyDrive file in an Office 2010 program

As anybody who has spent more than five minutes with an Office Web App knows, the Office Web Apps don't offer near as many features and doo-dads as their Office 2010 counterparts. If you want to create or edit a chart in Word

Web App, for example, you're out of luck because Word Web App doesn't provide charts. You can, however, open a Word file you keep on SkyDrive in Word 2010 and edit the file with your Word 2010 software.

If you get frustrated editing a file with the measly number of commands available in an Office Web App, you can open the file in Word 2010, Excel 2010, PowerPoint 2010, or OneNote 2010 and edit it there by using the techniques I explain forthwith.

Opening a file on SkyDrive in an Office 2010 program

Starting in an Office Web App, you can open an Office file from the preview window or the Home tab:

1. **Click the Open In button.**

   This button is found in the preview window and on the Home tab in all four Office Web Apps. The button is named after the Office Web App you are working in. For example, in PowerPoint Web App, the button is called Open In PowerPoint

   - *Preview window:* Click the Open In button (refer to Figure 6-9). To open a file's preview window, click the file's name in a folder. See "Opening and editing a file in an Office Web App," earlier in this chapter

   - *Office Web App:* On the Home tab, click the Open In button, or visit the File tab and choose Open In.

   The Open Document dialog box appears.

2. **Click OK to affirm that, although the file is located on the Internet, opening it is okay.**

   Word, Excel, PowerPoint, or OneNote 2010 opens on your computer and you see the Connecting To dialog box.

3. **Enter your Windows Live ID and password; then click OK.**

   Word, Excel, PowerPoint, or OneNote opens and you see your file in an Office 2010 program. Depending on your Windows settings, you may have to click the Enable Editing button before you can start editing the file.

Although the file looks as though it is located on your computer, the file is actually on a Web server at SkyDrive. All editorial changes you make are saved to the file on the Web server, not to a file located on your computer's hard drive.

Notice that the Save button (in Word, Excel, and PowerPoint) looks a little different when you open an Office file that is stored on SkyDrive in an Office 2010 program. (OneNote doesn't have a Save button.) The Save button looks different to remind you that your editorial changes, when you save your file, are sent to a server on the Internet at SkyDrive, and that changes made by others are downloaded to your file. When you click the Save button, notice the message on the status bar that says "Uploading to Server."

Editing an Office file on SkyDrive with an Office 2010 program has one big disadvantage if the file is being shared. Editing the file in Word, Excel, and PowerPoint 2010 (not OneNote) shuts out all others from editing the file at the same time. Chapter 7 explains how to get around the problem of being locked out of a file you want to edit.

Saving a file from Office 2010 to SkyDrive

Sharing is caring, and you can save a Word, Excel, PowerPoint, or OneNote 2010 file on your computer to a SkyDrive folder starting in Word, Excel, PowerPoint, or OneNote and thereby share your file with other people. Others who have access to the folder on SkyDrive can open the file in an Office Web App or in an Office 2010 program (if Office 2010 is installed on their computers).

Follow these steps to save a file to a SkyDrive folder by starting in an Office 2010 program:

1. **In Word, Excel, PowerPoint, or OneNote 2010, open the file you want to share with others on a SkyDrive folder.**

2. **On the File tab, choose Save & Send.**

   The Save & Send window opens.

3. **Choose Save to Web.**

   Save to Windows Live options appear.

4. **Click the Sign In button, enter your Windows Live ID and password, and click OK.**

   As shown in Figure 6-10, a list of folders you keep on Windows Live appears in the Save & Send window.

5. **Select the folder where you want to store the Office 2010 file.**

6. **Click the Save As button.**

   The Save As dialog box appears. In the top of the dialog box, notice the path to the folder where the file will be saved. The path shows a Web address followed by the name of the folder you selected in Step 4. You are about to save the file to a SkyDrive folder on the Internet.

Figure 6-10:
The Save
& Send
window
with options
for saving
an Office
2010 file to
a SkyDrive
folder.

 7. **Click the Save button.**

Although the file appears in Excel, Word, PowerPoint, or OneNote 2010
and looks to be stored on your computer, it is stored in a SkyDrive folder.
The Save button looks a little different because clicking the Save button
saves your editorial changes to a SkyDrive folder, not to a folder on your
computer's hard disk. In fact, when you click the Save button, a message
on the status bar says "Uploading to Server."

When you save an Excel, Word, PowerPoint, or OneNote 2010 file on
SkyDrive, you create a second copy of the file. The original remains on your
computer. Try this experiment: After saving an Office 2010 file to SkyDrive,
go to the File tab and click Recent. You see a list of files you recently opened.
Notice that the name of the file you saved to SkyDrive appears twice, once at
a Web address on SkyDrive and once at a folder on your computer.

Later in this chapter, "Uploading files to a folder on SkyDrive" explains
another way to place an Office 2010 file from your computer on SkyDrive —
by uploading it.

Working on files that originated in Office 2010

As "Saving a file from Office 2010 to SkyDrive" and "Uploading files to a folder on SkyDrive" explain, you can put Office 2010 files into a SkyDrive folder. But whether you can open these files in an Office Web App is another matter.

The Office Web Apps don't have all the editing capabilities of their Office 2010 namesakes. When you open a document that originated in Word 2010 in the Word Web App, for example, you can't edit the parts of the file that the Word Web App can't handle. For example, you can't draw shapes. You can see shapes that originated in the Word 2010 file, but you can't alter the shapes or change their positions in the Office Web App.

What's more, a handful of sophisticated Office 2010 features cause the Office Web Apps to gasp and wheeze. If you try to view a PowerPoint presentation with comments in the PowerPoint Web App, for example, a message tells you that "this presentation contains reviewing comments that cannot be viewed." Items that are beyond the ability of the Office Web Apps to handle remain in the file — you just can't do anything to them.

Managing Your Files on SkyDrive

SkyDrive is first and foremost a means of organizing and managing files. You can take advantage of commands in SkyDrive to upload files, download files from SkyDrive to your computer, and delete, rename, move, and copy files. Better keep reading.

Making use of the Properties window

As shown in Figure 6-11, the Properties window is the place to go when you want to do this, that, or the other thing to a file. The window offers commands for downloading, editing, deleting, moving, renaming, and copying files.

Opening the Properties window

To open a file's Properties window, use one of these techniques:

- ✔ In an Office Web App or the preview window (the window you see when you click a file's name in a folder), go to the File tab and choose Properties.

Do file-related tasks   Open a different file in the folder

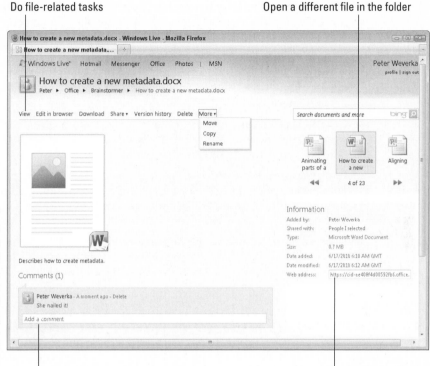

Figure 6-11:
The
Properties
window,
where you
do all things
relating to a
file.

Read and write a description and comments   Get the Web address

✔ In a folder in Details view (click the View link and choose Details on the drop-down list), move the pointer over a file, click the file's More link, and choose Properties on the drop-down list.

✔ In the Office window (on the Windows Live taskbar, move the pointer over the Office link and choose Recent Documents), move the pointer over a file, click the file's More link, and choose Properties on the drop-down list.

Properties window activities

Take heed of the activities you can do in the Properties window:

✔ **View or edit the file:** On the taskbar, click View to examine the file in the preview window; click Edit in Browser to open the file in an Office Web App.

✔ **Do other file-related tasks:** Visit the File window taskbar to download, share, delete, move, copy, or rename a file.

✔ **Read and enter a description and comments:** Especially if you share the file with others, enter a description of the file so that others know what it is. You can also enter and read comments about the file.

✔ **Examine a different file in the folder:** Click the Scroll Back or Scroll Forward button in the upper-right corner of the window to see the names of other files in the folder. Click a file's icon to open it in the Properties window.

✔ **Get file information:** Glance at the right side of the File window to see who created the file, whether it is shared, and other information. (You may have to scroll down to see this information.)

✔ **Copy the file's Web address:** One way to share a file is to copy its Web address and send it to other people. Under Information, you can copy the file's address from the Web Address box. For more information, see Chapter 7.

✔ **Copy code for embedding:** You can also share a public file by embedding code on a Web page so that others can click a hyperlink and go to the file on SkyDrive. See Chapter 7 for more information.

Uploading files to a folder on SkyDrive

A file must be smaller than 50MB to upload it to a folder on SkyDrive. Follow these steps to upload files from your computer to a folder you keep on SkyDrive:

1. **On SkyDrive, open the folder where you want to store the files.**

2. **Click the Add Files link.**

   The Add Documents window appears.

3. **Upload files by dragging and dropping or selecting files in the Open dialog box.**

   Choose which technique suits you best:

   • *Dragging and dropping:* Open Windows Explorer, drag its window to the right side of the screen, locate the files you want to upload, and select them. You can select more than one file. Then drag and drop the files into the Add Documents window.

   • *Choosing files in the Open dialog box:* Click the Select Documents from Your Computer link. The Open dialog box appears. Select files and click the Open button.

   The Add Documents window lists the files you want to upload.

4. **Click the Continue button.**

   The file or files are uploaded to the folder you selected in SkyDrive.

You can also upload an Excel 2010, Word 2010, PowerPoint 2010, or OneNote 2010 file by opening it in an Office 2010 program and saving it to a SkyDrive folder. See "Saving a file from Office 2010 to SkyDrive," earlier in this chapter.

Downloading files from SkyDrive to your computer

SkyDrive gives you the choice of downloading files one at a time or downloading all the files in a folder in a zip file.

- **Downloading a file:** In the file's Properties window, click the Download link. You see the standard dialog box for downloading files from the Internet. Choose to open or save the file after you download it and click OK. (Earlier in this chapter, "Making use of the Properties window" explains how to open the Properties window.)

- **Downloading all the files in a folder:** Open a folder and click the Download as .Zip File link. In the standard dialog box for downloading files, click the Save File option button and click OK.

Moving, copying, renaming, and deleting files

Starting in a Properties window (see "Making use of the Properties window" and refer to Figure 6-11, earlier in this chapter), use these techniques to move, copy, rename, or delete a file:

- **Moving a file:** Click the More link and choose Move on the drop-down list. You see a window that lists your SkyDrive folders. Select a folder name and then choose the Move This File command.

- **Copying a file:** Click the More link and choose Copy on the drop-down list. Then select a folder name and choose the Copy This File command.

- **Renaming a file:** Click the More link and choose Rename on the drop-down list. Then enter a name in the New Name text box and click the Save button.

- **Deleting a file:** Click the Delete link and then click OK in the confirmation dialog box.

Chapter 7

Collaborating, or Coauthoring, with Others on SkyDrive

*O*ne of the great advantages of SkyDrive is being able to share and work on Office files with other people. Microsoft uses the term *coauthoring* to describe what happens when more than one person works on a file that is stored on SkyDrive. As long as all parties have Windows Live accounts and all have permission to edit a file, they can edit it.

This chapter explores ways to share folders on Windows Live. It shows you how to determine who does and doesn't get into a folder you keep on SkyDrive and how to invite others to coauthor files in your folders. It describes what coauthoring a file means and what to do when you get locked out of a file and can't edit it.

Ways of Sharing Folders

This is the first thing you need to know if you want to share and coauthor files with others on SkyDrive: Only people who have signed up with Windows Live can edit files.

Here is the second thing you need to know: The owner of a folder decides whether the folder is public, shared, or private, and for anyone besides the owner to work on a file, it must be in a public or shared folder.

Here is the third thing: The owner of a folder can choose between different ways of sharing a folder and files inside it:

- ✔ **Sharing with friends on Windows Live:** The owner makes the folder available to his friends on Windows Live. These friends can go to the owner's profile page, where they see all public and shared folders. Friends can open these folders, view the files, and if they have permission, edit the files. (See "Making Friends on Windows Live," the next topic in this chapter, for information about making friends.)

- ✔ **Sending out e-mail invitations:** The owner decides he doesn't want to fool around with making friends on Windows Live. When he wants to share a file, he sends an e-mail invitation to visit the folder. A guest who gets the e-mail can go to the owner's SkyDrive page, where he sees the owner's public folders and the shared folder he was invited to open. The guest can open the owner's public folders or shared folder and see a file's contents. If the guest wants to edit a file, he must sign in with Windows Live. (See "Sending out e-mail invitations," later in this chapter.)

- ✔ **Posting hyperlinks on the Internet:** The owner creates a hyperlink to a folder and posts it on a Web page or blog. Anyone who clicks the hyperlink goes, after signing in to Windows Live, to the owner's SkyDrive page, where all public folders and the shared folder are visible. The guest can open all public folders and open the shared folder targeted by the hyperlink, if the guest has permission to enter the shared folder. (See "Posting hyperlinks on the Internet," later in this chapter.)

Kind of confusing, isn't it? And it's not as though you have to choose one of the methods described here. You can use a combination of folder-sharing methods or use all three methods. Get together with the people with whom you will share folders and decide which folder-sharing method or methods are best for you.

Making Friends on Windows Live

As the previous topic in this chapter, "Ways of Sharing Folders," explains, one way to share folders on SkyDrive is to rely on friends you make in Windows Live. Using this method, your circle of Windows Live friends can visit your profile page, open public and shared folders if you give them permission to do so, and open the files in those folders.

If you want to use the friends method of sharing files, you need to know what a Windows Live friend is, how to choose your friends, and how to reply when someone asks to be your friend. Heave a deep sigh and keep reading.

Friend invitations on Windows Live are sent with Hotmail, the Windows Live e-mail service. If you want to share folders and files with friends, your friends on Windows Live must sign up to use Hotmail. Moreover, you must get their e-mail addresses so that you can send them invitations to be your friend.

The two types of friends

It used to be that a friend in need was a friend indeed, but Facebook, MySpace, and now Windows Live have changed the meaning of "friend." Now a friend is something less intimate. A friend is somebody you designate as your friend on a social networking Website on the Internet.

To muddy the waters even further as to what a friend is, Windows Live makes a distinction between two types of friends:

✔ **Limited-access friend:** This friend can't send you instant messages, see your photo files, or get your contact information, but this friend can get information about your activities on Windows Live. As shown in Figure 7-1, when someone on Windows Live asks to be your friend, you can select the Limit the Access This Person Has to My Stuff and My Info check box to make your newfound friend a limited-access friend.

✔ **Friend:** This friend has full privileges to your Windows Live information and will be your friend till your dying day, through thick or thin.

For the purposes of sharing files, the two types of friends matter in that you can admit friends into a shared folder but keep limited-access friends out of it, as "Establishing a Folder's Share With Permissions" explains later in this chapter.

Fielding an invitation to be someone's friend

As shown at the top of Figure 7-1, invitations to be friends with someone else arrive in the form of e-mail messages. (To make friends on Windows Live, you must sign up for Hotmail, the Windows Live e-mail service.) To open the Inbox, click the Hotmail link on the Windows Live taskbar. Accept or decline the invitation by following these steps:

1. **Click the "Added you as a friend on Windows Live" message to open it.**

   The message window opens.

2. **Click the Add As Friend button.**

   Click this button whether or not you want a new friend. A profile window for the person who sent the invitation appears, as shown at the bottom of Figure 7-1. You can click the Details button in this window to discover more about the person who wants to be your friend.

3. **Click the Accept button to accept the invitation, click the No Thanks button to decline it, or delete the message to ignore the invitation altogether.**

   To be a limited-access friend, select the Limit the Access This Person Has to My Stuff and My Info check box. The previous topic in this chapter, "The Two Types of Friends," explains what a limited-access friend is.

And if you don't want to be friends with someone anymore? Click the Profile link to go to your Profile page, and click the Your Friends link to see a list of your friends. Then select your friend's name and click the Delete link.

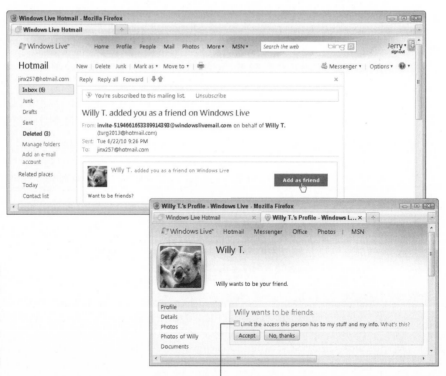

Figure 7-1:
Befriending someone on Windows Live.

Click Limit the Access to This Person to make yourself a limited-access friend

Inviting someone to be your friend

To add a friend, get his or her Hotmail e-mail address and send an invitation by following these steps:

1. **Click the Profile link.**

   This link is located in the upper-right corner of the screen below your name. You land on your Profile page.

2. **Click the Your Friends link to see your list of friends.**

3. **On the left side of the window, under "Your Network," click the Add People link.**

4. **Enter your prospective friend's e-mail address in the text box and click the Next button.**

5. **In the window that appears, jot down a note to your prospective friend.**

6. **Click the Invite button.**

   If your friend accepts your invitation, you are alerted by e-mail in your Hotmail account.

To see a list of your friends, click the Profile link (located below your name in the upper-right corner of the window). The names of your friends appear on the right side of your Profile page. You can click a friend's name to go to his or her Profile page.

Understanding the Folder Types

Whether coworkers can open a folder on SkyDrive, view its files, and edit its files depends on what kind of folder it is. In some types of folders, you can do tasks such as renaming and deleting files.

These pages explain the different types of folders. They also spell out which tasks you can do in private, public, shared, and linked folders. You need to know about folder types if you intend to collaborate with others on files that are stored in SkyDrive folders.

Types of folders

Table 7-1 describes the four types of folder — private, shared, public, and linked. Which Share With permission is assigned to a folder determines what kind of folder it is. Later in this chapter, "Establishing a Folder's Share With Permissions" explains how to assign a Share With permission to a folder.

Table 7-1	Types of SkyDrive Folders
Folder Type	**Description**
Private	Only the folder's owner — its creator — sees the folder on SkyDrive and can open the folder, view its files, and edit its files. The default My Documents folder is an example of a private folder.
	Store files in a private folder if you don't want anybody else to be able to see or open the files.
Shared	Friends on Windows Live and guests whom the owner invites to a shared folder can see the shared folder, open the folder to see the names of files inside it, open the files, and edit the files. Friends and guests can do other file-management tasks as well.
	Store files in a shared folder to collaborate with others online.
Public	Friends on Windows Live and guests whom the owner invites to his or her SkyDrive page can see and open all public folders and view the files in all public folders. However, guests can't edit files or do most file-management tasks.
	Don't store files in a public folder unless you don't care at all whether anybody sees them.
Linked	Anybody who has been invited to open the folder can open it, whether or not they have a Windows Live account. Invitations to open the folder are sent by e-mail. After opening the folder, a guest can see the names of files in the folder, open a file, and view the contents of a file. To edit a file after opening it, however, the guest must have a Windows Live account.
	Store files in a Linked folder to allow people who don't have Windows Live accounts to view files' contents.

Knowing what kind of folder you're dealing with

You can tell which type of folder you're dealing with by glancing at its icon in the SkyDrive widow. As shown in Figure 7-2, private folders have the lock symbol, shared folders the people symbol, public folders the globe symbol, and linked folders the e-mail symbol.

Figure 7-2:
Left to right:
A private
folder,
shared
folder, pub-
lic folder,
and linked
folder.

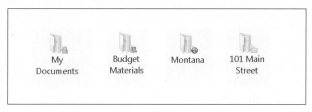

As Figure 7-3 shows, you can also tell whether a folder is private, shared, public, or linked by opening its Folder window (click a folder's icon to open its Folder window). Next to the words "Shared With," these words tell you what type of folder you're dealing with:

"Just Me"   Private folder

"Friends"   Shared folder

"Everyone (public)"   Public folder

"People with a link"   Linked folder

Figure 7-3:
In the Folder
window,
the "Shared
With" words
tell you
what type of
folder it is.

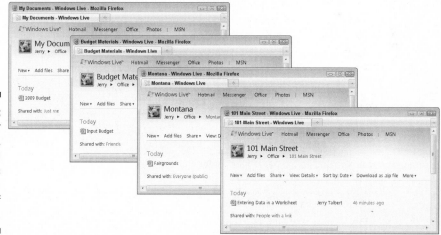

You can click the words next to "Shared With" to open the Permissions window and find out who owns the folder as well as who is sharing it (if anybody is allowed to share it).

Public and shared folder tasks

Table 7-2 lists tasks that Windows Live friends and guests of public folders and shared folders can do. The owner of a public folder or shared folder — the person who created the folder in the first place — can do all the tasks listed in Table 7-2.

Table 7-2	Tasks in Public and Shared Folders		
Task		**Public Folder**	**Shared Folder**
View Office files		Yes	Yes
Create new Office files		No	Yes
Edit an Office file with an Office Web App		No	Yes
Edit an Office file with an Office 2010 program (Word, Excel, PowerPoint, or OneNote)		No	Yes*
Establish permissions (decide who can view and edit files)		No	No
View permissions (see who owns and who can view and edit files)		Yes	Yes
Do folder-management tasks (delete, rename, and move the folder)		No	No
Do subfolder-management tasks (create, delete, rename, and move a subfolder within the folder)		No	Yes
Upload files to the folder		No	Yes
Download an individual file from the folder		Yes	Yes
Download all the files in the folder in a .ZIP file		No	Yes
Delete files		No	Yes
Rename files		No	Yes
Move files to a subfolder within the folder		No	Yes
Copy files to a subfolder within folder		No	Yes

*To edit an Office file stored on SkyDrive with Word 2010, Excel 2010, PowerPoint 2010, or OneNote 2010, that program must be installed on your computer.

Establishing a Folder's Share With Permissions

When you create a new top-level folder, SkyDrive asks you to choose a Share With option to determine whether the folder is private, shared, or public (see "Understanding the Folder Types," earlier in this chapter, for a description of private, shared, and public folders). At any time, however, you can follow these steps to establish or change a top-level folder's Share With permissions:

1. **Open the folder.**

   To open a folder window, click its name in the SkyDrive window.

2. **Click the Share With link and choose Edit Permissions on the drop-down list.**

   You see the Edit Permissions window, shown in Figure 7-4.

Shared folder

Public folder

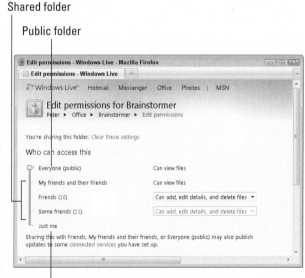

Figure 7-4:
Click a folder name on the SkyDrive Navigation bar to open a folder.

Private folder

3. **Drag the Who Can Access slider up or down to determine the folder's Share With permissions.**

Choose whether to make the folder public, shared, or private. Earlier in this chapter, "Types of folders" explains the three folder types.

- *Public folder:* Choose Everyone (Public).

- *Shared folder:* Choose one of the Friends settings:

    My Friends and Their Friends allows your Windows Live friends and friends you have in common with your Windows Live friends to access the folder.

    Friends allows all your Windows Live friends, including your limited-access friends, to access the folder. Earlier in this chapter, "The two types of friends" explains the difference between friends and limited-access friends.

    Some Friends allows your Windows Live friends but not friends with limited-access to access the folder.

- *Private folder:* Choose Just Me.

As "Ways of Sharing Folders" explains earlier in this chapter, you can share files on SkyDrive without having Windows Live friends. With this method, you invite colleagues by e-mail to share the files in a folder. If you want to use this method of sharing files, choose the Friends setting in the Edit Permissions window (and see "Sending out e-mail invitations," later in this chapter).

Be careful about making a folder public. Anyone who comes to your SkyDrive profile page or who is invited to share a folder with you can open any public folders you have and see their contents. Your public folders (and all their subfolders) are exposing themselves! I just thought you'd like to know.

4. **Optionally, if you choose Friends or Some Friends, you can open the drop-down list and choose Can View Files if you want your friends to be able to view the files in the folder but not edit them.**

    If you choose Can View Files, friends who visit your shared folder have the same privileges as visitors to a public folder. In other words, they have a narrower set of privileges. For example, they can't edit files in Office 2010 programs. Table 7-2, which appears earlier in this chapter, describes tasks you can do in public and private folders.

5. **Click the Save button.**

Share With permissions are assigned to top-level folders on SkyDrive. Subfolders inside these top-level folders inherit their permissions from their parent folders. For example, if a top-level folder called Planner is a shared folder, all subfolders that you or others create inside the Planner folder are shared folders as well.

Sharing on a Public or Shared Folder

Earlier in this chapter, "Ways of Sharing Folders" explains the different methods of sharing top-level folders on SkyDrive. You can create a circle of friends and share folders with them, bring others to a SkyDrive folder by invitation, or post hyperlinks that colleagues can click to get to a shared SkyDrive folder. All three techniques are explained forthwith.

Sharing with friends on Windows Live

Earlier in this chapter, "Making Friends on Windows Live" shows you how to invite someone on Windows Live to be your friend. It also explains how to field invitations from others who want to make friends with you. If a friend on Windows Live is sharing his or her folders, how do you get to your friend's folders? Good question. Follow these steps to navigate to a friend's folders:

1. **Click the Profile link to open your Profile page.**

   This link is located in the upper-right corner of the window. The right side of the Profile page lists your friends.

2. **Click the name of the friend who is sharing folders.**

   You land in your friend's Profile page, as shown at the top of Figure 7-5.

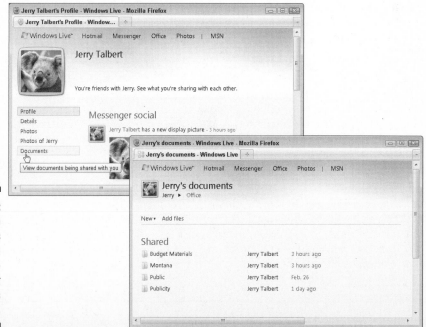

Figure 7-5: Click the Documents link to see a list of folders your friend is sharing.

3. **Click the Documents link (on the left side of the screen).**

   Folders that your friend is sharing appear in Details view in the Documents window, also shown in Figure 7-5.

4. **Click a folder name to open a folder.**

5. **Click a filename to open a file.**

   Whether you can edit as well as open a file in the folder depends on the Share With settings its owner, your friend, chose for the folder.

Sending out e-mail invitations

To share folders on Windows Live without making friends on the site, you can send out e-mail invitations to folders. The left side of Figure 7-6 shows an e-mail invitation to visit a SkyDrive folder. By clicking the View Folder button in the invitation, also shown in Figure 7-6, the recipient of the e-mail can go straight to a folder on SkyDrive. These invitations can be sent to people who are enrolled in Windows Live as well as people who aren't members of that exclusive club.

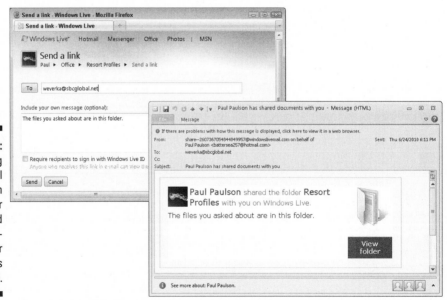

Figure 7-6: Composing an e-mail invitation to a folder (left), and the invitation after it arrives (right).

Follow these steps to send an e-mail invitation to someone to collaborate at a public or shared SkyDrive folder:

1. **Open the public or shared folder with the files that you want to share.**

2. **On the taskbar, click the Share link and choose Send a Link on the drop-down list.**

   The Send a Link window opens, as shown on the left side of Figure 7-6.

3. **Enter the e-mail address of the person you want to invite.**

   If you maintain a Contacts List at Windows Live, you can click the To button and select names from your Contacts List. To enter more than one address, separate the addresses with a colon or semicolon.

4. **If you want, enter a note to accompany the invitation.**

   I suggest telling recipients to bookmark the folder after they visit it the first time. Except by keeping the e-mail invitation on hand and clicking the View Folder button to visit the folder (refer to Figure 7-6), recipients won't be able to visit the folder without bookmarking it. By bookmarking the folder, they can select the bookmark in their browsers and go to the folder without having to reopen the e-mail message. Chapter 3 explains bookmarking.

5. **Optionally, select the Require Recipients to Sign In with Windows Live ID check box if you want to share this folder only with people who have a Windows Live account.**

   If you don't select the check box, guests can open the folder without first signing in to Windows Live. They can open and view files in the folder, but they can't edit the files unless they provide a Windows Live ID.

   If you select the check box, guests have to enter their Windows Live ID before they can see much less open the folder.

6. **Click the Send button.**

If you don't select the Require Recipients to Sign In with Windows Live ID check box, your folder becomes a linked folder. Anybody who has the link can see its files. Linked folders are marked with the e-mail icon (see "Understanding the Folder Types," earlier in this chapter, for a detailed explanation of linked folders). If you prefer that your linked folder be another kind of folder, open the folder, click the Share With Link on the toolbar, and choose Edit Permissions on the drop-down list to go to the Edit Permissions page. Then deselect the Don't Require Sign-In to View This Folder check box.

Posting hyperlinks on the Internet

Yet another way to attract people to a SkyDrive folder with files you want to share is to obtain the folder's hyperlink and either give the hyperlink to other people or make it part of a Web page by pasting it into the Web page's HTML code.

Obtaining a folder's URL link

To direct guests to a public or shared folder, you can obtain the folder's Web address, copy it, and send it to guests or use it to create a hyperlink. Guests who follow the link go to the folder. Follow these steps to obtain the Web address of a public or shared folder:

1. **Open the folder with the files you want to share.**

2. **In the Folder window, click the Share link on the toolbar and choose Get a Link on the drop-down list.**

   The Get a Link window opens, as shown in Figure 7-7. It offers two hyperlinks if your folder is shared (or one if it is private).

Figure 7-7: Copy a URL from this window to create a hyperlink.

People who click the first hyperlink have to enter their Windows Live ID to view the folder you want to share.

People who click the second hyperlink (or the first and only link, if your folder is public) can open the folder without providing a Windows Live ID, but they can only view the files, not edit them. (Click the Create Link button to create the second hyperlink.)

Your folder becomes a linked folder when you create a hyperlink to a Public folder or click the Create Link button to create a hyperlink to a shared folder such that people can visit the folder without entering a Windows Live ID. Anyone who has its hyperlink can visit a linked folder (earlier in this chapter, "Understanding the Folder Types" describes linked folders). To turn a linked folder into another kind of folder, open the folder, click the Share With Link on the toolbar, choose Edit Permissions on the drop-down list, and deselect the Don't Require Sign-In to View This Folder check box on the Edit Permissions page.

3. **Click in a Web Address box to select its hyperlink.**

   The text in the box is highlighted.

4. **Right-click and choose Copy on the shortcut menu that appears.**

   The hyperlink is copied to the Clipboard. Now you can paste the address in an e-mail message or use it to create a hyperlink that directs guests to the folder.

5. **Click the Done button.**

Obtaining HTML code for a public folder hyperlink icon

If you know your way around HTML codes, you can obtain code that creates a hyperlink icon that directs users to a public folder, and you can embed the code in a Web page or blog. Guests can click the hyperlink icon on the Web page or blog to open the public folder without having to enter a Windows Live ID. The icon appears in the form of a folder icon that looks just like a folder icon in the SkyDrive window.

Follow these steps to obtain the HTML code:

1. **Open the public folder with the files you want to share.**

2. **In the Folder window, click the Share link and choose Embed on the drop-down list.**

   The Share window opens, as shown in Figure 7-8. The code you see in this window, after it is embedded in a Web page or blog, creates the icon hyperlink shown on the right side of the window.

3. **Click the code to select it.**

   The code is highlighted.

4. **Right-click and choose Copy on the shortcut menu that appears.**

   The HTML code is copied to the Clipboard. Now you can paste the code in a Web page or blog.

5. Click the Done button.

You return to the Folder window.

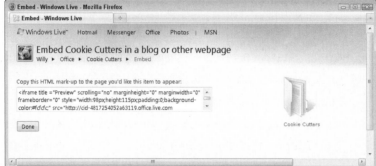

Figure 7-8:
The HTML
code (left)
creates the
icon hyper-
link (right).

Writing File Comments and Descriptions

If you share a file with others, be sure to enter comments and a description in the file's Properties window. Comments are the only way to record when changes were made and what the changes were. You owe it to the people with whom you share files to describe your editorial changes. While you're at it, you can also enter a description of the file in the Properties window to help you collaborators understand what the file is all about.

Figure 7-9 shows a Properties window with a description and comments. To open the Properties window, open the folder where the file is located and switch to Details view (click the View link and choose Details). Then move the pointer over the file's name, click More on the toolbar, and choose Properties.

Follow these instructions to enter a description or comments in the File window:

- **A description:** Click where the description or the words "Add a Description" are and enter a description. You can change a file's description at any time by clicking the description, which makes the description box appear, and entering a new description.

- **Comments:** Enter a comment in the Add a Comment box and click the Add button. Along with the commenter's name and the time of the comment, comments appear below the Comments box. You can delete a comment by clicking its Delete link.

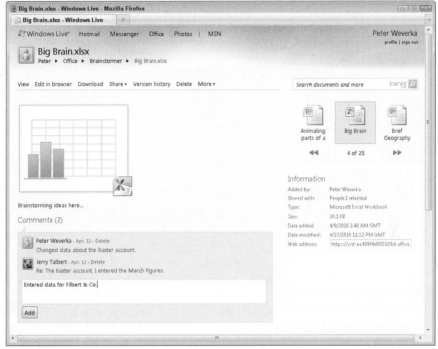

Figure 7-9:
The
Properties
window
offers
places for
writing a
description
and
comments.

Coauthoring Files Shared on SkyDrive

Microsoft uses the word *coauthor* to describe what happens when two people work on the same file simultaneously. Depending on which Web App you're working in, it isn't always possible to work on the same file with someone else. Sometimes you have to open the file in an Office 2010 program, not a Web App, to coauthor a file. These pages explain how you can coauthor files that are stored on SkyDrive and find out who else is coauthoring a file. You also discover what to do when you get locked out of a file.

The particulars of coauthoring Word documents are examined in Chapter 10, Excel worksheets in Chapter 12, PowerPoint presentations in Chapter 14, and OneNote notebooks in Chapter 16.

When you can and can't coauthor

Whether and how you coauthor files depends on the Office Web App you're working in. Sometimes you can't coauthor a file in an Office Web App and have to coauthor it in an Office 2010 program instead. Table 7-3 describes when you can and can't coauthor files in Office Web Apps and Office 2010 programs.

Table 7-3		Coauthoring Files Stored on SkyDrive	
User #1	*User #2*	*Description*	*Coauthoring?*
Word			
Word Web App	Word Web App	More than one person can't coauthor the same document in Word Web App.	No
Word Web App	Word 2010	One person in Word Web App and the other in Word 2010 can't coauthor the same document.	No
Word 2010	Word 2010	Two people both working in Word 2010 can coauthor the same document.	Yes
Excel			
Excel Web App	Excel Web App	More than one person can coauthor the same worksheet in PowerPoint Web App.	Yes
Excel Web App	Excel 2010	One person in Excel Web App and the other in Excel 2010 can't coauthor the same worksheet.	No
Excel 2010	Excel 2010	Two people, both editing in Excel 2010, can't coauthor the same worksheet.	No
PowerPoint			
PowerPoint Web App	PowerPoint Web App	Two people can't coauthor the same presentation in PowerPoint Web App.	No
PowerPoint Web App	PowerPoint 2010	One person in PowerPoint Web App and the other in PowerPoint 2010 can't coauthor the same presentation.	No
PowerPoint 2010	PowerPoint 2010	Two people, both working in PowerPoint 2010, can coauthor the same presentation.	Yes
OneNote			
OneNote Web App	OneNote Web App	More than one person can coauthor the same notebook in OneNote Web App.	Yes

User #1	User #2	Description	Coauthoring?
OneNote			
OneNote Web App	OneNote 2010	One person in OneNote Web App and the other in OneNote 2010 can coauthor the same notebook.	Yes
OneNote 2010	OneNote 2010	Two people, both working in OneNote, 2010 can coauthor the same workbook.	Yes

Finding out who your coauthors are

Except when you're working in OneNote Web App or OneNote 2010, it's easy to find out who is coauthoring a file with you. Follow these instructions to see who is coauthoring a file:

- ✔ **In Excel Web App:** The lower-right corner of the Office Web App window tells you how many people are coauthoring a file. As shown in Figure 7-10, you can click this notice to see a pop-up window that lists the Windows Live IDs of the other coauthors.

- ✔ **In Word 2010 and PowerPoint 2010:** On the status bar, the number next to the Authors icon tells you the number of coauthors. Click the Authors icon to see a pop-up list with coauthors' names, as shown in Figure 7-10. You can also go to the File tab, choose Info, and see your coauthors' names in the Information About window.

You can't find out who is currently editing a OneNote notebook, but you can get the names of people who wrote notes. In OneNote Web App, go to the View tab and choose Show Authors to see who authored notes. The name of its author appears beside each note. In OneNote 2010, authors' initials appear beside their notes. (Go to the View tab and click the Hide Authors button if you don't see authors' initials.) By moving the pointer over initials, you can read the author's name and when the note was written or edited last.

Getting locked out of a shared file

As Table 7-3 (earlier in this chapter) explains, you can coauthor files in Excel Web App and OneNote Web App, but not in Word Web App or PowerPoint Web App. And you can coauthor files in Word 2010, PowerPoint 2010, and OneNote 2010, but not Excel 2010.

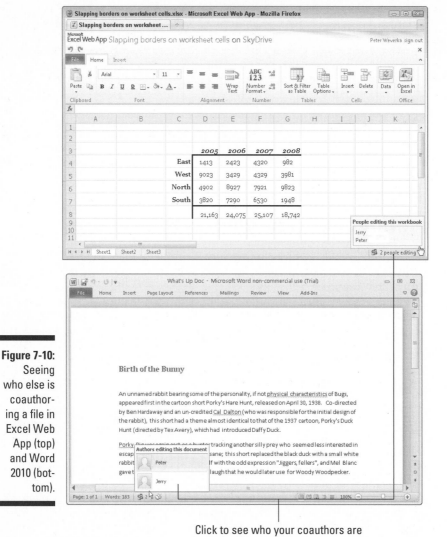

Figure 7-10: Seeing who else is coauthoring a file in Excel Web App (top) and Word 2010 (bottom).

Click to see who your coauthors are

Here are scenarios for what happens if you try to open a file on SkyDrive that is already open in an incompatible program:

> ✔ **Want to open in Word, Excel, or PowerPoint Web App; already open in Word, Excel, or PowerPoint 2010:** In this scenario, the file you want to open in an Office Web App is already open in an Office 2010 program. You see the message box at the top of Figure 7-11. All you can do is click

OK in the message box and come back later when your colleague finishes working on the file in Word, Excel, or PowerPoint 2010.

✔ **Want to open in Word 2010, Excel 2010, or PowerPoint 2010; already open in Word Web App, Excel Web App, or PowerPoint Web App:** In this scenario, the file you want to open in an Office 2010 program is already open in an Office Web App, and you can't open it in an Office 2010 program.

If the file is already open in your browser window and you try to open it by clicking the Open In button, you see the message box in the middle of Figure 7-11. All you can do is click OK and keep editing in your browser.

If you try to open the file in an Office 2010 from the get-go, you see the File In Use message box shown at the bottom of Figure 7-11. Choose an option and click OK:

- *View a Read-Only Copy:* The file opens in read-only mode. You can examine but not edit the file unless you click the Save As button and save it under a different name.

- *Save and Edit a Copy of the File:* The Save As dialog box opens so that you can save a copy of the file to work on. The copy is saved in the same SkyDrive folder as the original.

Figure 7-11: Locked out! What's a person to do?

Chapter 8

Sharing Files in SharePoint

SharePoint 2010 is a software product by which people who work together can collaborate and share information. Coworkers can share files, list tasks that need to be done, and discuss their work with one another. Think of SharePoint as a digital office. Rather than gather in the conference room to share files and ideas, you share them on a Web site. Coworkers in different states, countries, and continents — but not different planets — can work conveniently together.

If you're reading this in an office or cubicle, ask the person nearest you whether your company shares files via SharePoint. If your coworker answers "yes," ask your coworker whether the Office Web Apps are installed on the company's SharePoint site. If your coworker answers "yes" again, you're in luck because you can collaborate and even coauthor documents using either the Office programs or the Office Web Apps on your company's SharePoint site, which by coincidence happens to be the subject of this chapter.

Whether your SharePoint Web site offers the Office Web Apps depends on its administrator. Administrators have the option of making Office Web Apps available on a SharePoint Web site. Before trying your hand with the Office Web Apps, make sure they are available on your company's Web site.

Getting Equipped and Getting Started

To use SharePoint, you must have access to a SharePoint Web site similar to the one shown in Figure 8-1. These Web sites are maintained on a company intranet or on the Internet. Each Web site has an *administrator,* the person responsible for letting people into the Web site or barring the door, as well as for handing out passwords and giving permission to do different tasks.

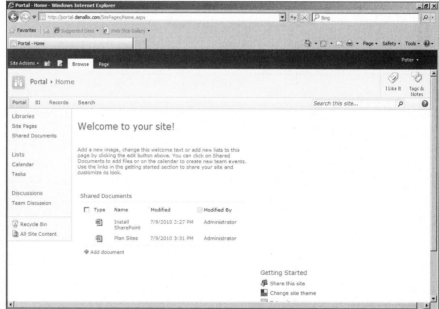

Figure 8-1:
The Home page of a SharePoint Web site.

To visit a SharePoint Web site and share files, you must first obtain the following from the administrator. Usually you get this information in an e-mail message.

> ✔ **The address of the SharePoint Services site:** The URL of the SharePoint site. Typically, the address is `http://companyweb` if the site is located on a company intranet. If it's located on the Internet, the address typically ends with `.com`, `.net`, or `.org`.

> ✔ **A username:** A name that identifies you to the Web site.

> ✔ **A password:** A password for gaining admission.

Often, the username and password that you use to log in to the SharePoint site are the very same username and password that you use to log in to your computer.

Visiting a SharePoint Web Site

If you received an e-mail invitation to join the SharePoint site, click the hyperlink in the e-mail to visit the site. Otherwise, follow these steps to gain entry to a SharePoint Web site:

1. **Open your Web browser.**

2. **Enter the address of the SharePoint site in the Address box and press Enter.**

3. **If a Connect To dialog box appears, enter your username and password and then click OK.**

Provided that you entered the correct username and password, you land on the Web site's Home page (refer to Figure 8-1).

Getting from Place to Place on the Web Site

Figure 8-2 shows a typical SharePoint Web site with a Navigation bar along the top of the site and, on the left side, links to libraries, lists, and discussions. SharePoint makes it pretty easy for administrators to customize these sites, so your SharePoint Web site may look different from this one.

Use these techniques to find the documents you want to work with:

- **Navigation bar:** Look for and open or select a menu or link on the Navigation bar.

- **Department URL:** Enter a URL that includes your department's name in your Web browser's address box. For example, if your company's portal is *www.mycompany.com*, and you work in the Human Resources Department, your department's URL could be *www.mycompany.com/HR/*.

- **Search box:** Enter a search term in the Search box and press Enter. You arrive at a Search results page, where you may be able to click a link to find the document you want to work on. The Search box is always available in the upper-right corner of the screen, no matter where you go in the SharePoint Web site.

Navigation bar

Libraries

Search box

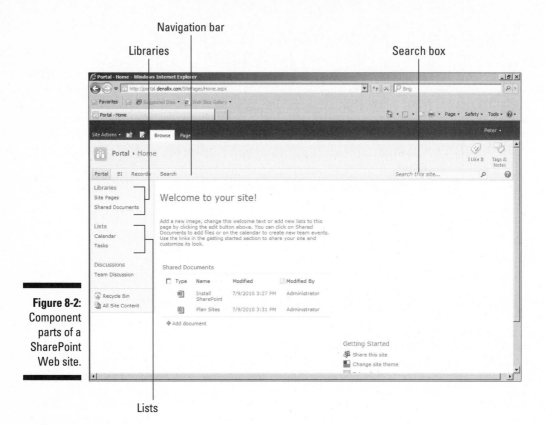

Lists

Figure 8-2:
Component
parts of a
SharePoint
Web site.

Uploading Documents to the SharePoint Library

Uploading means to send a file across an intranet or the Internet to a Web server so that others can view, open, and download it. Starting in the Shared Documents folder (or one of its subfolders), use one of these techniques to upload a file or files from your computer to a folder on the SharePoint site:

✔ **Uploading one file:** Click the Add Document link (located below the last document) or, on the Ribbon (click the Documents tab to see it), click the Upload Document button. In the Upload Document window, click the Browse button. You see the Choose File to Upload dialog box, which presents folders and files on your computer. Locate the file you want to upload, select it, and click the Open button. Click OK in the Upload Document window.

✔ **Uploading many files:** Open the drop-down list on the Upload Document button and choose Upload Multiple Documents. You go to the Upload Document window, as shown in Figure 8-3. Drag files into the Drag Files and Folders Here portion of the dialog box. You can also click the Browse For Files Instead link and choose the files to upload in a dialog box.

✔ **Uploading from inside an Office 2010 program:** On the File tab, choose Save & Send and then choose Save to SharePoint in the Save & Send window. Choose a location (or click the Browse for a Location button) and then click the Save As button. The Save As dialog box appears. If the Office program asks for them, enter your username and password. Then select Shared Documents in the dialog box and click the Save button.

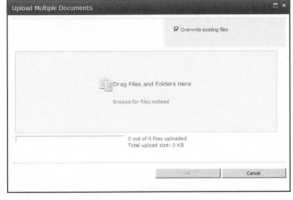

Figure 8-3:
You can upload several files by dragging their icons into this dialog box.

Opening Office Files in a SharePoint Site

To open an Office 2010 file from a SharePoint site, locate the document in the Document Library and open its drop-down list, as shown in Figure 8-4. Then choose one of these options:

✔ **View in Browser:** Opens the file in an Office Web App. You can view the file but not edit it (unless you click the Open In or Edit in Browser button).

✔ **Edit in Browser:** Opens the file in an Office Web App so that you can edit it.

✔ **Edit in Microsoft Word, Excel, PowerPoint, or OneNote:** Opens the file in Word 2010, Excel 2010, PowerPoint 2010, or OneNote 2010.

If you don't see the View in Browser or Edit in Browser options, your administrator hasn't installed the Office Web Apps on your company's SharePoint Web site.

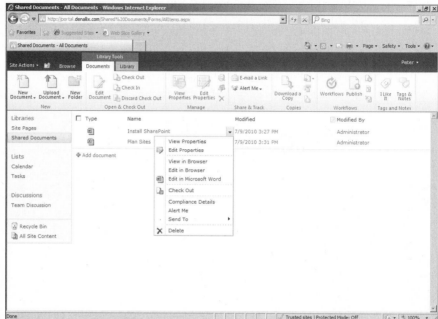

Coauthoring Files on a SharePoint Site

Microsoft uses the word *coauthor* to describe what happens when two or more people work on the same file at the same time. Working alongside others takes some getting used to. In the case of Excel worksheets and OneNote notebooks, words and numbers appear on-screen as if by magic. Who is entering those words or numbers? A colleague who is working right along with you on the file, that's who.

These pages look at whether more than one user can coauthor a file stored on a SharePoint site and how to tell who your coauthors are.

When you can and can't co-author

Some Office Web Apps are better than others in the matter of coauthoring files. Table 8-1 looks at whether and how two or more people can coauthor a file using the Office Web App and Office 2010 programs.

Table 8-1   Coauthoring Files Stored on a SharePoint Web Site

User #1	User #2	Description	Coauthoring?
Word			
Word Web App	Word Web App	Users can't coauthor the same document in Word Web App.	No
Word Web App	Word 2010	One person in Word Web App and the other in Word 2010 can't coauthor the same document.	No
Word 2010	Word 2010	Two people, both working in Word 2010, can coauthor the same document.	Yes
Excel			
Excel Web App	Excel Web App	Users can coauthor the same worksheet in PowerPoint Web App.	Yes
Excel Web App	Excel 2010	One person in Excel Web App and the other in Excel 2010 can't coauthor the same worksheet.	No
Excel 2010	Excel 2010	Two people, both editing in Excel 2010, can't coauthor the same worksheet.	No
PowerPoint			
PowerPoint Web App	PowerPoint Web App	Users can't coauthor the same presentation in PowerPoint Web App.	No
PowerPoint Web App	PowerPoint 2010	One person in PowerPoint Web App and the other in PowerPoint 2010 can't coauthor the same presentation.	No
PowerPoint 2010	PowerPoint 2010	Two people, both working in PowerPoint 2010, can coauthor the same presentation.	Yes
OneNote			
OneNote Web App	OneNote Web App	Users can coauthor the same notebook in OneNote Web App.	Yes
OneNote Web App	OneNote 2010	One person in OneNote Web App and the other in OneNote 2010 can coauthor the same notebook.	Yes
OneNote 2010	OneNote 2010	Two people, both working in OneNote 2010, can coauthor the same workbook.	Yes

If you try to open a file but it is checked out, you receive an error message like the one in Figure 8-5. You can tell when a document is checked out because its icon changes to indicate that it's currently checked out.

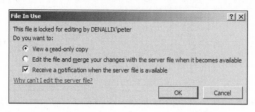

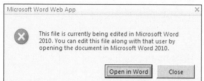

Figure 8-5:
This file is checked out.

Finding out who your collaborators are

No doubt you want to know who is coauthoring alongside you in Office Web Apps and Office 2010 programs. Follow these instructions to see who is coauthoring a file:

- ✔ **In Excel Web App:** Glance at the lower-right corner of the window to see a notice that tells you how many people are working on the file. By clicking the notice, you can see a pop-up message like the one in Figure 8-6 with the names of your coauthors.

- ✔ **In Word 2010 and PowerPoint 2010:** Look to the status bar to see how many people are editing the file. As shown in Figure 8-6, you can click the status bar notice to see a pop-up message with your collaborators' names.

In OneNote, you can find out who wrote or last edited a note, but you can't see who is coauthoring a file. On the View tab in OneNote Web App, click the Show Authors button to see who authored notes. You see author names next to notes. In OneNote 2010, only the authors' initials appear beside their notes, but by moving the pointer over initials, you can see the author's name in a pop-up box. (Go to the View tab and click the Hide Authors button if you don't see authors' initials).

The Require Check Out setting must be set to No for coauthoring to work. This setting is located in the Versioning Settings page (which you can get to by clicking a link on the Library Settings main page). If you don't see the Versioning Settings page, ask your administrator to check the setting for you.

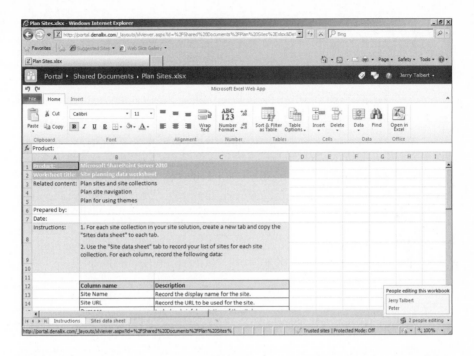

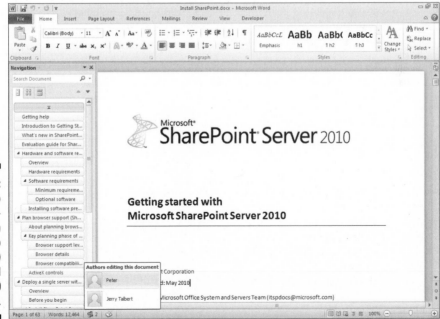

Figure 8-6:
Seeing who the coauthors are in Excel Web App (top) and Word 2010 (bottom).

Other Ways to Collaborate at a SharePoint Site

Besides file sharing, SharePoint offers these amenities to people who live far apart but want to work closely together:

- **Pictures:** Use the Picture Libraries to share photographs with coworkers. Upload, download, and view photographs by using the same techniques that you use to share files.

- **Lists:** Use announcement, calendar, link, and task lists to manage your work and deadlines better. The Links list is for listing Web sites that are of use to the people you work with.

- **Discussions:** Hold newsgroup-style discussions to iron out the problems that engage you at work. No gossiping is allowed.

- **Surveys:** Conduct a survey of coworkers to gauge people's opinions and establish goals and objectives.

- **Sites:** Use the Sites window to create more workspaces for sharing files and otherwise collaborating. For example, you can create a Document, Meeting, Decision Meeting, Social Meeting, or Multipage Meeting workspace. Wiki and Blog sites are also available.

- **People and Groups:** Use this window to store and obtain your coworkers' contact information.

Part III
Word Web App

"I love the way this program justifies the text in my resume. Now if I can just get it to justify my asking salary."

In this part . . .

Word Web App, a cousin of Microsoft Word, is the official word processor of the Office Web Apps. In Part III, you explore the nooks and crannies of Word Web App.

Part III tells you how to create documents with Word Web App, use styles, and create tables. Coauthoring with Word Web App is a bit trickier than coauthoring is with the other Office Web Apps, and Part III explains all you need to know about coauthoring.

Chapter 9

Up and Running with Word Web App

*E*lsewhere in this book, I lament how the Office Web Apps aren't nearly as useful as their namesakes in Office 2010. I'm sorry to report that Word Web App, of all the Office Web Apps, has the most shortcomings. If you have even a brushing acquaintance with Word 2010 (or earlier editions of Word), you will be disappointed by Word Web App. I thought of calling this chapter "Word Web App: Making the Best of It."

To make the best of it, this chapter introduces you to Word Web App, examines the differences between it and Word 2010, and takes you on a tour of the Word Web App screen. You also find out how to switch between Editing and Reading View. (Tools that Word Web App has in common with the other Office Web Apps are described in Chapter 4.)

Creating Documents with Word Web App

Chapter 2 describes how to create new files with Word Web App and the other Office Web Apps. It also describes how to open and close files. For readers who don't care to make the long, arduous journey to Chapter 2, here are short, to-the-point instructions for creating a document with Word Web App:

1. **Click the New link and choose Word Document on the drop-down list.**

   The New Microsoft Word Document window opens.

2. **Enter a name for your document.**

3. **Click the Save button.**

   A pristine, new document opens just for you.

Comparing Word Web App to Word 2010

Word Web App doesn't offer anywhere near the number of features as Word 2010, as a glance at Figure 9-1 shows. In the figure, you can see the same document in Word Web App (top) and Word 2010 (bottom). Notice that Word Web App offers a mere four tabs on its Ribbon, whereas Word 2010 offers eight.

So that you know what you're missing, Table 9-1 lists features in Word 2010 that aren't available in Word Web App. Except by clicking the Open In Word button in Word Web App and opening your document in Word 2010, you can't use any of the features listed in Table 9-1 to edit a Word document.

Figure 9-1:
Word Web
App (top)
and Word
2010
(bottom).

Table 9-1 Word 2010 Features Not Available in Word Web App

Feature	Description
Home tab	
Line Spacing	Change the amount of space between lines of text
Sort	Sort lists in alphabetical or numeric order
Show/Hide	Display hidden formatting symbols
Replace	Find words or phrases and replace them with other words or phrases
Selection Pane	Select items in the Selection and Visibility pane
Insert tab	
Pages	Create cover, blank pages, and page breaks
Shapes	Draw lines, arrows, rectangles, ovals, and other shapes
SmartArt	Create diagrams
Charts	Create a chart for displaying data
Screenshot	Take a picture of a screen or a portion of a screen
Bookmark	Mark parts of a document with bookmarks
Cross-reference	Create cross-references to headings, pages, and text
Headers and Footers	Create header and footer text for pages
Page Number	Number the pages in documents
Text Box	Draw a text box for framing text
Quick Parts	Enter document properties, fields, and building-block text
WordArt	Display a WordArt image on a page
Drop Cap	Create a drop capital letter
Date & Time	Enter the current date and time
Object	Create OLE links
Equation	Draw an equation with the Equation Editor tools
Symbol	Enter a symbol or foreign character in text
Page Layout	
Themes	Choose an all-encompassing look for a document
Page Setup	Establish the margin size, page size, and page orientation
Breaks	Insert page breaks
Line Numbers	Number the lines on the page
Hyphenation	Hyphenate words
Page Background	Create watermarks, choose background colors for pages, and put borders on pages

(continued)

Table 9-1 *(continued)*

Feature	Description
Page Layout	
Paragraph	Indent and determine the space between paragraphs
Arrange	Position, wrap, align, group, and rotate objects
References	
Table of Contents	Create a table of contents
Footnotes	Insert footnotes
Citations & Bibliography	Create a bibliography
Captions	Caption figures and other objects
Index	Create an index
Table of Authorities	Mark citations for tables
Mailings	
Envelopes and Labels	Print addresses on envelopes and labels
Mail Merge	Print addresses and greetings for mass mailings on documents, envelopes, and labels
Review and Edit	
Research	Use the Research task pane services — the dictionaries, thesauruses, and search engines
Thesaurus	Find a synonym for a word
Translate	Translate text from one language to another
Word Count	Count the words in a document or text selection
Comments*	Enter comments in text
Tracking	Track editorial changes to documents
Changes	Accept and reject editorial changes
Compare	Examine and compare edits made by different people to the same document
Protect document	Prevent edits from being made
View	
Web Layout view	See how a document looks in a Web browser
Outline view	See headings only
Show/Hide	Display and hide the ruler, gridlines, and document map
Window	Open secondary windows or split the screen as you work on a presentation
Macros	Record and play macros

* Comments don't appear in Word Web App under any circumstances, even if the comments were created first in Word 2010.

Introducing the Word Web App Screen

Figure 9-2 shows you the different parts of the Word Web App screen. Here are descriptions of these screen parts:

✔ **Quick Access toolbar:** This toolbar offers the Save, Undo, and Redo buttons. Wherever you go in Word Web App, you see the Quick Access toolbar. Word Web App is the only Office Web App that has a Save button and requires you to click the Save button to save your work.

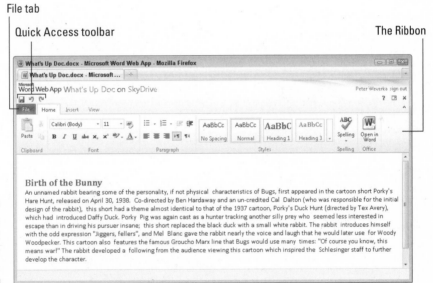

✔ **File tab:** Go to the File tab to take care of file-management tasks.

✔ **The Ribbon:** Select a tab on the Ribbon — Home, Insert, View — to undertake a new task.

✔ **Scroll bars:** The scroll bars help you get from place to place in a document.

File tab

Quick Access toolbar   The Ribbon

Figure 9-2:
The Word
Web App
screen.

Getting Around in Documents

To get from place to place in a document, use the scrollbars, turn the mouse wheel (if your mouse has a mouse wheel), or press these keyboard shortcuts:

Key to Press	Where It Takes You
PgUp	Up the length of one screen
PgDn	Down the length of one screen
Ctrl+Home	To the top of the document
Ctrl+End	To the bottom of the document

Changing Views

On the View tab, Word Web App offers two views, one for editing and one for seeing a document with all its data intact, including images, tables, charts, and the like. Figure 9-3 demonstrates the differences between the two views. Switch views early and often as you work on your document to see how it is shaping up:

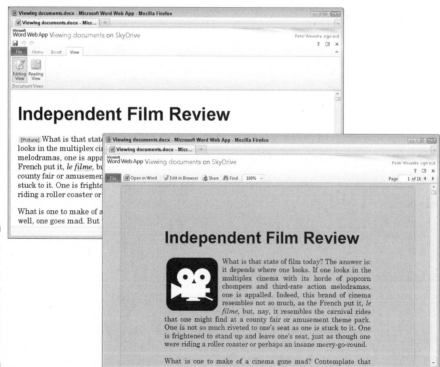

Figure 9-3: Change views on the View tab: Editing View (left) and Reading View (right).

✔ **Editing View:** Click the Editing View button (or the Edit in Browser button if you're starting in Reading View). The Ribbon appears and you can make edits. Vector graphics such as drawings and shapes don't appear but are instead indicated by placeholders — that is, by words enclosed by brackets, such as [Drawing] or [Shape].

✔ **Reading View:** Click the Reading View button to proofread your document. The document appears as it looks when printed; you see drawings, pictures, and objects as well as the text. The Ribbon doesn't appear and you can't make any edits. To return to Editing View, click the Edit in Browser button.

Chapter 10

Advanced Word Web App Techniques

In This Chapter

▶ Selecting text and paragraphs

▶ Applying a style to text

▶ Creating and editing tables

▶ Coauthoring documents alongside others in Word 2010

As I mention at the start of the previous chapter, Word Web App has a number of shortcomings. Realistically, you can use it only to touch up documents that you created in Word 2010 and view document online.

This chapter explains a couple of tasks that Word Web App is good at doing. I tell you how to assign styles to text and work with tables. You also find a bit of gratuitous advice about how to select text. This chapter also looks at how to coauthor a file with someone else in Word 2010.

Selecting Text

Before you can do much of anything to text — apply a style, delete text, move text — you have to select it. Use these techniques to select text:

To Select . . .	Do This . . .
A word	Double-click the word.
A few words	Drag over the words.
A block of text	Click the start of the text, hold down the Shift key, and click the end of the text.
All text	Press Ctrl+A.

All about Styles

A *style* is a collection of formatting commands assembled under one name. When you apply a style, you give many formatting commands simultaneously, and you spare yourself the trouble of choosing many different commands to format text. Styles save time and make documents look more professional. Headings assigned the same style — Heading1, for example — all look the same. When readers see that headings and paragraphs are consistent with one another across all the pages of a document, they get a warm, fuzzy feeling.

Sorry, you can't create a new style or modify styles in Word Web App, as you can in Word. But applying a style that's already built in is easy enough. (You can find more about built-in styles in the upcoming section "Styles and templates.")

Types of styles

Word Web App (and Word 2010) makes a distinction between three types of styles:

- **Paragraph styles:** Determine the formatting of entire paragraphs. Choosing a paragraph style changes font settings and text layouts throughout the paragraph where the cursor is (or for more than one paragraph, if you select — that is, highlight — more than one before choosing a paragraph style).

- **Character styles:** Apply to text, not to paragraphs. You select text before you apply a character style, and your style choice applies only to the text you selected.

- **Linked (paragraph and character) styles:** Apply paragraph formats as well as text formats throughout a paragraph (or more than one paragraph if you select more than one before choosing a paragraph style).

In Word 2010, you can tell right away whether a style is a paragraph, character style, or linked style because symbols in the Styles gallery tell you as much. Word Web App isn't that sophisticated. Its Style gallery doesn't tell you which styles are paragraph, character, or linked styles. All you can do is take a hint from the style's name (maybe) to understand what kind of style you're dealing with. For example, a style called "emphasis" is likely to be a character style that italicizes words, whereas "Heading 3" is almost certainly a style that applies to entire paragraphs. It would certainly be nice if Word Web App were more forthcoming in telling you what styles do.

Styles and templates

Documents are created from *templates,* and every document comes with built-in styles that it inherits from the template with which it was created. Documents you create with the Word Web App are made from the Normal template. This is the same vanilla-flavored template that is used to create documents in Word 2010 when you create a new document by pressing Ctrl+N or choosing Blank Document in the Available Templates window.

Documents that you upload from your computer to SkyDrive or a SharePoint Web site retain their styles. (In SharePoint, new Word documents are created with the template associated with the Document Library.) When you upload a document and open it in Word Web App, you see the same styles on the Style gallery that you saw when you opened the document in Word 2010. You see the same styles — and you also see styles from the Normal template that Word Web App loaded in the Styles gallery. Word Web App places its own styles in the Styles gallery alongside styles that are native to the document.

As mentioned previously, you can't create or change any of these styles in Word Web App.

Applying a style

Enough already about style types and templates. By now you must be aching to apply a style to part of your document. Follow these steps:

1. **Select the part of your document that you want to apply the style to.**

   What you select depends on the type of style you want to apply.

   - *A word or phrase (character style)*: Select the word or phrase. Earlier in this chapter, "Selecting Text" explains how. The style you choose will be applied only to the word or phrase you selected.

   - *A paragraph (paragraph or linked style)*: Click in the paragraph. Paragraph and linked styles apply to the entire paragraph that the cursor is in. All you have to do is click in a paragraph to apply a paragraph or linked style throughout.

   - *More than one paragraph(paragraph or linked style)*: Select all or part of the paragraphs. Because paragraph and linked styles apply throughout a paragraph, you can select part of a paragraph. You don't have to select all of it.

2. **Select a style.**

   Word Web App gives you two ways to select a style:

   - *Styles gallery:* On the Home tab, open the Styles gallery and choose a style, as shown in Figure 10-1.

- *Apply Styles dialog box:* On the Home tab, open the Styles gallery and choose Apply Styles. The Apply Styles dialog box appears. Select a style and click OK.

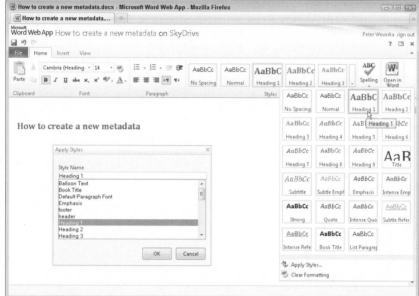

Figure 10-1:
Apply styles with the Apply Styles dialog box (left) or Styles gallery (right).

Don't like the style you selected? Click the Undo button and start all over.

To clear a paragraph of all style formatting, go to the Home tab and click the Clear All button. The Clear All command is also available in the Styles gallery. Choosing Clear All applies the Normal style to text and removes all character styles such as boldface and italics.

Determining which style is in use

How can you tell which style has been applied to a paragraph or text? Sometimes you need to know which style is in play before you decide whether applying a different style is necessary.

To find out which style has been applied to text, click in the text, go to the Home tab, and open the Styles gallery. Whichever style is selected in the gallery is the one that has been applied to the text.

All about Tables

The best way to present a bunch of data at one time is to do it in a table. Viewers can compare and contrast the data. They can compare Elvis sightings in different cities or income from different businesses. They can contrast the number of socks lost in different washing machine brands. A table is a great way to plead your case or defend your position. Readers can refer to a table to get the information they need.

As everyone who has worked on tables knows, however, tables are a chore. Getting all the columns to fit, making columns and rows the right width and height, and editing the text in a table isn't easy. This chapter explains how to create tables, enter text in tables, change the number and size of columns and rows, lay out tables, and format tables.

Creating a table

Follow these steps to create a table:

1. **Click in your document where you want the table to be.**

2. **On the Insert tab, click the Table button.**

   A drop-down table appears, as shown in Figure 10-2.

3. **Point in the table to indicate how many columns and rows you want.**

4. **Click and release the mouse button.**

   After you create your table, the (Table Tools) Layout tab appears, as shown in Figure 10-3. Go to this tab to format your table, insert rows and columns, and delete rows and columns.

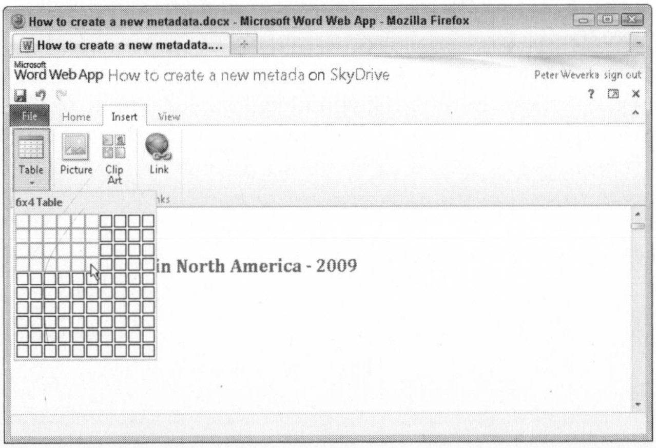

Figure 10-2: Point and click to choose how many columns and rows you want in your table.

Entering the text and numbers

After you've created the table, you can start entering text and numbers. All you have to do is click in a cell and start typing.

Here are some shortcuts for moving the cursor in a table:

Press	*Moves the Cursor to*
Tab	Next column in row
Shift+Tab	Previous column in row
↓	Row below
↑	Row above

Selecting different parts of a table

It almost goes without saying, but before you can reformat, alter, or diddle with table cells, rows, or columns, you have to select them. On the (Table Tools) Layout tab (refer to Figure 10-3), use these techniques to select parts of a table:

✔ **Selecting cells:** Click in a cell to select it. You can select several adjacent cells by dragging over them.

✔ **Selecting rows:** Click in the row and click the Select Row button. To select more than one row, select cells in the rows before clicking the Select Row button. You can also right-click and choose Select⇨Select Row on the shortcut menu that appears.

 ✔ **Selecting columns:** Click in the column and click the Select Column button. To select more than one column, select cells in the columns before clicking the Select Column button. You can also right-click and choose Select⇨Select Column on the shortcut menu that appears.

 ✔ **Selecting a table:** Click the Select Table button. You can also right-click and choose Select⇨Select Table on the shortcut menu.

Inserting and deleting columns and rows

 The trick to inserting and deleting columns and rows is to correctly select part of the table first. You can insert more than one column or row at a time by selecting more than one column or row before giving the Insert command. To insert two columns, for example, select two columns and click the Insert Left or Insert Right button.

On the (Table Tools) Layout tab (refer to Figure 10-3), use these techniques to insert and delete columns and rows:

✔ **Inserting columns:** Select a column or columns and click the Insert Left or Insert Right button. You can also right-click, choose Insert, and choose an Insert Column command on the submenu.

✔ **Inserting rows:** Select a row or rows and click the Insert Above or Insert Below button. You can also right-click, choose Insert on the shortcut menu that appears, and choose an Insert Row command on that shortcut menu.

 To insert a row at the end of a table, move the pointer into the last cell in the last row and press the Tab key.

 ✔ **Deleting columns:** Click in the column you want to delete and click the Delete Column button. You can also right-click and choose Delete⇨Delete Column on the shortcut menu that appears.

 ✔ **Deleting rows:** Click in the row you want to delete and click the Delete Row button. You can also right-click and choose Delete⇨Delete Row on the shortcut menu.

 ✔ **Deleting a table:** Click in the table and then click the Delete Table button.

Changing the width of columns and the table

Word Web App makes columns wider to accommodate text as you enter it in a table. You can't change the height of a row (although that happens automatically if you add enough text to a cell in a row), but you can widen or narrow columns and the table itself by dragging. Move the pointer onto a column or table border, and when the pointer changes into a double-headed arrow, click and start dragging. Tug and pull, tug and pull until the column or table is the right size.

Aligning text in columns

Aligning text in columns is a matter of selecting a column and clicking an Alignment button — Align Left, Center, or Align Right. You can find these buttons on the (Table Tools) Layout tab.

Coauthoring Word Documents

Microsoft uses the term *coauthor* to describe when two people work on a file simultaneously at Windows Live or a SharePoint Web site. As far as the simultaneous coauthoring of Word documents goes, you can do it, but only if both authors have opened the document in Word 2010. Microsoft does not permit two people to coauthor a file at the same time in Word Web App. The remainder of this chapter looks at some peculiarities of coauthoring Word documents with colleagues at Windows Live or a SharePoint Web site. (Chapter 2 explains how to open a Word document in Word Web App and Word 2010; Chapters 6 and 7 explain Window Live; Chapter 8 explains SharePoint.)

Seeing who your coauthors are

To see who your coauthors are in a Word document that you have opened in Word 2010 or a SharePoint Web site, use one of these techniques:

✔ Move the pointer over the Authors icon on the status bar. A pop-up box tells you the name of people who are also working on the document.

✔ On the File tab, choose Info. The Information About window lists the names of your coauthors.

Later in this chapter, "Communicating with a coauthor" tells you how to get in touch with someone who is editing a Word document simultaneously with you.

Synchronizing a Word document

When one of your coauthors makes changes to a paragraph in a file that you're also working on, Word 2010 marks the change by putting the name of the coauthor who made it to the left of the paragraph, as shown in Figure 10-4. While this name appears in the left margin, you can't make changes to the paragraph unless you synchronize your version of the document with your coauthor's version.

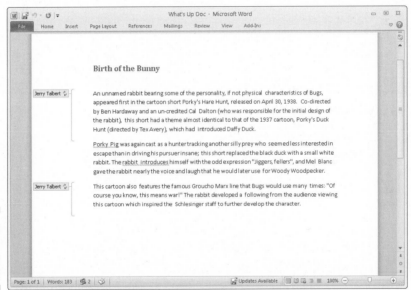

Figure 10-4:
This docu-
ment needs
updating.

Seeing names to the left of a paragraph is your cue to synchronize your document with your coauthor's by following these steps:

1. **If necessary, switch to Print Layout view to see coauthors' names next to paragraphs they edited.**

   Coauthors' names do not appear to the left of paragraphs unless you are in Print Layout view. To switch to this view, click the Print Layout button on the status bar or go to the View tab and click the Print Layout button.

Blocking others from editing a paragraph

A coauthor who doesn't want others to edit a paragraph can block it from being edited. You can tell when a paragraph has been blocked for editing because the blocked symbol appears next to the coauthor's name to the left of the paragraph.

Follow these instructions to block and unblock paragraphs:

✔ **Blocking paragraphs:** Select all or part of the paragraphs you want to block, go to the Review tab, and click the Block Authors button.

✔ **Unblocking paragraphs:** Select all or part of the paragraphs you want to unblock, and on the Review tab, click the Block Authors button. (This button functions as a toggle, and clicking it a second time unblocks the paragraphs.)

✔ **Unblocking all paragraphs:** Open the drop-down list on the Block Authors button and choose Release All of My Blocked Areas.

Click the Save button to send your block instructions to the Web server.

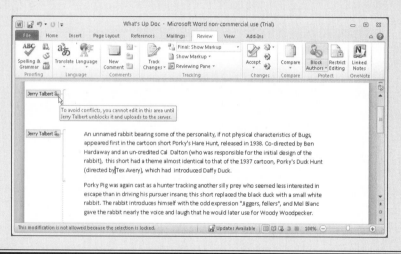

Besides seeing coauthors' names beside paragraphs, you can tell whether your document needs synchronizing by looking on the right side of the status bar. If you see the message "Updates Available," your document is out of sync with your coauthors'.

2. **Click the Save button (or press Ctrl+S).**

    After you click the button, a message on the status bar says, "Word is refreshing the document," and the document on your computer is synchronized with your coauthors'. Green highlights appear in the document to show where your coauthors made their changes. Your document is up-to-date.

Revisiting an earlier version of a Word document

Suppose you don't like what your coauthors did to a document and you want to see an earlier, unrevised (or less revised) copy. Follow these steps to open an earlier version of a document:

File

1. **Go to the File tab and choose Info.**

   The Information About window opens, as shown in Figure 10-5.

2. **In the Versions area at the bottom of the window, click the name of an earlier version of a document.**

   Earlier versions are date- and time-stamped so that you can identify them. After you click the version's name, it opens in Word 2010.

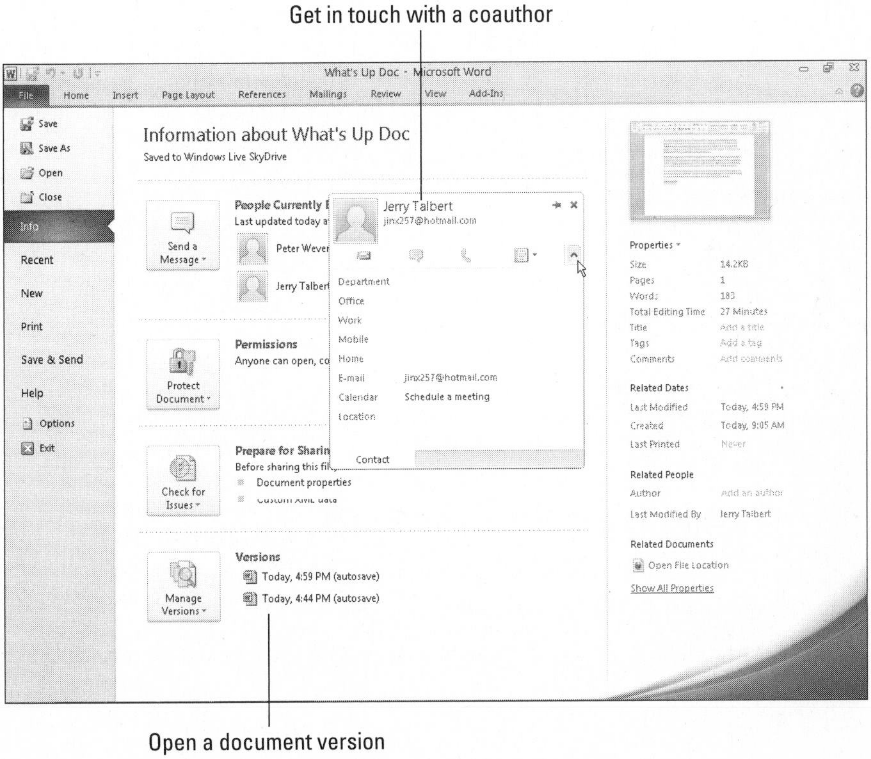

Get in touch with a coauthor

Figure 10-5: Go to the Information About window to communicate with coauthors or open an earlier version of a document.

Open a document version

Reviewing a document with change marks

Reviewing a document with change marks isn't easy. The marks can get in the way. Fortunately, Word offers the Display for Review menu on the Review tab for dealing with documents that have been scarred by change marks. Choose options on the Display for Review drop-down list to get a better idea of how your changes are taking shape:

- **See more clearly where text was deleted from the original document:** Choose Final: Show Markup. In Print Layout view, deleted material appears in balloons on the right side of the screen and insertions are underlined.

- **See what the document would look like if you accepted all changes:** Choose Final. All change marks are stripped away and you see what your document would look like if you accepted all changes made to it.

- **See more clearly where text was inserted in the document:** Choose Original: Show Markup. In Print Layout view, insertions appear in balloons on the right side of the screen and a line appears through text that has been deleted.

- **See what the document would look like if you rejected all changes:** Choose Original. You get the original, pristine document back.

The best way to handle change marks is to go through the document, reject the changes you don't care for, and when you have finished reviewing, accept all the remaining changes.

That way, reviewing changes is only half as tedious.

Whatever your preference for accepting or rejecting changes, start by selecting a change. To do so, either click it or click the Previous or Next button on the Review tab to locate it in your document. With the change selected, do one of the following:

- **Accept a change:** Click the Accept button or open the drop-down list on the Accept button and choose Accept Change or Accept and Move to Next. You can also right-click and choose Accept Change.

- **Reject a change:** Click the Reject button or open the drop-down list on the Reject button and choose Reject Change or Reject and Move to Next. You can also right-click and choose Reject Change.

- **Accept all changes:** Open the drop-down list on the Accept button and choose Accept All Changes in Document.

- **Reject all changes:** Open the drop-down list on the Reject button and choose Reject All Changes in Document.

By way of the Accept and Reject buttons, you can also accept or reject all changes made by a single reviewer. First, isolate the reviewer's changes by clicking the Show Markup button, choosing Reviewers, and selecting a reviewer's name. Then open the drop-down list on the Accept or Reject button, and choose Accept All Changes Shown or Reject All Changes Shown.

What you see on-screen is a different Word document, a precursor to the one that was on-screen when you visited the File tab. The top of the window offers commands for comparing and restoring this document:

✔ **Comparing:** Click the Compare button to compare the precursor document to the most recent one. The Review tab opens, and you can see the earlier version, the current document, and a comparison document on-screen at the same time. If you know your way around the Track Changes feature in Word, you can study the change marks, and choose what parts of the document to keep and discard, and then save the document under a different name.

✔ **Restoring:** Click the Restore button to make the version you opened the official version of the document. Clicking the Restore button overwrites the version of the document that was on-screen when you opened the File tab and opened an earlier version.

Communicating with a coauthor

Sometimes it's necessary to trade a word or two with coauthors as you put together a Word document. Word 2010 offers a shortcut to getting in touch with a coauthor:

File

1. **Go to the File tab and choose Info.**

   The Information About window opens. In the People Currently Editing area of the window, you see the names of your coauthors.

2. **Click a coauthor's name to open his or her contact card.**

3. **Click the Expand button on the contact card.**

   You see whatever information your coauthor has chosen to divulge about him- or herself (refer to Figure 10-5). You can get a phone number or e-mail address from the contact card.

Part IV
Excel Web App

The 5th Wave   By Rich Tennant

Spreadsheet
Creation
.50¢-Min.

In this part . . .

Part IV is for number crunchers. It describes how to crunch numbers and construct worksheets with Excel Web App.

This part explains what a worksheet is, how to enter data in a worksheet, and how to make worksheets easier to read and understand. You also discover how to write formulas, use functions in formulas, sort data, and filter data.

Chapter 11

Entering the Data

This chapter introduces Excel Web App, the official Office Web App number cruncher. The purpose of Excel Web App is to track and tabulate numbers. Use the program to project profits and losses, formulate a budget, or analyze Elvis sightings in North America. Doing the setup work takes time, but after you enter the numbers and tell Excel Web App how to tabulate them, you're on Easy Street. Excel Web App does the math for you. All you have to do is kick off your shoes, sit back, and see how the numbers stack up.

This chapter explains what a workbook and a worksheet are, and how rows and columns on a worksheet determine where cell addresses are. You also discover tips and tricks for entering data in a worksheet and making a worksheet easier to understand and read. And in case you're a fan of Excel 2010, this chapter outlines the differences between the Excel Web App and its cousin Excel 2010.

Creating Workbooks with Excel Web App

Chapter 2 explains in excruciating detail how to create an Excel workbook with Excel Web App and how to open workbooks you already created. In case you haven't visited Chapter 2, here are shorthand instructions for opening a workbook with Excel Web App:

1. **Click the New link and choose Excel Workbook on the drop-down list.**

   You see the New Microsoft Excel Workbook window.

2. **Enter a name for your workbook.**

3. Click the Save button.

A new workbook opens, ready for you to fill it with numbers.

Comparing Excel Web App to Excel 2010

Excel Web App is an abridged version of Excel 2010. It doesn't have nearly as many features as Excel 2010, as Figure 11-1 demonstrates. You can find but three tabs — File, Home, and Insert — on the Ribbon in the Excel Web App; Excel 2010 offers no fewer than eight tabs on its Ribbon.

Table 11-1 lists features in Excel 2010 that aren't available in Excel Web App. If you want to use one of these features, you're out of luck unless you open your workbook in Excel 2010.

Don't fret if you need one of the features listed in Table 11-1 for your Excel workbook. If Excel 2010 is installed on your computer, you can edit a workbook in Excel 2010 by going to the Home tab in Excel Web App and clicking the Open in Excel button. Chapter 2 explains how to open and edit Excel workbooks in Excel 2010.

Table 11-1	Excel 2010 Features Not Available in the Excel Web App
Feature	*Description*
Home tab	
Cell Styles	Apply a different look to selected cells
Conditional Formats	Highlight and color-code cells that meet criteria
Format As Table	Format part of a worksheet so it looks and works like a table
Insert tab	
Charts	Create a chart for displaying data
Clip Art	Place clip-art images in worksheets
Equation	Draw an equation with the Equation Editor tools
Picture	Insert a picture or graphic image
PivotTable	Create a PivotTable
Screenshot	Take a picture of a screen or a portion of a screen
Shapes	Draw lines, arrows, rectangles, ovals, and other shapes
SmartArt	Create a SmartArt graphic
Sparklines	Insert a mini-chart within a single cell
Symbol	Enter a symbol or foreign character in text

Feature	Description
Insert tab	
Text Box	Insert a text box in a worksheet
WordArt	Display a WordArt image on a worksheet
Page Layout	
Background	Choose an image for the worksheet background
Gridlines	Hide and display gridlines
Print Area	Choose which part of a worksheet to print
Scale to Fit	Scale a worksheet to make it fit on the page
Slide Orientation	Display worksheets in portrait as well as landscape mode
Themes	Choose an all-encompassing look for a worksheet
Formulas	
Auditing	Trace precedents and dependents in formulas; error-check formulas
Cell-range Names	Name cell ranges
Functions	Use a function from the Function Library in a formula
Data	
Data Validation	Establish data-validation rules
Duplicates	Remove duplicate rows
External Data	Obtain data from sources outside the workbook
Group	Group data for quick analyses
What-If Analysis	Use the Scenario Manager and Goal Seek commands
Review	
Comments*	Enter comments about slides
Compare	Examine and compare edits made by different people to the same workbook
Language	Proof foreign-language text
Research	Use the Research task pane services — the dictionaries, thesauruses, and search engines
Spelling	Spell-check the worksheet
Thesaurus	Find a synonym for a word
Translate	Translate text from one language to another
View	
Macros	Play macros
Show	Display the ruler and gridlines
Views	Switch to Normal or Page Layout view; create a custom view
Window	Freeze panes, split the window, and arrange window
Zoom	Zoom in and out

* Comments don't appear in Excel Web App under any circumstances, even if the comments were created first in Excel 2010.

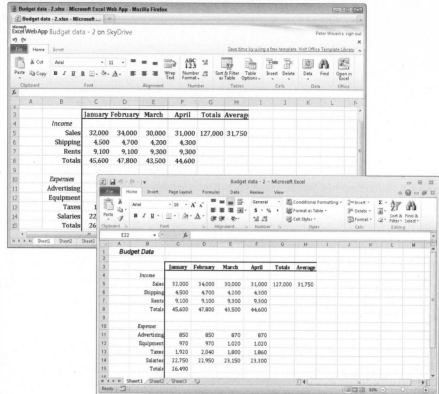

Figure 11-1:
Excel Web
App (top)
and Excel
2010
(bottom).

Getting Acquainted with the Excel Web App

An Excel file is called a *workbook*. Each workbook comprises one or more worksheets. A *worksheet,* also known as a *spreadsheet,* is a table where you enter data and data labels. Figure 11-2 shows a worksheet with data about rainfall in different counties in Excel Web App.

A worksheet works like an accountant's ledger — only it's much easier to use. Notice how the worksheet is divided by gridlines into columns (A, B, C, and so on) and rows (1, 2, 3, and so on). The rectangles where columns and rows intersect are *cells,* and each cell can hold one data item, a formula for calculating data, or nothing at all. At the bottom of the worksheet are tabs — Sheet1, Sheet2, and Sheet3 — for visiting the other worksheets in the workbook.

Formula bar   Active cell

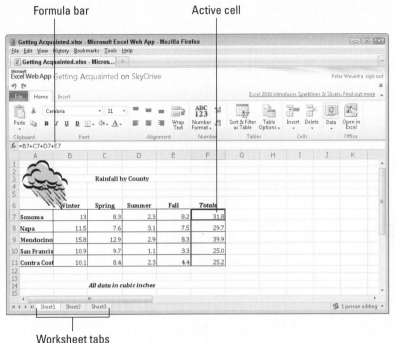

Figure 11-2:
The Excel
Web App
screen.

Worksheet tabs

Each cell has a different cell address. In Figure 11-1, cell B7 holds 13, the amount of rain in inches that fell in Sonoma County in the winter. Meanwhile, as the Formula bar at the top of the screen shows, cell F7, the *active cell,* holds the formula =B7+C7+D7+E7, the sum of the numbers in cells — you guessed it — B7, C7, D7, and E7.

The beauty of Excel is that the program does all the calculations and recalculations for you after you enter the data. If I were to change the number in cell B7, Excel would instantly recalculate the total amount of rainfall in Sonoma County in cell F7. People like myself who struggled in math class will be glad to know that you don't have to worry about the math because Excel Web App does it for you. All you have to do is make sure that the data and the formulas are entered correctly.

Rows, columns, and cell addresses

Not that anyone except an Enron accountant needs all of them, but a worksheet has numerous columns and over 1 million rows. The rows are numbered, and columns are labeled A to Z, then AA to AZ, then BA to BZ, and so on. The important thing to remember is that each cell has an address whose name comes from a column letter and a row number. The first cell in row 1 is A1, the second is B1, and so on. You need to enter cell addresses in formulas to tell the Excel Web App which numbers to compute.

To find a cell's address, make note of which column and row it lies in. The currently selected cell is called the active cell. You can tell which cell is active because a black frame appears around it.

Workbooks and worksheets

When you create a new Excel file, you open a *workbook,* a file with three worksheets in it. The worksheets are called Sheet1, Sheet2, and Sheet3. To get from worksheet to worksheet, click tabs along the bottom of the Excel Web App window. Why three worksheets? Because you might need more than one worksheet for a single project. Think of a workbook as a stack of worksheets. Besides calculating the numbers in cells across the rows or down the columns of a worksheet, you can make calculations throughout a workbook by using numbers from different worksheets in a calculation.

Entering Data in a Worksheet

Entering data in a worksheet is an irksome activity. Fortunately, Excel Web App offers a few shortcuts to take the sting out of it. These pages explain how to enter data in a worksheet, how the Excel Web App displays data in cells, and how to enter data in the form of a text label, number, date, or time value.

The basics of entering data

No matter what type of data you're entering, the basic steps are the same:

1. **Click the cell where you want to enter the data or text label.**

   As shown in Figure 11-3, a square appears around the cell to tell you that the cell you clicked is now the active cell.

2. **Type the data in the cell.**

   If you find typing in the Formula bar easier, click and start typing there.

3. **Press the Enter key to enter the number or label.**

   Besides pressing the Enter key, you can also press Tab or an arrow key (←, ↑, →, ↓).

   If you change your mind about entering data, press Esc to delete what you entered and start over.

Enter the data here . . .   or here

Elvis Sightings in North America

			2006	2007	2008	2009	2010
Top Five Cities							
	Memphis		23	24			
	New York		18				
	New Orleans		44				
	St. Louis		16				
	Chicago		16				

Figure 11-3:
Entering
data.

How data displays in worksheet cells

Sometimes a data entry is too long to fit in a cell. How Excel Web App accommodates these wide-load entries depends on whether data is in the cell to the right and whether you entered text or a number:

✔ **Text:** If the cell to the right is empty, Excel Web App lets the text spill into the next cell; if the cell to the right contains data, the entry gets cut off.

✔ **Numbers:** Excel Web App displays the number in scientific notation, and if the number still doesn't fit in the cell, you see pound signs (###).

Nothing gets lost when it can't be displayed on-screen. You just can't see the text or numbers except by glancing at the Formula bar, where the contents of the active cell can be seen in its entirety.

To solve the problem of text that doesn't fit in a cell, widen or shorten the column (Chapter 12 explains how) or wrap the contents of the cell. *Wrapping* means to run the text down to the next line, much the way the text in a paragraph runs to the next line when it reaches the right margin. Excel Web App makes rows taller to accommodate wrapped text in a cell. To wrap text in cells, select the cells, go to the Home tab, and click the Wrap Text button.

Formatting numbers, dates, and other values

Formats matter in worksheets because they make numbers and text easier to read and understand. What's more, for Excel Web App to perform calculations correctly, you must choose the correct format for data. For example, before Excel Web App can calculate the number of days between two dates, the data for the calculation must be entered in the Date format.

These pages explain the different formats and how to choose a format for data in a worksheet.

Understanding data formats

Table 11-2 describes the data formats. These formats are available on the Number Format drop-down list on the Home tab.

Excel Web App assigns a format automatically when you enter a number in a format it recognizes. Enter 45%, for example, and the Excel Web App assigns the Percentage format. Enter $4.25 and you get the Currency format. Table 11-2 also explains how to enter a number so that Excel Web App formats it for you.

Table 11-2		Number Formats	
Format	*Example*	*Explanation*	*Automatic Format*
General	44	No specific number format. (Choose this option to strip formats from numbers.)	Enter a number. This is the default format for numbers.
Number	44.00	Number to two decimal places.	None.
Currency	$44.00	Number with dollar sign and two decimal places.	Enter a dollar sign and then enter the number.
Accounting	$ 44.00	Number with dollar sign and two decimal places, with the dollar signs and decimal points lined up with other numbers in the column.	None.

Format	Example	Explanation	Automatic Format
Short Date	31-Jul-09	Date expressed as a day, month, and year.	Enter the date in *m/d/yy*, *m-d-yyyy*, or *d-mmm-yy* format. If you don't enter a year, Excel Web App enters the current year.
Long Date	Saturday, July 31, 2010	Date expressed as day of the week, month, day, and year.	Enter the date in *m/d/yy*, *m-d-yyyy*, or *d-mmm-yy* format. If you don't enter a year, Excel Web App enters the current year.
Time	12:00:00 AM	Time expressed in the hour, minute, and seconds.	Enter the time in *h:mm* AM/PM or *h:mm:ss* AM/PM format. Separate hours, minutes, and seconds with a colon (:). Enter AM or PM.
Percentage	44.00%	Number as percentage with two decimal places and percent sign.	Enter a percent sign (%) after the number.
Fraction	3/4	Number expressed as a fraction.	Enter a 0 or a whole number, a blank space, and the fraction. For example, to enter ⅜, type a **0**, press the spacebar, and type **3/8**.
Scientific	4.44E+03	Number in scientific notation.	None.
Text	Total	For text and for numbers to be treated as text. (Use this format for ZIP Codes and other labels that are composed of numbers.)	Enter text. This is the default format for text.

Assigning a format to data

Follow these steps to choose a format for data you entered or will enter in worksheet cells:

1. Select the cells.

To select one cell, click it; to select several cells, drag across them with the mouse. Later in this chapter, "Selecting cells in a worksheet" describes all the techniques for selecting cells.

2. On the Home tab, click the Number Format button.

As shown in Figure 11-4, a drop-down list with formats appears.

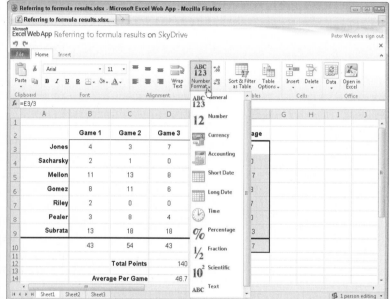

Figure 11-4: Choosing a format for a data entry.

3. Choose a format on the drop-down list.

Earlier in this chapter, Table 11-1 explains the formats.

Here's a shortcut for formatting cells: Select a cell with the format you want to copy, click the Copy button on the Home tab, select the cell or cells that need a formatting change, open the drop-down list on the Paste button, and choose Paste Formatting.

Displaying decimal places in numbers

Select cells and click these buttons on the Home tab to determine how many decimal places appear in numbers:

- ✔ **Increase Decimal:** Increases the number of decimal places by one.
- ✔ **Decrease Decimal:** Decreases the number of decimal places by one.

Editing Worksheet Data

Creating the perfect worksheet is more of a wrestling match than a stroll through the park. These pages explain how to be a better wrestler. They tell you how to edit a data entry, move around in a worksheet, and select, delete, move, and copy data.

Editing data entries

Not everyone enters data correctly the first time. To edit data you entered in a cell, do one of the following:

- **Double-click the cell.** Doing so places the cursor squarely in the cell, where you can start deleting or entering numbers and text.

- **Click the cell and press F2.** This technique also lands the cursor in the cell.

- **Click the cell you want to edit.** With this technique, you edit the data on the Formula bar.

Selecting cells in a worksheet

Before you can format, copy, move, delete, or format numbers and words in a worksheet, you have to select the cells in which the numbers and words are found. Here are ways to select cells and the data inside them:

- **Adjacent cells in a row or column:** Drag across the cells.

- **A block of cells:** Drag diagonally across the worksheet from one corner of the block of cells to the opposite corner. You can also click in one corner and Shift+click the opposite corner.

- **A row or rows:** Click a row number to select an entire row. Click and drag down the row numbers to select several adjacent rows.

- **A column or columns:** Click a column letter to select an entire column. Click and drag across letters to select adjacent columns.

Press Ctrl+Spacebar to select the column that the active cell is in; press Shift+Spacebar to select the row where the active cell is.

Deleting, copying, and moving data

In the course of putting together a worksheet, it is sometimes necessary to delete, copy, and move cell contents. Here are instructions for doing these chores:

- ✔ **Deleting cell contents:** Select the cells and then press the Delete key. (Avoid the Delete button on the Home tab for deleting cell contents. Clicking that button deletes cells as well as their contents.)

- ✔ **Copying and moving cell contents:** Select the cells and, on the Home tab, click the Cut or Copy button. Then click where you want the first cell of the block of cells you're copying or moving to go and click the Paste button. To copy or move formula results without copying the formulas themselves, open the drop-down list on the Paste button and choose Paste Values.

Moving around in a worksheet

Going from place to place gets progressively more difficult as a worksheet gets bigger. Luckily for you, Excel Web App offers keyboard shortcuts for jumping around. Table 11-3 describes these keyboard shortcuts.

Table 11-3	Keyboard Shortcuts for Getting around in Worksheets
Press . . .	*To move . . .*
Home	To column A
Ctrl+Home	To cell A1, the first cell in the worksheet
Ctrl+End	To the last cell in the last row with data in it
←, →, ↑, ↓	To the next cell
PgUp *or* PgDn	Up or down one screen's worth of rows

As well as pressing keys, you can use these techniques to get from place to place in a worksheet:

- ✔ **Scroll bars:** Use the vertical and horizontal scroll bars to move to different areas. Drag the scroll box to cover long distances.

- ✔ **Scroll wheel on the mouse:** If your mouse is equipped with a scroll wheel, turn the wheel to quickly scroll up and down.

✔ **The Find command:** On the Home tab, click the Find button, and in the Find dialog box, enter a search term, select the Up or Down option button, and click Find Next.

Making a Worksheet Easier to Read and Understand

Especially if others will see your worksheet, you may as well dress it in its Sunday best. And you can do a number of things to make worksheets easier to read and understand. You can change character fonts. You can align the data in cells in different ways. You can draw borders around cells. You can resize columns and rows. This part of Chapter 11 is dedicated to the proposition that a worksheet doesn't have to look drab and solemn.

Experimenting with text formats

One of the easiest ways to make a worksheet easier to understand is to change the text formats. For example, make data labels bold and choose a different font and font size for them. Or make negative numbers red or another color apart from black. Chapter 4 explains in detail how to change the appearance of text.

Aligning numbers and text in columns and rows

To start with, numbers in worksheets are right-aligned in cells, and text is left-aligned. Numbers and text sit squarely on the bottom of cells. You can, however, change the way that data is aligned. For example, you can make data float at the top of cells rather than rest at the bottom, and you can center or justify data in cells.

Figure 11-5 illustrates different ways to align text and numbers. How text is aligned helps people make sense of worksheets. In Figure 11-5, for example, Income and Expenses are left-aligned so that they stand out and make clearer what the right-aligned column labels below are all about.

Select the cells whose alignment needs changing and follow these instructions to realign data in the cells:

✔ **Changing the horizontal (side-to-side) alignment:** On the Home tab, click the Align Text Left, Center, or Align Text Right button.

Wrapped

Left-aligned

Right-aligned   Centered

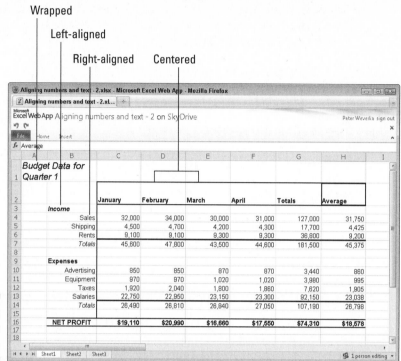

Figure 11-5:
Ways to
align data.

✔ **Changing the vertical (top-to-bottom) alignment:** On the Home tab, click the Top Align, Middle Align, or Bottom Align button.

As Figure 11-5 demonstrates, you can also wrap text in a cell to realign it. To wrap text, click the cell in question, go to the Home tab, and click the Wrap Text button.

Inserting and deleting rows and columns

At some point, everybody has to insert new columns and rows and delete ones that are no longer needed. Make sure before you delete a row or column that you don't delete data that you really need. Do the following to insert and delete rows and columns:

✔ **Deleting rows or columns:** Drag across the row numbers or column letters of the rows or columns you want to delete; then, on the Home tab, open the drop-down list on the Delete button and select Delete Rows or Delete Columns.

✔ **Inserting rows:** Select the row below the row you want to insert; then, on the Home tab, open the drop-down list on the Insert button and choose Insert Rows. For example, to insert a new row above row 11, select the current row 11 before choosing Insert Rows. You can insert more than one row at a time by selecting more than one row before giving the Insert Rows command.

✔ **Inserting columns:** Select the column to the right of where you want the new column to be; then, on the Home tab, open the drop-down list on the Insert button and choose Insert Columns. You can insert more than one column this way by selecting more than one column before giving the Insert command.

To insert more than one row or column at a time, select more than one row number or column letter before giving the Insert command.

Changing the size of columns and rows

Columns and rows inevitably need resizing. Make columns wider to accommodate letters and numbers that aren't displayed in their entirety. Make rows taller when you want to make data labels or other information stand out.

Before you change the size of columns or rows, select them (or select it if you want to change the size of a single column or row). Click or drag across row numbers to select rows; click or drag across column letters to select columns. (See "Selecting cells in a worksheet," earlier in this chapter, if you need help selecting columns or rows).

Adjusting the height of rows

By default, the Excel Web App makes rows taller to accommodate letters with large font sizes. Here are ways to change the height of rows:

✔ **One at a time:** Move the mouse pointer onto the boundary between row numbers and, when the pointer changes to a cross, drag the boundary between rows up or down.

✔ **Several at a time:** Select several rows and drag the boundary between one of the rows; all rows change height.

Adjusting the width of columns

Here are ways to make columns wider or narrower:

✔ **One at a time:** Move the mouse pointer onto the boundary between column letters, and when the pointer changes to a cross, drag the border between the columns.

✔ **Several at a time:** Select several columns and drag the boundary between one of the columns; all columns adjust to the same width.

Slapping borders on worksheet cells

Put borders on worksheet cells to box in cells, draw lines beneath cells, or draw lines along the side of cells. Borders can direct people who review your worksheet to its important parts. Typically, for example, a line appears above the Totals row of a worksheet to separate the Totals row from the rows above and help readers locate cumulative totals.

Follow these steps to draw borders on a worksheet:

1. **Select the cells around which or through which you want to place borders.**

   Earlier in this chapter, "Selecting cells in a worksheet" explains how to select cells.

2. **On the Home tab, click the Borders button.**

   As shown in Figure 11-6, a drop-down list appears.

3. **Choose a border.**

To remove the border from cells, select the cells, open the drop-down list on the Borders button, and choose No Border.

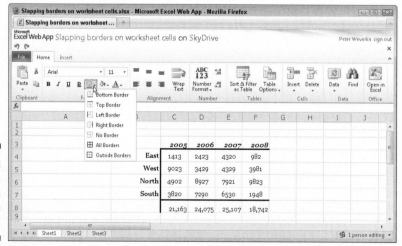

Figure 11-6:
Drawing a border with the Borders button.

Chapter 12

Crunching the Numbers

This chapter explains how to construct formulas and analyze data with the Sort and Filter commands.

Formulas are where it's at as far as Excel Web App is concerned. After you know how to construct formulas, and constructing them is pretty easy, you can truly put Excel Web App to work. You can make the numbers speak to you. You can turn a bunch of unruly numbers into meaningful figures and statistics.

This chapter explains what a formula is, how to enter a formula, and how to enter a formula quickly. You also discover how to copy formulas from cell to cell and keep formula errors from creeping into your workbooks. This chapter also explains how to make use of the hundred or so functions that the Excel Web App offers. Finally, you discover how to sort and filter data to locate the information you need in a worksheet.

How Formulas Work

A *formula,* you may recall from the sleepy hours you spent in math class, is a way to calculate numbers. For example, 2+3=5 is a formula. When you enter a formula in a cell, Excel Web App computes the formula and displays its results in the cell. Click in cell A3 and enter **=2+3**, for example, and the Excel Web App displays the number 5 in cell A3.

Referring to cells in formulas

As well as numbers, Excel formulas can refer to the contents of different cells. When a formula refers to a cell, the number in the cell is used to compute the formula. In Figure 12-1, for example, cell A1 contains the number 2; cell A2 contains the number 3; and cell A3 contains the formula =A1+A2. As shown in cell A3, the result of the formula is 5. If I change the number in cell A1 from 2 to 3, the result of the formula in cell A3 (=A1+A2) becomes 6, not 5. When a formula refers to a cell and the number in the cell changes, the result of the formula changes as well.

Formula in the Formula bar

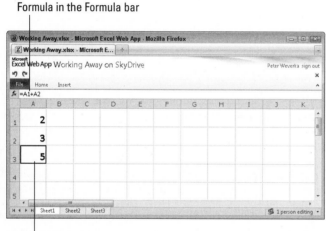

Figure 12-1:
A simple
formula.

Result of the formula

To see the value of using cell references in formulas, consider the worksheet shown in Figure 12-2. The purpose of this worksheet is to track the budget of a school's Parent Teacher Association (PTA):

- ✔ Column C, Actual Income, lists income from different sources.

- ✔ Column D, Projected Income, shows what the PTA members thought income from these sources would be.

- ✔ Column E, Over/Under Budget, shows how actual income compares to projected income from the different sources.

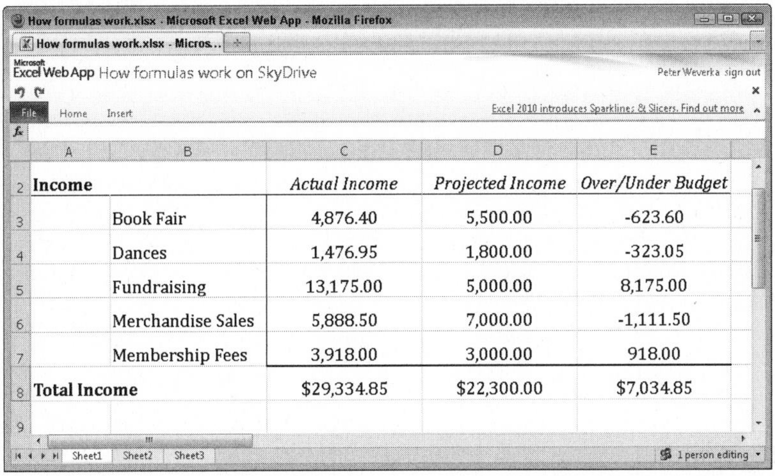

Figure 12-2:
Using formulas in a worksheet.

	A	B	C	D	E
2	Income		Actual Income	Projected Income	Over/Under Budget
3		Book Fair	4,876.40	5,500.00	-623.60
4		Dances	1,476.95	1,800.00	-323.05
5		Fundraising	13,175.00	5,000.00	8,175.00
6		Merchandise Sales	5,888.50	7,000.00	-1,111.50
7		Membership Fees	3,918.00	3,000.00	918.00
8	Total Income		$29,334.85	$22,300.00	$7,034.85

As the figures in the Actual Income column (column C) are updated, figures in the Over/Under Budget column (column E) and the Total Income row (row 8) change instantaneously. These figures change instantaneously because the formulas refer to the numbers in cells, not to unchanging numbers (known as *constants*).

Excel Web App is remarkably good about updating cell references in formulas when you move cells. To see how good Excel Web App is, consider what happens to cell addresses in formulas when you delete a row in a worksheet. If a formula refers to cell C1 but you delete row B, row C becomes row B, and the value in cell C1 changes addresses from C1 to B1. You would think that references in formulas to cell C1 would be out-of-date, but you would be wrong. Excel Web App automatically adjusts all formulas that refer to cell C1. Those formulas now refer to cell B1 instead.

Referring to formula results in formulas

Besides referring to cells with numbers in them, you can refer to formula results in a cell. Consider the worksheet shown in Figure 12-3. The purpose of this worksheet is to track scoring by the players on a basketball team over three games:

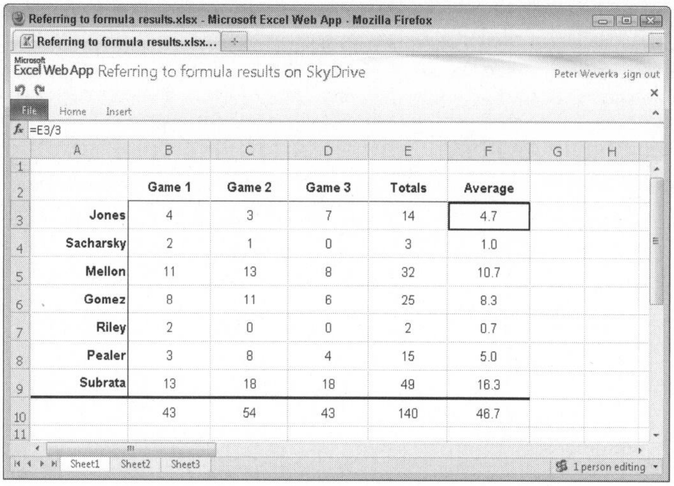

Figure 12-3:
Using formula results as other formulas.

✔ The Totals column (column E) calculates the total points each player scored in the three games.

✔ The Average column (column F), using the formula results in the Totals column (column #), determines how much each player has scored on average. The Average column does that by dividing the results in column E by 3, the number of games played.

In this case, Excel Web App uses the results of the total-calculation formulas in column E to compute average points per game in column F.

Operators in formulas

Addition, subtraction, and division aren't the only operators you can use in formulas. Table 12-1 explains the arithmetic operators you can use and the key you press to enter each operator. In the table, operators are listed in the order of precedence. (See the sidebar "The order of precedence" to see what this means.)

Table 12-1	Arithmetic Operators for Use in Formulas		
Precedence	*Operator*	*Example Formula*	*Returns*
1	% (Percent)	=50%	50 percent, or 0.5
2	^ (Exponentiation)	=50^2,	50 to the second power, or 2500
3	* (Multiplication)	=E2*4	The value in cell E2 multiplied by 4

Precedence	Operator	Example Formula	Returns
3	/ (Division)	`=E2/3`	The value in cell E2 divided by 3
4	+ (Addition)	`=F1+F2+F3,`	The sum of the values in those cells
4	– (Subtraction)	`=G5-8,`	The value in cell G5 minus 8
5	& (Concatenation)	`="Part No.: "&D4`	The text *Part No.:* and the value in cell D4
6	= (Equal to)	`=C5=4,`	If the value in cell C5 is equal to 4, returns TRUE; returns FALSE otherwise
6	<> (Not equal to)	`=F3<>9`	If the value in cell F3 is *not* equal to 9, returns TRUE; returns FALSE otherwise
6	< (Less than)	`=B9<E11`	If the value in cell B9 is less than the value in cell E11, returns TRUE; returns FALSE otherwise
6	<= (Less than or equal to)	`=A4<=9`	If the value in cell A4 is less than or equal to 9, returns TRUE; returns FALSE otherwise
6	> (Greater than)	`=E8>14`	If the value in cell E8 is greater than 14, returns TRUE; returns FALSE otherwise
6	>= (Greater than or equal to)	`=C3>=D3`	If the value in cell C3 is less than or equal to the value in cell D3, returns TRUE; returns FALSE otherwise

The order of precedence

When a formula includes more than one opera-tor, the order in which the operators appear in the formula matters a lot. Consider this formula:

=2+3*4

Does this formula result in 14 (2+[3*4]) or 20 ([2+3]*4)? The answer is 14 because the Excel Web App performs multiplication before addi-tion in formulas. In other words, multiplication takes precedence over addition.

The order in which calculations are made in a formula that includes different operators is called the *order of precedence*. Be sure to remember the order of precedence when you construct complex formulas with more than one operator:

1. Percent (%)

2. Exponentiation (^)

3. Multiplication (*) and division (/); leftmost operations are calculated first

4. Addition (+) and subtraction (-); leftmost operations are calculated first

5. Concatenation (&)

6. Comparison (<, <=, >,>=, and <>)

To get around the order of precedence prob-lem, enclose parts of formulas in parenthe-ses. Operations in parentheses are calculated before all other parts of a formula. For example, the formula =2+3*4 equals 20 when it is written this way: =(2+3)*4.

Another way to compute a formula is to make use of a function. As "Working with Functions" explains later in this chapter, a function is a built-in formula that comes with Excel Web App. SUM, for example, adds the numbers in cells; AVG finds the average of different numbers.

The Basics of Entering a Formula

No matter what kind of formula you enter, no matter how complex the for-mula is, follow these basic steps to enter it:

1. **Click the cell where you want to enter the formula.**

2. **Click in the Formula bar if you want to enter the data there rather than the cell.**

3. **Enter the equals sign (=).**

You must be sure to enter the equals sign before you enter a formula. Without it, the Excel Web App thinks you're entering text or a number, not a formula.

4. **Enter the formula.**

   For example, enter **=B1*.06**. Make sure that you enter all cell addresses correctly. By the way, you can enter lowercase letters in cell references. Excel Web App changes them to uppercase after you finish entering the formula. The next section in this chapter explains how to enter cell addresses quickly in formulas.

5. **Press Enter, press an arrow key, or click in a different cell.**

   The result of the formula appears in the cell.

Speed Techniques for Entering Formulas

Entering formulas and making sure that all cell references are correct is a tedious activity, but fortunately for you, Excel Web App offers a few techniques to make entering formulas easier. Read on to find out how ranges make entering cell references easier and how you can enter cell references in formulas by pointing and clicking. You also find instructions here for copying formulas.

Clicking cells to enter cell references

The hardest part about entering a formula is entering the cell references correctly. You have to squint to see which row and column the cell you want to refer to is in. You have to carefully type the right column letter and row number. However, rather than type a cell reference, you can click the cell you want to refer to in a formula.

In the course of entering a formula, simply click the cell on your worksheet that you want to reference. As shown in Figure 12-4, a blue box appears around the cell that you clicked so that you can clearly see which cell you're referring to. The cell's reference address, meanwhile, appears in the Formula bar. In Figure 12-4, I clicked cell F3 rather than entered its reference address on the Formula bar. The reference F3 appears on the Formula bar, and the blue box appears around cell F3.

Get in the habit of pointing and clicking cells to enter cell references in formulas. Clicking cells is easier than typing cell addresses, and the cell references are entered more accurately.

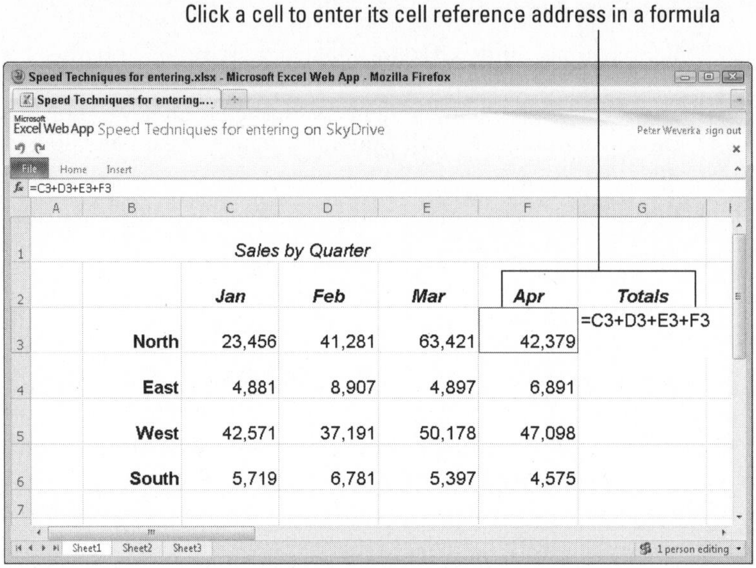

Click a cell to enter its cell reference address in a formula

Figure 12-4:
Clicking to
enter a cell
reference.

Entering a cell range

A *cell range* is a line or block of cells in a worksheet. Rather than type cell reference addresses one at a time, you can simply select cells on your worksheet. In Figure 12-5, I selected cells C4, D4, E4, and F4 to form cell range C4:F4. This spares me the trouble of entering the cell addresses one at a time: C4, D4, E4, and F4. The formula in Figure 12-5 uses the "SUM" function to total the numeric values in cell range C4:F4. Notice the box (which is blue on-screen) around the range C4:F4. The box shows precisely which range you're selecting. Cell ranges come in especially handy where functions are concerned (see "Working with Functions" later in this chapter).

To identify a cell range, the Excel Web App lists the outermost cells in the range and places a colon (:) between cell addresses:

- ✔ A cell range comprising cells A1, A2, A3, and A4 is listed this way: A1:A4.

- ✔ A cell range comprising a block of cells from A1 to D4 is listed this way: A1:D4.

You can enter cell ranges on your own without selecting cells. To do so, type the first cell in the range, enter a colon (:), and type the last cell.

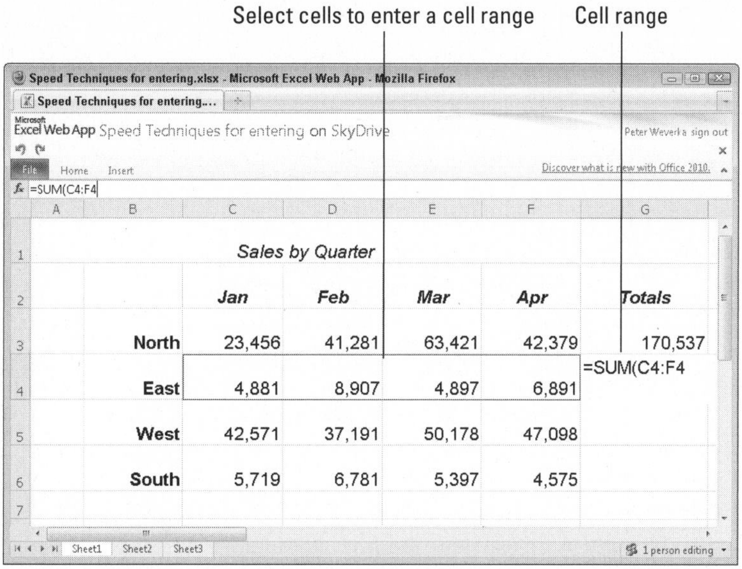

Select cells to enter a cell range   Cell range

Figure 12-5:
Using a cell
range in a
formula.

Copying formulas from cell to cell

Often in worksheets, the same formula but with different cell references is used across a row or down a column. For example, in the worksheet shown in Figure 12-6, column F totals the rainfall figures in rows 6 through 10. To enter formulas for totaling the rainfall figures in column F, you could laboriously enter formulas in cells F6, F7, F8, F9, and F10. But a faster way is to enter the formula once in cell F6 and then copy the formula in F6 to cells F7, F8, F9, and F10.

When you copy a formula to a new cell, Excel Web App adjusts the cell references in the formula so that the formula works in the cells to which it has been copied. Astounding! Opportunities to copy formulas abound on most worksheets. And copying formulas is the fastest and safest way to enter formulas in a worksheet.

Follow these steps to copy a formula:

1. Select the cell with the formula you want to copy.

2. On the Home tab, click the Copy button (or press Ctrl+C).

Broken lines appear around the cell you selected to indicate that its formula is the one being copied.

Choose Paste Formulas

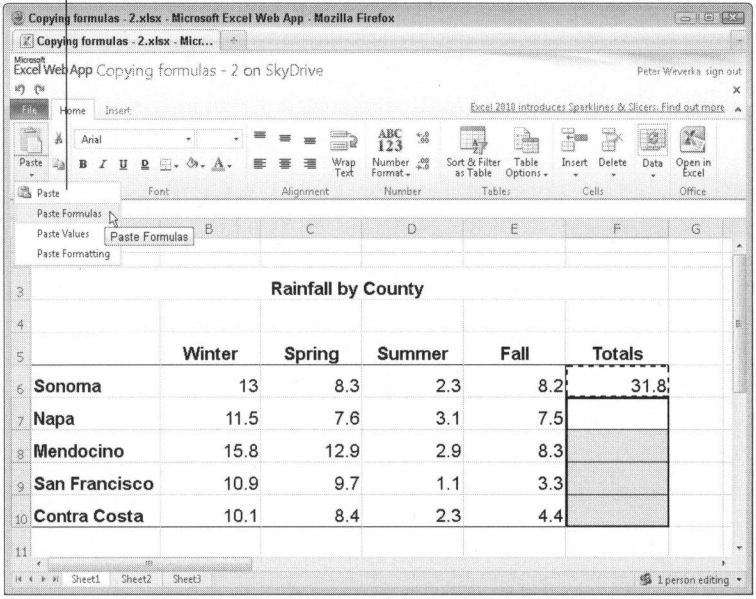

Figure 12-6:
Copying a
formula.

3. **Click in the cell where you want to copy the formula; to copy a formula to several different cells, select them.**

4. **On the Paste button, click the arrow to open the drop-down list; then choose Paste Formulas.**

If I were you, I would click in the cells to which you copied the formula and glance at the Formula bar to make sure that the formula was copied correctly. I'd bet you it was, but it's best to be sure.

Working with Functions

A *function* is a canned formula. Excel Web App offers hundreds of functions, some of which are very obscure and fit only for use by rocket scientists and securities analysts. Other functions are very practical. For example, you can use the SUM function to quickly total the numbers in a range of cells. Rather than enter **=C2+C3+C4+C5** on the Formula bar, you can enter **=SUM(C2:C5)**, which tells Excel Web App to total the numbers in cell C2, C3, C4, and C5. To obtain the product of the number in cell G4 and the number .06, you can use the PRODUCT function and enter **=PRODUCT(G4,.06)** on the Formula bar.

Table 12-2 lists common functions. The pages that follow explain how to use functions in formulas.

Table 12-2	Common Functions and Their Use
Function	*Returns*
AVERAGE(*number1*, *number2,. . .*)	The average of the numbers in the cells listed in the arguments.
COUNT(*value1*, *value2,. . .*)	The number of cells that contain the numbers listed in the arguments.
MAX(*number1*, *number2,. . .*)	The largest value in the cells listed in the arguments.
MIN(*number1*, *number2,. . .*)	The smallest value in the cells listed in the arguments.
PRODUCT(*number1*, *number2,. . .*)	The product of multiplying the cells listed in the arguments.
STDEV(*number1*, *number2,. . .*)	An estimate of standard deviation based on the sample cells listed in the arguments.
STDEVP(*number1*, *number2,. . .*)	An estimate of standard deviation based on the entire sample cells listed in the arguments.
SUM(*number1*, *number2,. . .*)	The total of the numbers in the arguments.
VAR(*number1*, *number2,. . .*)	An estimate of the variance based on the sample cells listed in the arguments.
VARP(*number1*, *number2,. . .*)	A variance calculation based on all cells listed in the arguments.

Using arguments in functions

Every function takes one or more *arguments*. Arguments are the cell references or numbers, enclosed in parentheses, that the function acts upon. In this example, the AVERAGE function returns the average of the numbers in the cell range B1 through B4:

```
=AVERAGE(B1:B4)
```

In this example, the PRODUCT function returns the product of multiplying the number 6.5 by the number in cell C4:

```
=PRODUCT(6.5,C4)
```

When a function requires more than one argument, enter a comma between the arguments. (Enter a comma without a space.)

Writing a formula with a function

Follow these steps to make use of a function in a formula:

1. **Select the cell where you want to enter the formula.**

2. **In the Formula bar, type an equals sign (=).**

   Please, please, please be sure to start every formula by entering an equals sign (=). Without it, Excel Web App thinks you're entering text or a number in the cell.

3. **Type the function's name.**

   If you type the function's name in the cells, not the Formula bar, you see a drop-down list with functions you can choose from.

   You can enter function names in lowercase. Excel Web App converts function names to uppercase after you complete the formula.

   Table 12-2 (earlier in this chapter) lists common functions. To get an idea of the numerous functions that Excel offers, open Excel 2010, go to the Formulas tab, and click the Insert Function button. You see the Insert Function dialog box. Choose a function category in the dialog box, choose a function name, and read the description. You can click the Help on This Function link to open the Excel Help window and get a thorough description of the function and how it's used.

4. **Enter arguments for the function.**

   Earlier in this chapter, "Using arguments in functions" explains arguments. Be sure to enclose the function's argument or arguments in parentheses. Don't enter a space between the function's name and the first parenthesis. Likewise, don't enter a comma and a space between arguments; enter a comma, nothing more:

   ```
   =SUM(F11,F14,23)
   ```

5. **Press the Enter key to finish entering the formula.**

   Did your formula compute correctly? I certainly hope it did. If you enter a function name incorrectly, #NAME? appears in the cell where the result of the formula should be.

Sorting and Filtering Data

Excel Web App offers commands for sorting and filtering data in table form. Use the Sort command to arrange data in a different way. Filter data to isolate data of a certain kind or exclude data that isn't necessary to you.

Before you can sort or filter data in a worksheet, you must arrange the data correctly into a table. How to do that, sort a table, and filter a table are the subjects of the following pages, and I invite you to quit your yawning and keep reading.

Understanding what sorting and filtering are

Sorting means to rearrange the rows in a table on the basis of data in one or more columns. Sort a table on the Last Name column, for example, to arrange rows in the table in alphabetical order by last name. Sort a table on the ZIP Code column to arrange the rows in numerical order by ZIP code. Sort a table on the Birthday column to arrange it chronologically from earliest born to latest born.

Filtering means to scour a table for certain kinds of data. To filter, you tell the Excel Web App what kind of data you're looking for, and the program assembles rows with that data to the exclusion of rows that don't have the data. You end up with a shorter table with only the rows that match your filter criteria. Filtering is similar to using the Find command except that you can find more than one item. For example, in a table of addresses, you can filter for addresses in California. In a price-list table, you can filter for items that fall within a certain price range.

Presenting data for the table

To sort or filter data in a worksheet, start by arranging the data in the form of a table, as shown at the top of Figure 12-7. Make sure that your table has these characteristics:

- ✔ **Column labels in the header row:** The row along the top of the table where the column labels are is called the *header row*. I recommend entering labels in the header row to help Excel Web App identify and be able to sort or filter the data in the rows below. Give each label a different name.

- ✔ **No empty rows or columns:** Sorry, but the table can't include any empty rows or columns if you intend to use your table to sort data. Excel Web App is incapable of sorting a table if a row or column is blank.

- ✔ **No Total row:** Don't include a total row (a last row that totals figures in the other rows) if you intend to sort or filter data in your table. The total row presents cumulative data and is therefore not appropriate for sorting or filtering.

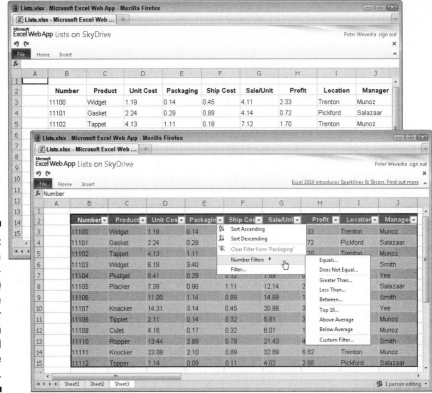

Figure 12-7:
Table data
in a work-
sheet (top)
and the
table after
it has been
designated
as a table
(bottom).

Creating the table

After you arrange data for the table and make sure the data is presented properly, you can tell Excel Web App that the data is indeed a table by follow-ing these steps:

1. Select the data.

You can do so by dragging from the northwest to the southeast corner of the table.

2. On the Insert tab, click the Table button.

The Create Table dialog box appears, as shown in Figure 12-8. It lists the cell range you selected in Step 1. You can also display this dialog box by clicking the Sort & Filter As Table button on the Home tab.

Figure 12-8:
The Create
Table
dialog box.

3. **Declare whether your table has a header row by selecting or deselecting the My Table Has Headers check box; then click OK.**

The header row is the row at the top of the table with labels that describe what is in each column. You can't sort and filter a table that doesn't have a header row. If your table doesn't have a header row (and you deselect the My Table Has Headers check box), Excel Web App provides a generic header row for you with columns named Column1, Column2, and so on.

As shown previously in Figure 12-7, a drop-down list appears beside each column header. Open a drop-down list to sort or filter your table.

Excel Web App doesn't have a command for unmaking a table. After you declare that data in a worksheet belongs in a table, you can't remove the table from the data except by clicking the Undo button.

Sorting a table

After the preliminaries are over, you can sort a table by following these steps:

1. **On the column that you want to use for sorting, open the drop-down list on the column header.**

For example, to sort a table in alphabetical order by last name, open the drop-down list on the Last Name column header. Earlier in this chapter, Figure 12-7 shows a drop-down list on a column header.

If you don't see column headers in your table, go to the Home tab, click the Table Options button, and choose Toggle Header Row on the drop-down list.

2. **Choose Sort Ascending or Sort Descending on the drop-down list.**

Which command you choose depends on whether you want an ascending sort or a descending sort:

- *Ascending sort:* Arranges text entries in alphabetical order from A to Z, numbers from smallest to largest, and dates chronologically from earliest to latest.

- *Descending sort:* Arranges text entries from Z to A, numbers from largest to smallest, and dates chronologically from latest to earliest.

You can tell whether a table has been sorted by glancing at the column header buttons. If the table has been sorted, the button on the column used for sorting shows an arrow. The arrow points up if the table was sorted in ascending order; it points down if the table was sorted in descending order. Move the pointer over the button and you see the "Sorted Ascending" or "Sorted Descending" pop-up message.

Filtering a table

Filter a table to isolate the data you want to examine and exclude all other data. Filtering is especially useful in long tables when you need to see only a few table entries.

Excel Web App offers two means of filtering. You can filter by exclusion to prune entries you don't want from the table, or filter by criteria to see entries that meet search criteria. Both techniques are described here. You also find out how to "unfilter" a table and see all the entries in the table again after you finish filtering it.

You can tell when a table has been filtered because the Filtered symbol appears on the column that was used for the filtering operation. If you move the pointer over the Filtered symbol, the word "Filtered" appears in a pop-up message. To find out how a table was filtered, open the column button, choose Filters on the drop-down list, and note which filtering option is selected on the submenu.

Filtering by exclusion

Filter by exclusion to select only the entries you want to examine in a table. For example, you can filter an Address table to see only addresses in Boston, Chicago, and Miami, and exclude all other addresses. Follow these steps to filter by exclusion:

1. **On the column that you want to use for filtering, open the drop-down list on the column header and choose Filter.**

   The Filter dialog box appears, as shown in Figure 12-9. It lists all values in the column.

2. **Deselect the Select All check box.**

3. **Select the check box next to each item you *don't* want to filter out.**

   For example, to filter an Address table to see only addresses in Illinois, Indiana, and Ohio, select the check boxes next to those cities' names.

4. **Click OK.**

   Your table shows only the entries you selected in Step 3. Later in this chapter, "Unfiltering a table" explains how to see all table entries again.

Figure 12-9:
The Filter
dialog box.

Filter by criteria

Filter by criteria to display table entries that meet a certain criteria. In the case of a table with a column of numbers, for example, you can filter the table to find numbers in the 100 to 150 range. In the case of text, you can find table entries that begin with the same two or three letters. In the case of dates, you can find entries before or after a certain date. What's more, you can filter by criteria on more than one column. For example, in a table that tracks house sales in different counties, you can filter for houses sold in one county and filter a second time to find houses sold in the county in a certain price range.

Follow these steps to filter by criteria:

1. **On the column that you want to use for filtering, open the drop-down list on the column header and choose Number Filters, Date Filters, or Text Filters.**

   Which option you see — Number Filters, Date Filters, or Text Filters — depends on what kind of data you're dealing with. A submenu with options appears.

2. **On the submenu, choose a filtering option or choose Custom Filter at the bottom of the submenu.**

   Table 12-3 describes filtering options. On the submenu, options that are followed by an ellipsis (. . .) require you to enter a filtering criterion. Choosing one of these options opens the Custom Filter dialog box.

   If you choose an option on the submenu that isn't followed by an ellipsis (. . .), Excel Web App filters the table immediately. You don't have to enter filtering criteria. You're finished with this filtering business.

3. **In the Custom Filter dialog box, choose a Show Items Where option, if necessary.**

   Choose an option if you chose Custom Filter in Step 2 or you want to choose a different option than the one you chose in Step 2.

4. **Enter a criterion for filtering the table.**

   Table 12-3 describes filtering options and filtering criteria.

5. **Click OK in the Custom Filter dialog box.**

   Only table entries that meet your filtering criteria appear in the table. Later in this chapter, "Unfiltering a table" shows how to see all table entries again.

To narrow your search for table entries even further, filter the table again on another column.

Table 12-3	Filtering Options and Criteria
Option(s)	*Example Criteria and Explanation*
Number Filters	
Equals...	10, ten — not any other number
Does Not Equal...	10, all numbers except ten
Begins With...	46, any number beginning with the numerals *46*
Does Not Begin With...	46, all numbers except those beginning with the numerals *46*
Ends With...	28, any number ending with the numerals *28*
Does Not End With...	28, all numbers except those ending with the numerals *28*
Contains...	546, any number that includes the numerals *546* (in that order)
Does Not Contain...	546, all numbers except those that include the numerals *546* (in that order)
Is Greater Than...	10, any number larger than ten
Is Greater Than Or Equal To...	10, ten as well as any number larger than ten
Is Less Than...	10, any number smaller than ten
Less than or equal to...	10, ten as well as any number smaller than ten
Is Between...	10 *and* 15, a number between 10 and 15 or equal to 10 or 15
Is Not Between...	10 *and* 15, any number except 10, 15, and all numbers between 10 and 15

Option(s)	Example Criteria and Explanation
Above Average	Determines the average of numbers in the column and displays entries with above-average numbers only
Below Average	Determines the average of numbers in the column and displays entries with below-average numbers only
Date Filters	
Equals...	4/27/11, the day April 27, 2011
Before...	5/3/09, all days prior to May 3, 2009
After...	12/31/09, all days after December 31, 2009
Between...	4/3/09 *and* 4/21/10, April 3, 2009 and April 21, 2010, as well as all days between those days
Tomorrow	One day after the current day
Today	The current day
Yesterday	One day before the current day
Next Week, This Week, Last Week	The following, current, or previous week with respect to the current day (weeks begin on Sunday and end on Saturday)
Next Month, This Month, Last Month	The following, current, or previous month with respect to the current day
Next Quarter, This Quarter, Last Quarter	The following, current, or previous quarter with respect to the current day (the first quarter comprises January–March, the second April–June, the third July–September, and the fourth October–December)
Next Year, This Year, Last Year	The following, current, or previous year with respect to the current day
Year To Date	Days in the current year, previous to and including the current day
All Dates In This Period	A quarter or month (choose on the submenu); dates refer to any year or quarter (for example, choosing January finds dates in January 2011 and January 2012)
Text Filters	
Equals...	Mexico, all entries that match the criteria exactly (*Mexico* remains in the table because it is an exact match, but *New Mexico* is removed)
Does Not Equal...	Boston, all entries except those that match the criteria exactly (*Boston Baked Beans* remains in the table because it is not an exact match, but *Boston* is removed)

(continued)

Table 12-3 *(continued)*

Option(s)	Example Criteria and Explanation
Begins With. . .	`bow`, all entries beginning with the letters *bow* (*bowler* and *Bowdoin College* remain in the table, but *elbow* and *Medicine Bow* are removed)
Ends With. . .	`burgh`, all entries ending with the letters *burgh* (*Pittsburgh* and *van der Burgh* remain in the table, but *burgher* and *Burgh Castle* are removed)
Contains. . .	`nut`, all entries that contain the letters *nut*, in that order (*peanut butter* and *Nutley* remain in the table, but *Hunter* and *Tunis* are removed)
Does Not Contain. . .	`san`, all entries except those that contain the letters *san*, in that order (*red snapper* and *NASCAR* remain in the table, but *Santa Fe* and *Nissan* are removed)

Unfiltering a table

Look for the Filtered symbol on table columns to find out whether a table has been filtered. Follow these steps to unfilter a table and see more or all of its table entries:

1. **On a column that was used for filtering, open the drop-down list.**

2. **Choose Clear Filter From.**

   As shown in Figure 12-10, the Clear Filter From option is named after the column that was used for filtering. In a column called Cities, for example, the option is called Clear Filter From Cities.

If the table was filtered on more than one column, you may have to unfilter the column as well.

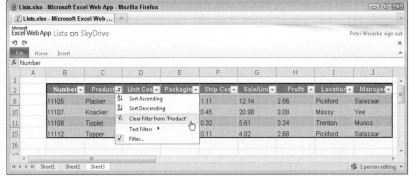

Figure 12-10: Unfiltering a table is pretty darn easy.

Part V
PowerPoint Web App

In this part . . .

Part V is dedicated to the proposition that anyone can create a PowerPoint presentation that makes the audience say "Wow!"

This part describes the PowerPoint Web App, what constitutes a good PowerPoint presentation, and how to connect with an audience. It also looks at creating lists, scribbling notes during presentations, and doing one or two other things to make your presentation stand out.

Chapter 13

Getting Acquainted with PowerPoint Web App

. . . .

In This Chapter

▶ Creating a new PowerPoint presentation

▶ Understanding PowerPoint terminology

▶ Finding your way around the PowerPoint Web App screen

▶ Persuading the audience to see it your way

▶ Looking at design considerations

▶ Examining how PowerPoint Web App and PowerPoint 2010 differ

. . . .

*T*his chapter lays the groundwork for you to create a persuasive presentation with PowerPoint Web App. It explains what the different parts of the PowerPoint Web App screen are. It also tells you what to consider when you design slides and how to bring the audience around to your point of view when you give a presentation.

In the next chapter, you apply the skills you discover here to create slides for a presentation. For instructions in opening PowerPoint Web App and creating a new presentation, see Chapter 2.

Creating a PowerPoint Presentation

Chapter 2 explains in detail how to create and open Office Web App files, including PowerPoint presentations, in an Office Web App. To keep you from having to make the long, arduous journey to Chapter 2, here are shorthand instructions for creating a new PowerPoint presentation in PowerPoint Web App:

1. **Click the New link and choose PowerPoint Presentation on the drop-down list.**

   You see the New Microsoft PowerPoint Presentation window.

2. **Enter a name for your presentation.**

3. **Click the Save button.**

   As shown in Figure 13-1, the Select Theme dialog box appears. A *theme* is a ready-made, canned slide design. Most themes come with sophisticated background patterns and colors.

4. **Select a theme and click the Apply button.**

   Congratulations — you just created a PowerPoint presentation in PowerPoint Web App.

Sorry, but you can't select a different theme for a presentation in PowerPoint Web App. To select a different them, you have to open your presentation in PowerPoint 2010.

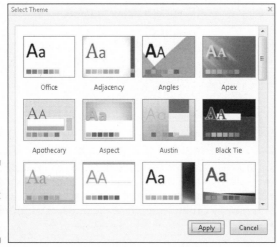

Figure 13-1:
The Select Theme dialog box.

Talking PowerPoint Lingo

Figure 13-2 (top) shows the PowerPoint Web App window. That thing in the middle is a *slide,* PowerPoint's word for an image that you show your audience. Surrounding the slide are tools for entering text and formatting slides.

When the time comes to show your slides, you dispense with the tools and make the slide fill the screen, as shown in Figure 13-2 (bottom). Throughout this chapter and the next, you find instructions for making slides and for constructing a *presentation,* the PowerPoint word that describes all the slides, from first to last, that you show to your audience.

Here's another PowerPoint word you need to know — *notes*. The audience doesn't see notes. You, the speaker, can write notes so that you know what to say during a presentation.

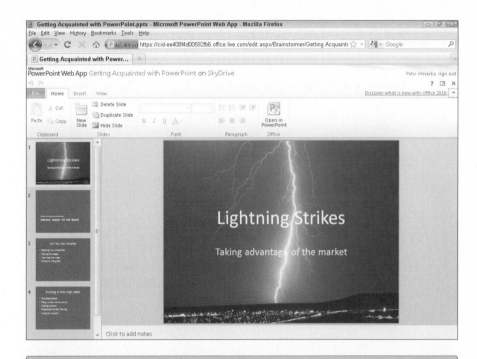

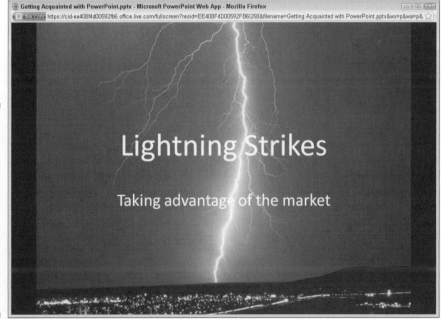

Figure 13-2: A slide in the PowerPoint Web App window (top) and the same slide the way it looks during a presentation (bottom).

A Brief Geography Lesson

Here is a brief geography lesson about the different parts of the PowerPoint Web App screen. I'd hate for you to get lost in PowerPoint Land. Figure 13-3 shows the different parts of the screen. Fold down the corner of this page so that you can return here if screen terminology confuses you:

- ✔ **Title bar:** The stripe along the top of your browser window. It lists your presentation's name.

- ✔ **Quick Access toolbar:** A toolbar with two buttons — Undo and Repeat. You see this toolbar wherever you go in the PowerPoint Web App.

- ✔ **File tab:** The tab that offers commands for opening a PowerPoint presentation in PowerPoint 2010, printing a presentation, closing a presentation, and doing other file-related tasks.

- ✔ **Ribbon:** The place where the tabs are located. Click a tab — Home, Insert, or View — to start a task. Chapter 2 explains the Ribbon and its tabs in detail.

- ✔ **Slides pane:** In Editing view, the place on the left side of the screen where you can see the slides in your presentation. The slides are numbered. Scroll in the Slides pane to move backward and forward in a presentation.

- ✔ **Slide window:** Where the slide you're working on is displayed.

- ✔ **Notes pane:** In Editing view, where you can type notes that you can refer to when giving your presentation or hand out to audience members. The audience can't see these notes — they are for you and you alone. On the View tab, click the Notes button to hide or display the Notes pane.

Advice for Building Persuasive Presentations

As nice as PowerPoint is, it has its detractors. If the software isn't used properly, it can come between the speaker and the audience. In a May 28, 2001, *New Yorker* article titled "Absolute PowerPoint: Can a Software Package Edit Our Thoughts?" Ian Parker argued that PowerPoint might actually be more of a hindrance than a help in communicating. PowerPoint, Parker wrote, is "a social instrument, turning middle managers into bullet-point dandies." The software, he added, "has a private, interior influence. It edits ideas . . . . It helps you make a case, but also makes its own case about how to organize information, how to look at the world."

File tab

Quick Access toolbar   Ribbon

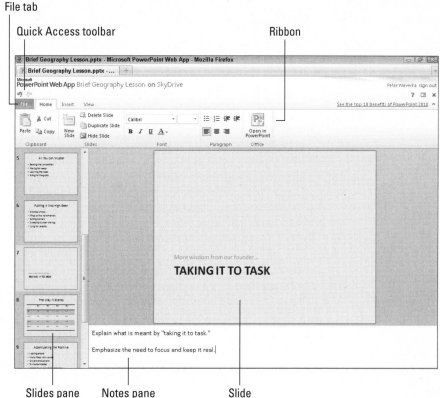

Figure 13-3:
The different parts
of the
PowerPoint
Web App
screen.

Slides pane   Notes pane   Slide

Before you create any slides with the PowerPoint Web App, think about what you want to communicate to your audience. Your goal is not to dazzle the audience with your PowerPoint skills, but to communicate something — a company policy, the merits of a product, the virtues of a strategic plan. Your goal is to bring the audience around to your side.

To that end, the following pages offer practical advice for taking your presentation from the drawing-board stage to the next stage, the one in which you actually start creating slides.

Want to see a great example of a bad PowerPoint presentation? Try visiting the Gettysburg PowerPoint Presentation, a rendering of Lincoln's Gettysburg Address in PowerPoint. Yikes! You'll find it here:

```
www.norvig.com/Gettysburg
```

Start by writing the text

Here's one of the best pieces of advice you'll ever get about creating a PowerPoint presentation: Write the text of the presentation first. Focus on the words to begin with. This way, you focus on what you want to communicate, not slide layouts or graphic designs or fonts.

I suspect that people actually enjoy doodling with PowerPoint slides because it distracts them from focusing on what really matters in a presentation — what's meant to be communicated. Building an argument is hard work. People who can afford it pay lawyers and ghostwriters to do the job for them. Building an argument requires thinking long and hard about your topic, putting yourself in the place of an audience member who doesn't know the topic as well as you, and convincing the audience member that you're right. You can do this hard work better in Word, where the carnival atmosphere of PowerPoint isn't there to distract you.

Make clear what the presentation is about

In the early going, state very clearly what your presentation is about and what you intend to prove with your presentation. In other words, state the conclusion at the beginning as well as the end. This way, your audience will know exactly what you're driving at and be able to judge your presentation according to how well you build your case.

Start from the conclusion

Try writing the end of the presentation first. A presentation is supposed to build to a rousing conclusion. By writing the end first, you have a target to shoot for. You can make the entire presentation service its conclusion, the point at which your audience says, "Ah-ha! She's right."

Personalize the presentation

Make the presentation a personal one. Tell the audience what *your* personal reason for being there is or why *you* work for the company you work for. Knowing that you have a personal stake in the presentation, the audience is more likely to trust you. The audience will understand that you're not a spokesperson, but a speaker — someone who has come before them to make a case for something that you believe in.

Tell a story

Include anecdotes in the presentation. Everybody loves a pertinent and well-delivered story. This piece of advice is akin to the previous one about personalizing your presentation. Typically, a story illustrates a problem for *people* and how *people* solve the problem. Even if your presentation concerns technology or an abstract subject, make it about people. "The people in Shaker Heights needed faster Internet access," not "the data switches in Shaker Heights just weren't performing fast enough."

Assemble the content

Finally, for a bit of practical advice, assemble the content before you begin creating your presentation. Gather together everything you need to make your case — photographs, facts, data, quotations. By so doing, you can have at your fingertips everything you need to get going. You don't have to interrupt your work to get more material, and having all the material on hand will help you formulate your case better.

Designing Your Presentation

Entire books have been written about how to design a PowerPoint presentation. I've read three or four. However, designing a high-quality presentation comes down to observing a few simple rules. These pages explain what those rules are.

Keep it simple

To make sure that PowerPoint doesn't upstage you, keep it simple. Make use of the PowerPoint features, but do so judiciously. A picture in the right place at the right time can serve a valuable purpose. It can highlight an important part of a presentation or jolt the audience awake. But stuffing a presentation with too many pictures turns a presentation into a carnival sideshow and distracts from your message.

On the subject of keeping it simple, slides are easier on the eyes if they aren't crowded. A cramped slide with too many words and pictures can cause claustrophobia. Leave some empty space on a slide so that the audience can see and read the slide better.

Studying others' presentations by starting at Google

How would you like to look at others' presentations to get ideas for your presentation? Starting at Google.com, you can search for PowerPoint presentations, find one that interests you, download it to your computer, open it, and have a look. Follow these steps to search online for PowerPoint presentations and land one on your computer:

1. **Start PowerPoint, if necessary, and open your Web browser.**

2. **Go to Google at this address:** `www.google.com`.

3. **Click the Advanced Search link.**

   You land on the Advanced Search page.

4. **Open the File Type drop-down list and choose Microsoft PowerPoint (.ppt).**

5. **In the All These Words text box, enter a descriptive term that describes the kind of PowerPoint presentations you're interested in.**

   For example, enter **succotash** if you have been charged with creating a PowerPoint presentation about a food dish made of green beans and corn.

6. **Click the Advanced Search button.**

   In the search results, you see a list of PowerPoint presentations.

7. **Select the name of a presentation that looks interesting and download it.**

   After you download the presentation, it opens in PowerPoint. Do you like what you see? Scroll through the slides to find out how someone else designed a presentation.

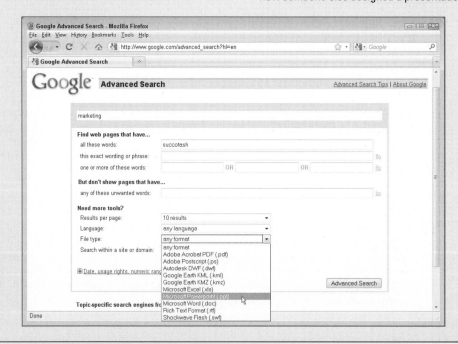

Be consistent from slide to slide

The surest sign of a professional, well-thought-out presentation is consistency from slide to slide. The titles are formatted the same way on all slides. The fonts and font sizes are consistent. Bulleted lists are formatted the same way. The capitalization scheme in titles is the same from slide to slide. If the title of one slide has a capitalized first word with the remaining words uncapitalized, titles on all the other slides appear the same way.

Choose colors that help communicate your message

The color choices you make for your presentation say as much about what you want to communicate as the words and graphics do. Colors set the tone. They tell the audience right away what your presentation is about. A loud presentation with a black background and red text conveys excitement; a light-blue background conveys peace and quiet. Use your intuition to think of color combinations that say what you want your presentation to say.

When fashioning a design, consider the audience

Consider who will view your presentation, and tailor the presentation design to your audience's expectations. The slide design sets the tone and tells the audience in the form of colors and fonts what your presentation is all about. A presentation to the American Casketmakers Association calls for a mute, quiet design; a presentation to the Cheerleaders of Tomorrow calls for something bright and splashy; a presentation about a daycare center requires light blues and pinks, the traditional little-boys and little-girls colors. Choosing colors for your presentation is that much easier if you consider the audience.

Beware the bullet point

Terse bullet points have their place in a presentation, and many PowerPoint slide layouts are made for bulleted lists, but if you put the lists in your presentation strictly to remind yourself what to say next, you're doing your audience a disfavor. An overabundance of bullet points can cause drowsiness. Bullets can be a distraction. The audience skims the bullets when it should be attending to your voice and the case you're making.

One way to get around the problem of putting too many bulleted lists in a presentation is to use diagrams in place of lists. Figure 13-4 demonstrates how the information in a bulleted list can be presented in a diagram. Chapter 5 explains how to handle diagrams in an Office Web App.

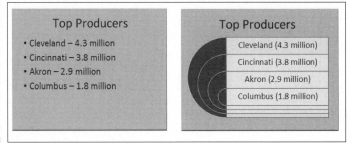

Figure 13-4: Rather than a bulleted list, you can present list information in a diagram.

Observe the one-slide-per-minute rule

At the very minimum, a slide should stay on-screen for at least one minute. If you have been given 15 minutes to speak, you are allotted no more than 15 slides for your presentation, according to the rule.

Rules, of course, are made to be broken, and you may break the rule if your presentation consists of vacation slides that can be shown in a hurry. The purpose of the one-slide-per-minute rule is to keep you from reading from your notes while displaying PowerPoint slides. Remember: The object of a PowerPoint presentation is to communicate with the audience. By observing the one-slide-per-minute rule, you make sure that the focus is on you and what you're communicating, not on PowerPoint slides.

Make like a newspaper

As you write slide titles and headings, take your cue from the editors who write newspaper headlines. A newspaper headline is supposed to serve two purposes. It tells readers what the story is about but it also tries to attract readers' attention or pique their interest. The title "Faster response times" is descriptive, but not captivating. An alternative slide title could be "Are we there yet?" or "Hurry up and wait." These titles aren't as descriptive as the first, but they are more captivating, and they hint at the slide's subject. Your talk while the slide is on-screen will suffice to flesh out the topic in detail.

Put a newspaper-style headline at the top of each slide, and while you're at it, think of each slide as a short newspaper article. Each slide should address a specific aspect of your subject, and it should do so in a compelling way. How long does it take to read a newspaper article? It depends on how long the article is, of course, but a PowerPoint slide should stay on-screen for roughly the time it takes to explore a single topic the way a newspaper article does.

Use visuals, not only words, to make your point

You really owe it to your audience to take advantage of the picture capabilities of the PowerPoint Web App. People understand more from words and pictures than they do from words alone. It's up to you as the speaker, not the slides, to describe topics in detail with words.

Figure 13-5 shows an example of how a few words and a picture can convey a lot. This slide comes from the beginning of a presentation. It tells the audience which topics will be covered. Instead of being covered through long descriptions, each topic is encapsulated in a word or two, and the picture in the middle shows plainly what the presentation is about. Chapter 5 explains how to insert pictures with an Office Web App.

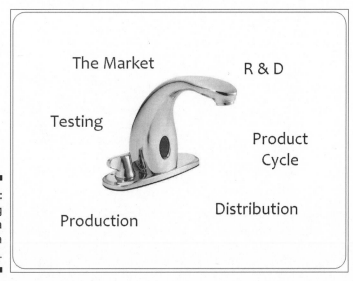

Figure 13-5:
Combining words and a picture in a slide.

Comparing PowerPoint Web App to PowerPoint 2010

As a glance at Figure 13-6 shows, PowerPoint Web App doesn't offer nearly as many features as its counterpart, PowerPoint 2010. PowerPoint Web App Ribbon has three measly tabs — Home, Insert, and View. In PowerPoint 2010, you can find no fewer than nine tabs on the Ribbon. The fact is, you can do far more to construct a presentation in PowerPoint 2010 than you can in PowerPoint Web App.

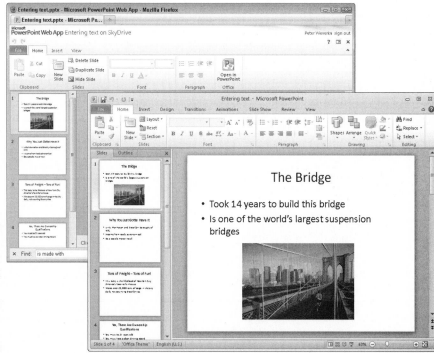

Figure 13-6:
PowerPoint
Web App
(top) and
PowerPoint
2010
(bottom).

To give you a clear understanding of how PowerPoint Web App and Power-Point 2010 differ, Table 13-1 lists PowerPoint 2010 features that aren't a part of PowerPoint Web App. In the table, features are listed according to the tab on which they are found in PowerPoint 2010.

Don't be discouraged if you need to use a feature listed in Table 13-1. As long as PowerPoint 2010 is installed on your computer, you can edit a PowerPoint presentation in PowerPoint 2010 by going to the Home tab in PowerPoint Web App and clicking the Open in PowerPoint button. Chapter 2 explains how to open a file you're editing in an Office Web App in Office 2010.

Table 13-1	PowerPoint 2010 Features Not Available in the PowerPoint Web App
Feature	*Description*
Home tab	
Find/Replace	Find words or phrases in slides, and replace them with other words or phrases
Line Spacing	Change the amount of space between lines of text
Selection Pane	Select items in the Selection and Visibility pane
Insert tab	
Audio	Play music or a voice narration during a presentation
Charts	Create a chart for displaying data
Clip Art	Place clip-art images in slides
Equation	Draw an equation with the Equation Editor tools
Headers and Footers	Create header and footer text for slides
Photo Album	Create a presentation featuring photos
Screenshot	Take a picture of a screen or a portion of a screen
Shapes	Draw lines, arrows, rectangles, ovals, and other shapes
Symbol	Enter a symbol or foreign character in text
Tables	Construct a table for presenting data
Video	Show a video on a slide
WordArt	Display a WordArt image on a slide
Design	
Background Styles	Choose a color, picture, text, or gradient pattern for slide backgrounds
Slide Orientation	Display slides in portrait as well as landscape mode
Themes	Choose an all-encompassing look for a presentation
Transitions	
Transitions	Make slides fade in, dissolve, or otherwise change as they arrive on-screen
Animations	
Animations	Make parts of a slide — a heading, bulleted list items, shapes — move on-screen

(continued)

Table 13-1 *(continued)*

Feature	Description
Slide Show	
Custom Slide Show	Create a secondary presentation with a portion of the slides in a presentation
Rehearse Timings	Make a slide show progress automatically with each slide appearing for a prescribed number of seconds
Set Up Slide Show	Create a user-run or kiosk-style presentation that runs on its own
Review	
Comments*	Enter comments about slides
Compare	Examine and compare edits made by different people to the same presentation
Language	Proof foreign-language text
Research	Use the Research task pane services — the dictionaries, thesauruses, and search engines
Thesaurus	Find a synonym for a word
Translate	Translate text from one language to another
View	
Color/Grayscale	Display slides in gray shades or black and white
Macros	Play macros
Master Views	On the Slide Master, Handout Master, and Notes Master, create a default look for slides, handouts, and notes
Show	Display the ruler, gridlines, and guides
Slide Sorter View	View all the slides in a presentation in thumbnail form
Window	Open secondary windows or split the screen as you work on a presentation
Zoom	Zoom in and out on slides

* Comments don't appear in PowerPoint Web App under any circumstances, even if the comments were created first in PowerPoint 2010.

Chapter 14

Constructing and Delivering a Presentation

This chapter picks up where the previous chapter left off and delves into the nitty-gritty of creating a presentation with PowerPoint Web App. It explains everything a body needs to know about creating slides, entering and formatting text on slides, positioning text, and changing the appearance of text. You also find information here about lists and writing notes.

Finally, turn to this chapter to find out how to give a PowerPoint presentation with PowerPoint Web App.

Understanding How Slides Are Constructed

When you create a slide, PowerPoint Web App asks you a very important question: "Which slide layout do you want?" You can choose from several different *slide layouts,* the preformatted slide designs that help you enter text, pictures, and other items on slides. Some layouts have text placeholder frames for entering titles and text. Some layouts come with icons that you can click to insert a diagram or picture.

When you create a slide, select the slide layout that best approximates the slide you have in mind for your presentation. These pages explain slide layouts.

Slide layouts

To make a wise choice about inserting slides, it helps to know how slide layouts are constructed. Figure 14-1 shows one of the simplest layouts, Title and Content, in three incarnations:

✔ The Title and Content layout as it appears in the New Slide dialog box. As you find out shortly, you create a slide by choosing a layout in the New Slide dialog box.

✔ The slide as it looked right after I selected it, before I entered any text (middle).

✔ The finished product, after I entered a bulleted list (right).

Figure 14-1:
A slide layout (left), the bare-bones slide (middle), and the finished slide (right).

Text frames and content frames

The Title and Content slide layout includes two *placeholder frames,* one for entering a title and one for entering either a bulleted list or "content" of some kind — a diagram or picture. Most slide layouts come with *text placeholder frames* to make entering text on a slide a little easier.

As Figure 14-2 shows, all you have to do to enter text in a text placeholder frame is "Click to add [the] title" or "Click to add [the] text." When you click in a text placeholder frame, these instructions disappear, and when you start typing, the text you enter appears in the frame where the instruction used to be.

Many slide layouts come with *content placeholder frames* as well as text placeholder frames. Content placeholder frames are designed to help you create diagrams and pictures. Figure 14-3 shows the Picture with Caption slide layout in three incarnations:

- The Picture with Caption layout as it appears on the New Slide dialog box (left).
- The slide as it looked right after I selected it, before I entered the picture and the text (middle).
- The finished product, after I entered the picture, title, and caption (right).

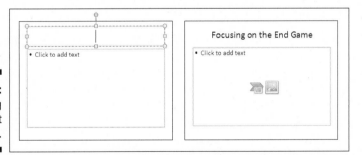

Figure 14-2: Entering text in a text frame.

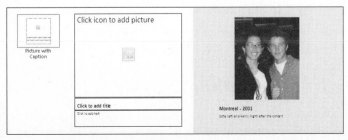

Figure 14-3: The Picture with Caption layout (left), the bare-bones slide (middle), and the finished slide (right).

Content placeholder frames come with icons that you can click to enter a diagram or picture. As the instruction in Figure 14-3 says, "Click icon to add picture." You click the icon that represents the item you want to create.

Creating New Slides for a Presentation

After you create a presentation, your next step on the path to glory is to start creating the slides. PowerPoint Web App has done its best to make this little task as easy as possible. These pages explain all the techniques for creating a new slide.

Adding a new slide

To add a slide to a presentation, choose a slide layout in the New Slide dialog box. Follow these steps to create a new slide for your presentation:

1. **Select the slide that you want the new slide to go after.**

    To select a slide, click it in the Slides pane. If you're unable to do that because you're in Reading view, click the Edit in Browser button.

2. **Go to the Home tab if you aren't already there.**

3. **Click the New Slide button.**

    The New Slide dialog box appears. It offers slide layouts for creating slides.

    Figure 14-4 shows what the slide layouts look like (left), what a slide looks like right after you insert it (middle), and finished slides (right). The previous topic in this chapter, "Understanding How Slides Are Constructed," explains what slide layouts are.

    The first slide layout, Title Slide, is designed to be the first slide in presentations; the Section Header slide layout is for changing the course of a presentation; and the other slide layouts are meant for presenting information in various ways.

4. **Select a slide layout.**

5. **Click the Add Slide button.**

    Your new slide appears in the Slide window.

Creating a duplicate slide

Creating a duplicate slide can save you the trouble of doing layout work. All you have to do is duplicate a slide and then go into the duplicate and change its title, text, or other particulars.

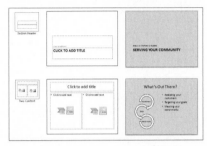

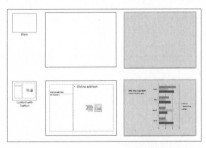

Figure 14-4:
The first step in creating a slide is to choose a slide layout. The left side of this figure shows the slide layouts in the New Slide dialog box.

Follow these steps to create a duplicate slide:

1. **Select the slide you want to duplicate.**

   In Editing view, click a slide in the Slides pane to select a slide.

2. **Go to the Home tab.**

3. **Click the Duplicate Slide button.**

   The duplicate slide appears after the slide you selected in Step 1. See "Selecting, Moving, and Deleting Slides," later in this chapter, if you need help moving the duplicate slide to another location.

Copying a slide

Similarly to duplicating a slide, you can create a new slide by copying one you already created. After you make the copy, you can change its title, text, or whatever needs changing and get yourself a brand-new slide. Copying a slide has an advantage over duplicating a slide: You can place the copy wherever you want.

Follow these steps to copy a slide:

1. **Select the slide you want to copy.**

   To select a slide, switch to Editing view and click the slide in the Slides pane.

2. **Go to the Home tab.**

3. **Click the Copy button (or press Ctrl+C).**

4. **In the Slides pane, select the slide that you want the copy to appear after.**

   For example, if you want to place the copied slide after the second slide, select slide number 2.

5. **Click the Paste button (or press Ctrl+V).**

   Your cloned slide appears after the slide you selected in Step 4.

Getting a Better View of Your Work

Depending on the task at hand, some views are better than others. Figure 14-5 illustrates the different ways of viewing a presentation. These pages explain how to change views and when to choose one view over another.

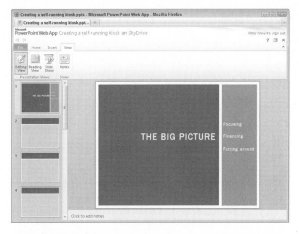

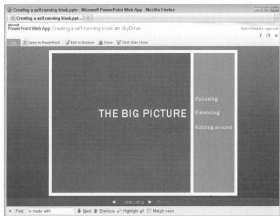

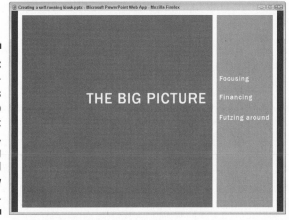

Figure 14-5: The different views (from top to bottom): Editing view, Reading view, and Slide Show view.

Changing views

Follow these steps to change views:

1. **Go to the View tab.**
2. **Click the Editing View, Reading View, or Slide Show button.**

   That's all there is to it.

Editing view: Moving from slide to slide

 Switch to Editing view (refer to Figure 14-5) and select a slide in the Slides pane when you want to enter text or content on a slide. In this view, thumbnail slides appear in the Slides pane, and you can see your slide in all its glory in the middle of the screen. Editing view in PowerPoint Web App is the equivalent of Normal view in PowerPoint 2010.

You can use the scrollbar in the Slides pane to scroll to a particular slide. You can also press the Home key to go to the first slide or the End key to go to the last slide in your presentation.

Reading view: Proofreading slides

 In Reading view (refer to Figure 14-5), you see a single slide. In Reading view, the Ribbon doesn't appear on-screen. Use Reading view to enlarge a slide and examine it closely or proofread it.

In Reading view, you can go from slide to slide by clicking buttons along the bottom of the screen:

- ✔ Click the Previous slide button to go to the previous slide in your presentation.
- ✔ Click the Next slide button to go to the next slide.
- ✔ Click the Slide Menu button and choose a slide on the pop-up list to jump forward or backward by several slides.

While you're in Reading view, you can read notes you entered by clicking the Notes button (it is located on the bottom of the screen). You can't enter notes in Reading view; you can only read notes.

To exit Reading view, click the Edit in Browser button.

Slide Show view: Giving a presentation

 In Slide Show view (refer to Figure 14-5), you see a single slide. Not only that, but the slide fills the entire screen (or most of the screen, depending on your browser settings). This is what your presentation looks like when you show it to an audience in a browser window. You can see what a slide really looks like at this size. To advance from slide to slide, click the screen. To quit Slide Show view, press the Esc key. Later in this chapter, "Giving a Presentation" explains how to deliver a presentation in Slide Show view.

Entering and Editing Text on Slides

No presentation is complete without a word or two at least, which is why the first thing you see when you add a new slide to a presentation are the words "Click to add [the] text." As soon as you click, those words of instruction disappear, and you are free to enter a title or text of your own. Most slides include a text placeholder frame at the top for entering a slide title. Many slides also have another, larger text placeholder frame for entering a bulleted list.

To enter text, simply wiggle your fingers over the keyboard. In case you need to edit text, these pages explain how to select, delete, copy, and move text on slides. (Chapter 4 explains how to change the look of text by choosing a font and font size for letters.)

Selecting text on a slide

Before you can reformat, delete text, copy, or move text, you have to select it. Here are techniques and shortcuts for selecting text:

To Select	Do This
A word	Double-click the word.
A few words	Drag over the words.
A paragraph	Triple-click inside the paragraph.
A block of text	Click at the start of the text you want to select, hold down the Shift key, and click at the end of the text.
All text in a text placeholder frame or text box	Press Ctrl+A.

Deleting text

To delete a bunch of text at one time, select the text you want to delete and press the Delete key. By the way, you can kill two birds with one stone by selecting text and then starting to type. The letters you type immediately take the place of and delete the text you selected.

You can always click the Undo button if you regret deleting text. You can find this button on the Quick Access toolbar in the upper-left corner of the screen.

Moving and copying text

As Chapter 4 explains in onerous detail, you can move and copy text in an Office Web App, PowerPoint Web App included, by using these techniques:

- ✔ **Drag and drop:** Select the text and drag it to a new location. To copy the text, hold down the Ctrl key while you drag.

- ✔ **Cutting and copying to the Clipboard:** Select the text, and on the Home tab, click the Cut button (or press Ctrl+X) to move the text or click the Copy button (or press Ctrl+C) to copy it. Then click where you want to move or copy the text and click the Paste button (or press Ctrl+V).

Aligning Text in Text Frames

Where text appears in a text frame is governed by how it is aligned, as shown in Figure 14-6. Use the Align buttons on the Home tab to align paragraphs and bulleted or numbered list items horizontally in a text frame. PowerPoint offers these Align buttons:

- ✔ **Align Text Left:** Lines up text along the left side of a frame. Typically, paragraphs and list items are left-aligned. Click the Align Text Left button (or press Ctrl+L).

- ✔ **Center:** Centers text, leaving an equal amount of space on both slides. Titles are often centered. Click the Center button (or press Ctrl+E).

- ✔ **Align Text Right:** Lines up text along the right side of a frame. Right-aligned text is uncommon but can be used artfully in titles. Click the Align Text Right button (or press Ctrl+R).

Indiana Sister Cities

Bloomington	Posoltega, Nicaragua
Fort Wayne	Gera, Germany
Gary	Fuixin, China
Indianapolis	Monza, Italy
South Bend	Czestochowa, Poland
Terre Haute	Tambov, Russia
Vincennes	Wasserburg, Germany

Figure 14-6: Ways of aligning text in text frames: Align text left, center, and align text right.

Handling Bulleted and Numbered Lists

What is a PowerPoint presentation without a list or two? It's like an emperor without any clothes on. This part of the chapter explains everything there is to know about bulleted and numbered lists, including how to remove the bullets or numbers and create a sublist, also known as a nested list.

In typesetting terms, a *bullet* is a black, filled-in circle or other character that marks an item on a list. As Figure 14-7 shows, bulleted lists are useful when you want to present the reader with alternatives or present a list in which the items are not ranked in any order. Use a numbered list to rank items in a list or present step-by-step instructions, as shown in Figure 14-8.

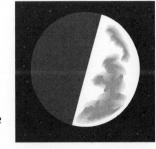

- Earth
- Jupiter
- Mars
- Mercury
- Neptune
- Saturn
- Uranus
- Venus

1. Mercury
2. Venus
3. Earth
4. Mars
5. Jupiter
6. Saturn
7. Uranus
8. Neptune

Figure 14-7: Items aren't ranked in a bulleted list (left); use a numbered list to show rank or chronology (right).

Creating a bulleted or numbered list

Many slide layouts include text frames that are already formatted for bulleted lists. All you have to do in these text frames is "click to add text" and keep pressing the Enter key as you enter items for your bulleted list. Each time you press Enter, PowerPoint Web App adds another bullet to the list.

Follow these instructions to create a bulleted or numbered list:

- ✔ **Creating a bulleted list:** Select the list if you've already entered the list items, go to the Home tab, and click the Bullets button.

- ✔ **Creating a numbered list:** Select the list if you've already entered the list items, go to the Home tab, and click the Numbering button.

- ✔ **Converting a numbered to a bulleted list (or vice versa):** Drag over the list to select it, go to the Home tab, and then click the Bullets or Numbering button.

Removing bullets and numbers from a list

Follow these steps to remove the bullets or numbers from a list:

1. **Select the list.**

2. **Go to the Home tab.**

3. **Click the Bullets or Numbering button.**

   Clicking the Bullets button removes the bullets and turns the paragraphs into standard paragraphs; clicking the Numbering button removes the numbers and turns the paragraphs into standard paragraphs.

Making sublists, or nested lists

A *sublist,* also known as a *nested list,* is a list that is found inside another list. Figure 14-8 shows a common type of sublist, a bulleted sublist inside a numbered list. Follow these steps to create a bulleted sublist:

1. **Create the parent list and number it.**

   In other words, make all entries in the list, including the entries you want for the sublist, and number the entries.

2. **Select the part of the numbered list that you want to make into a sublist.**

Rules of Engagement

1. Forge ahead without regard for life and limb.
2. Keep our shoulders to the wheel.
3. Watch out for these obstacles:
   – Brickbats
   – Flying objects
   – Misplaced foreign matter
4. Keep plugging away no matter what.
5. Never give up unless we have to.

Figure 14-8:
A numbered list with a bulleted sublist.

3. On the Home tab, click the Increase List Level button.

The list is intended.

4. Click the Bullets or Numbering button.

The indented portion of the list is marked with bullets, not numbers.

Click the Decrease List Level button if you want to return a sublist to the parent list.

Selecting, Moving, and Deleting Slides

As a presentation takes shape, you have to move slides forward and backward in the presentation. And sometimes you have to delete a slide. To turn your sow's ear into a silk purse, you have to wrestle with the slides. You have to make them do your bidding. These pages explain how to move and delete slides and how to select them. You can't move or delete slides unless you select them first.

Selecting slides

Switch to Editing view to select slides. After you switch to Editing view, click a slide in the Slides pane to select it. I'm sorry, but you can't select more than one slide at a time.

Moving slides

In Editing view, select the slide you want to move and use one of these techniques to move it:

> ✔ **Dragging and dropping:** Click the slide you selected and drag it up or down in the Slides pane to a new location. A horizontal line shows you where the slide will land when you release the mouse button.

> ✔ **Cutting and pasting:** On the Home tab, click the Cut button (or press Ctrl+X). Next, select the slide that you want the slide to appear after and then click the Paste button (or press Ctrl+V).

Deleting slides

Before you delete a slide, think twice about deleting. Short of clicking the Undo button, you can't resuscitate a deleted slide. Select the slide you want to delete and use one of these techniques for deleting slides:

> ✔ On the Home tab, click the Delete Slide button.

> ✔ Press the Delete key.

Hidden Slides for All Contingencies

Hide a slide when you want to keep it on hand "just in case" during a presentation. Hidden slides don't appear in presentations unless the presenter decides to show them. Create hidden slides if you anticipate having to turn your presentation in a different direction — to answer a question from the audience, prove your point more thoroughly, or revisit a topic in more depth.

The best place to put hidden slides is the end of a presentation where you know you can find them. Follow these steps to hide slides:

1. **Select the slide you want to hide.**

2. **Go to the Home tab.**

3. **Click the Hide Slide button.**

   Hidden slides' numbers are crossed through in the Slides pane in Editing view.

To "unhide" a slide, select the slide and click the Hide Slide button again.

WARNING! PowerPoint Web App doesn't offer commands for showing hidden slides during a presentation. You must show the presentation in PowerPoint 2010 to show hidden slides.

Scribbling Notes to Help with Presentations

Notes are strictly for the speaker. They aren't for the unwashed masses. Don't hesitate to write notes to yourself as you put together your presentation. The notes will come in handy when you're rehearsing and giving your presentation. They'll give you ideas for what to say and help you communicate better. I find when I'm constructing a slide that I often get ideas for the words I want to say while the slide is on-screen, and I jot down those words in the Notes pane.

Entering a note

Follow these steps to enter a note:

1. **Switch to Editing view.**

2. **Click the Notes button, if necessary, to display the Notes pane along the bottom of the Slide window.**

3. **Enter your note, as shown in Figure 14-9.**

   Treat the Notes pane like a page in a word processor. For example, press Enter to go to the next paragraph, and press the Tab key to indent. Be creative. Don't even bother to spell words correctly. Brainstorm and rain notes onto the Notes pane as you construct your presentation.

Reading notes

Use one of these techniques to read notes:

- **In Editing view:** Click the Notes button, if necessary, to view notes in the Notes pane.

- **In Reading view:** Click the Notes button, if necessary to display notes. This button is located along the bottom of the screen.

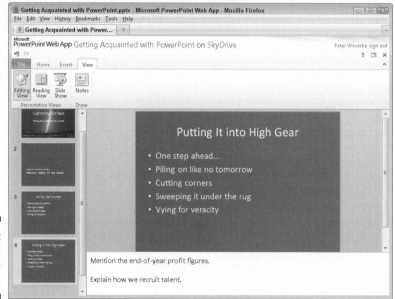

Figure 14-9:
Entering a
note in the
Notes pane.

Advice for Delivering a Presentation

As one who is terrified of speaking in public, I know that most advice about
public speaking is gratuitous advice. It's easy to say, "Don't be nervous in
front of the audience" or "Direct your nervous energy into the presentation,"
but not being nervous is easier said than done. Following are some tips — I
hope they aren't too gratuitous — to help you deliver your presentation and
overcome nervousness.

Rehearse, and rehearse some more

The better you know your material, the less nervous you will be. To keep
from getting nervous, rehearse your presentation until you know it backward
and forward. Rehearse it out loud. Rehearse it while imagining yourself in the
presence of an audience.

Remember that the audience wants you to succeed. The audience is rooting
for you. Audiences want to see good presentations.

Connect with the audience

Address your audience and not the screen where your presentation is being shown. Look at the audience, not the slides. Pause to look at your notes, but don't read notes word for word. You should know your presentation well enough in advance that you don't have to consult the notes often.

I have heard two different theories about making eye contact with an audience. One says to look over the heads of the audience and address your speech to an imaginary tall person in the back row. Another says to pick out three or four people in different parts of the room and address your words to them at various times as you speak. The main thing to remember is to keep your head up and look into the audience as you present your slides.

Anticipate questions from the audience

If you intend to field questions during a presentation, make a list of what those questions might be, and formulate your answers beforehand. You can "hide slides" in anticipation of questions you will be asked, as "Hidden Slides for All Contingencies" explains earlier in this chapter.

Take control from the start

Spend the first minute introducing yourself to the audience without running the PowerPoint Web App (or, if you do run it, put a simple slide with your company name or logo on-screen). Make eye contact with the audience. This way, you establish your credibility. You give the audience a chance to get to know you.

Giving Your Presentation

Compared to the preliminary work, giving a presentation can seem kind of anticlimactic. All you have to do is go from slide to slide and woo your audience with your smooth-as-silk voice and powerful oratory skills. Well, at least the move-from-slide-to-slide part is pretty easy.

These pages explain how to start and end a presentation, and how to advance or retreat from slide to slide.

Starting a presentation

Follow these steps to start a presentation:

1. **Go to the View tab.**

2. **Click the Slide Show button.**

   As shown in Figure 14-10, the slide fills the browser window. This is what the audience sees when you deliver your presentation in a Web browser.

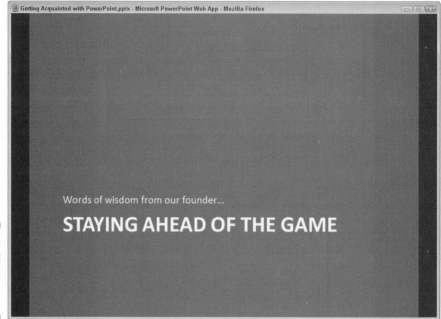

Figure 14-10: A slide as it looks during a presentation.

Going from slide to slide

To go forward from one slide to the following slide in a presentation, click on-screen. As soon as you click, the next slide appears. If all goes well, clicking is the only technique you need to know when giving a presentation, but you can also take advantage of these techniques:

- ✔ **Advancing the presentation:** Click the screen or press the spacebar, N (for next), PgDn, ↓, or → key on your keyboard.

- ✔ **Going backward in a presentation:** Press the P (or previous), PgUp, ↑, or ← key on your keyboard.

Ending a presentation

When you reach the end of a presentation, the screen turns black and you see the words "End of slide show, click to exit." Clicking returns you to Editing view.

To end a slide show at any time, whether you're at the start, middle, or end, click the Esc key.

Coauthoring a PowerPoint Presentation

The only way to coauthor a PowerPoint presentation — to work on it at the same time as someone else — is to open it in PowerPoint 2010. Microsoft doesn't permit two people to work on a presentation at the same time in PowerPoint Web App.

PowerPoint 2010 doesn't mark changes that coworkers make to a presentation. The changes just appear. In my experiments, it takes about 15 seconds after one coauthor saves changes to a presentation for the words "Updates Available" to appear on the other coauthor's PowerPoint status bar. When you see the words "Updates Available" on the status bar, click the Save button (or press Ctrl+S) to synchronize your presentation with the Web server and get an up-to-date presentation.

On the status bar, a number next to the Authors icon tells you how many coauthors are also working on your PowerPoint presentation. You can click the Authors icon to see a pop-up list with your coauthors' names.

Part VI
OneNote Web App

In this part . . .

Part VI takes you on a whirlwind tour of OneNote Web App, the Office Web App devoted to taking, organizing, and storing notes.

OneNote Web App is unique among the Office Web Apps in that sharing notebooks is very, very easy. Part VI describes the ins and outs of coauthoring notebooks and how to make sure your notebook is always in sync with your collaborators'.

Chapter 15

Writing and Storing Notes

*T*his chapter introduces OneNote Web App and describes how you can use it to take notes and organize them. You find out how to create units for storing notes — a notebook, sections, pages, and subpages. You also find out how to write notes and format the text on notes. Turn to this chapter to get the basics of using OneNote Web App.

Introducing OneNote Web App

Everybody who has been in a classroom or participated in a business meeting knows what note-taking is. What makes taking notes with OneNote Web App special is that the notes are digital, and for that reason, you can store, organize, and retrieve your notes in various ways. OneNote Web App adds another dimension to note taking. Because notes can be copied, moved, and combined with other notes, you can use notes as building blocks for different projects — for white papers and reports, for example.

A OneNote file is called a *notebook*. Within a notebook, you can write notes and organize your notes into sections, pages, and subpages. You can use OneNote Web App to refine your thinking about the work you want to do and the subjects you want to tackle. OneNote Web App helps you organize your ideas.

OneNote Web App is a little different from the other Office Web Apps. You can't open a Word, Excel, or PowerPoint file in Word Web App, Excel Web App, or PowerPoint Web App if somebody already has it open in Word, Excel, or PowerPoint 2010. But that isn't true of OneNote Web App. Two people, one using OneNote Web App and the other using OneNote 2010, can open the same OneNote notebook. They can work on the same notebook together. OneNote Web App doesn't have the same limitations as the other Office Web Apps when it comes to opening a file at the same time in an Office Web App and an Office 2010 program.

Creating Notebooks with OneNote Web App

Chapter 2 explains in detail how to create files with the Office Web Apps, as well as how to open and close files. To spare you a trip to Chapter 2, here are the basics of creating a new notebook with OneNote Web App:

1. **Click the New link and choose OneNote Notebook on the drop-down list.**

   The New Microsoft OneNote Notebook window opens.

2. **Enter a name for your notebook.**

3. **Click the Save button.**

   A new notebook opens, ready for you to fill it with notes.

As of this writing, you can't store OneNote notebooks in subfolders on SkyDrive.

Comparing OneNote Web App to OneNote 2010

OneNote Web App isn't as sophisticated as OneNote 2010, as Figure 15-1 demonstrates. This figure shows the same notebook in OneNote Web App (top) and OneNote 2010 (bottom). OneNote 2010 offers many more tabs, section tabs along the top of the page, and a page list on the right side of the screen.

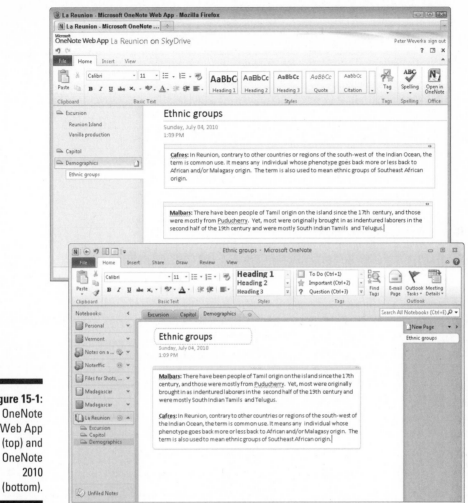

Figure 15-1:
OneNote
Web App
(top) and
OneNote
2010
(bottom).

Table 15-1 lists features in OneNote 2010 that aren't available in OneNote Web App. If you want to use one of the features listed in the table, you have to click the Open In OneNote button on the Home tab. Clicking this button opens your notebook in OneNote 2010.

Table 15-1	OneNote 2010 Features Not Available in OneNote Web App
Feature	*Description*
Home tab	
Outlook	Send notes by e-mail, assign notes to tasks, and insert a meeting from Outlook
Insert tab	
Insert Space	Insert and remove extra writing space
Screen clipping	Copy part of a screen into a note
Attach File	Attach a file to a note
File Printout	Insert a printed copy of a file in a note
Scanner Printout	Scan paper documents and insert them in notes
Time Stamp	Record the date and time on a note
Equation	Draw an equation with the Equation Editor tools
Symbol	Enter a symbol or foreign character in text
Share	
E-mail Page	Send a page by e-mail
Next Unread	Go to a page with an unread note
Mark As Read	Mark a page's notes as unread
Shared Notebook	Share a notebook with colleagues
Notebook Recycle Bin	Open the Recycle Bin to view and restore notes
Draw	
Tools	Draw notes by hand
Insert Shapes	Create shapes on the page
Edit	Rotate and handle overlapping shapes
Convert	Convert handwritten notes to text
Review	
Spelling	Spell-check notes
Research	Use the Research task pane services — the dictionaries, thesauruses, and search engines
Translate	Translate text from one language to another
Language	Declare what language a note is written in
Linked Notes	Link notes with a Web page or Office file

Feature	Description
View	
Full Page View	Switch to full-screen mode
Dock to Desktop	Place OneNote on the side of the Windows desktop
Page Setup	Specify how to show pages when printed
Zoom	Zoom in and out
Window	Open secondary windows; keep the OneNote window on top
Side Note	Write a side note that you can enter on a page later

OneNote Web App: A Geography Lesson

Figure 15-2 points out the different parts of the OneNote Web App screen. Here is a brief OneNote Web App geography lesson:

✔ **Quick Access toolbar:** This toolbar offers the Undo and Redo buttons. Click the Undo button to reverse your latest action; click the Redo button if you regret clicking the Undo button.

✔ **File tab:** Go to the File tab to open a notebook in OneNote 2010, view a notebook's Properties page, or close a notebook.

✔ **The Ribbon:** Select a tab on the Ribbon — Home, Insert, View — to undertake a new task.

✔ **Navigation bar:** Sections and pages you create for organizing your notes appear on the Navigation bar.

✔ **Sections, pages, and subpages:** Organize your notes into sections, pages, and subpages. The names of sections, pages, and subpages appear on the Navigation bar. The upcoming section "Units for Organizing Notes" explains sections, pages, and subpages.

File

Creating Storage Units for Notes

Before you write your first note, give a moment's thought to organizing notes in the notebook-section-pages-subpages hierarchy. Think of descriptive names for your notebook, sections, pages, and subpages. Then get to work creating the storage units you need for your notes. These pages explain what the storage units are and how to create sections, pages, and subpages.

File tab

Quick Access toolbar

Navigation bar

Ribbon

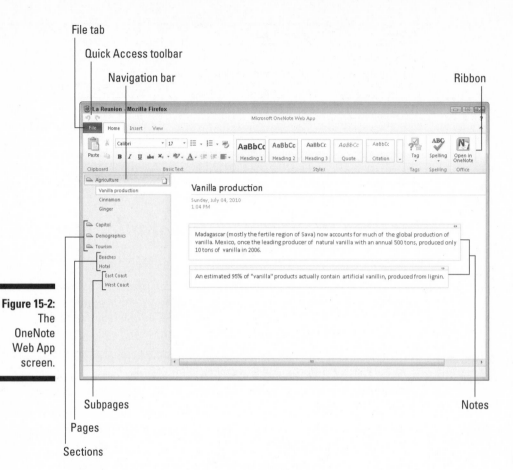

Figure 15-2:
The
OneNote
Web App
screen.

Subpages

Notes

Pages

Sections

Units for organizing notes

From largest to smallest, OneNote Web App offers these units for organizing notes:

✔ **Notebook:** Create a *notebook* for each important project you're involved in. Earlier in this chapter, "Creating Notebooks with OneNote Web App" describes how to create a notebook.

✔ **Sections:** A *section* is a subcategory of a notebook; it is used to store pages. Each notebook can have many different sections, and each section, in turn, can have many pages. Earlier in this chapter, Figure 15-2 shows four sections in a notebook: Agriculture, Capitol, Demographics, and Tourism.

✔ **Pages and subpages:** *Pages* and *subpages* are for writing and storing notes. Pages and subpages are stored in sections. As shown in Figure 15-2, the names of pages appear under section names. These section names are on *page tabs,* which are on the Navigation bar (look to the left side of the screen). Within a page, you can also create a *subpage*, as shown in Figure 15-2.

✔ **Notes:** Write your notes on pages. To write a note, all you have to do is click and begin typing.

If you've spent any time with OneNote 2010, you may notice a note storage unit missing from OneNote Web App: section groups. A section group is a means of organizing and quickly finding sections.

Creating a section

Follow these steps to create a new section for storing notes:

1. **On the Insert tab, click the New Section button (see Figure 15-3).**

   The New Section dialog box appears. You can also right-click in the Navigation bar and choose New Section to display this dialog box.

2. **Enter a name for the section.**

3. **Click OK.**

   After you create a new section, OneNote Web App automatically creates a new page to go with it. This page is called "Untitled Page." To rename this page, enter a name in the Title text box at the top of the page.

Creating a page

Follow these steps to create a new page for storing notes:

1. **In the Navigation bar, select the section where you want the new page to go.**

2. **Click the New Page button.**

   You can find this button on the Insert tab and Navigation bar.

   • **Insert tab:** The New Page button is the leftmost button on the Insert tab.

   • **Navigation bar:** Move the pointer onto the section name. The New Page button appears to the right of the name.

Click a button or right-click to create a page or section

Right-click to create a subpage

A new page appears. You can also right-click a section name in the Navigation bar and choose New Page to create a new page.

3. **Enter a name in the Title text box.**

The name you enter appears on a page tab in the Navigation bar.

The date and time you create a page appears under the page's name. You can use this information to help identify pages.

Creating a subpage

Within a page, you can create subpages to help organize your notes. Follow these steps to create a subpage:

1. **Create a page.**

   The previous topic in this chapter explains how to create a page.

2. **In the Navigation bar, right-click the page and choose Increase Indent on the shortcut menu.**

   The page is indented to indicate that it is a subpage. You can indent a page even further, if you want, by choosing the Increase Indent command again.

To promote a subpage to a page, right-click it and choose Decrease Indent on the shortcut menu that appears.

Renaming and deleting sections, pages, and subpages

Think the word "right-click" when you want to rename or delete a section or page. To rename or delete one of these items, right-click it in the Navigation bar and choose Rename or Delete on the shortcut menu (refer to Figure 15-3). After you choose Rename, enter a new name for your section or page.

Entering and Arranging Notes

After you create sections and pages for storing notes, you can begin entering notes. As shown in Figure 15-4, notes appear in note boxes. You can drag these boxes where you will on the page. You can also change a box's size and shape. These topics are explained forthwith.

Writing a note

Follow these steps to write a note:

1. **Double-click the spot on the page where you want the note box to be.**

   An empty note box appears.

2. **Type your note in the box.**

   You can also copy text into the box by clicking the Paste button (or pressing Ctrl+V).

To edit a note, click inside it and start entering or deleting text.

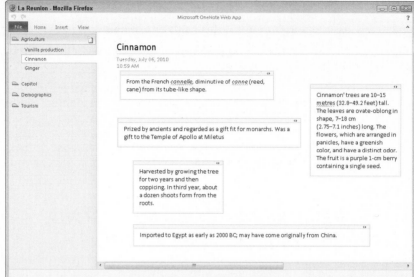

Figure 15-4:
Notes
appear in
note boxes.

Arranging and resizing notes

Arrange notes on the page to make them easier to read and understand. Follow these instructions to arrange notes:

- **Changing a note's position:** Move the pointer over the top of the note box, and when the pointer changes into a four-headed arrow, click and start dragging.

- **Changing a note's size:** Move the pointer over the right side of the note box, and when the pointer changes into a double arrow, click and drag to the left or right.

Formatting the Text in Notes

On the Home and Insert tabs, OneNote offers different commands for formatting the text in notes. If formatting note text makes reading and understanding notes easier, by all means format the text. You can do so with these techniques:

- **Basic text formatting:** On the Home tab, you can choose a font for text, change the size and color of text, and create bulleted and numbered lists. Chapter 4 explains commands for formatting text in Office Web Apps.

Revisiting (and restoring) an earlier version of a page

From time to time, OneNote Web App saves a copy of the page in case you want to revisit or restore it. To read an earlier version of a page, follow these steps:

1. **Go to the View tab.**

2. **Click the Page Versions button.**

   The names of page versions appear on the Navigation bar below the name of the page you right-clicked. These page versions are dated with an author's name. You can also see page versions on the Navigation bar by right-clicking a page's name and choosing Show Versions on the shortcut menu.

3. **Click a page version's name to open and read an earlier version of a page.**

To make an earlier version of a page the one you want for your notes, click the top of the page to open a drop-down list with options for re-hiding, deleting, and restoring the page. Then choose Restore on the drop-down list.

To hide page versions, click the Page Versions button a second time or right-click a page's name in the Navigation bar and choose Hide Versions on the shortcut menu.

To delete a page version, right-click it and choose Delete.

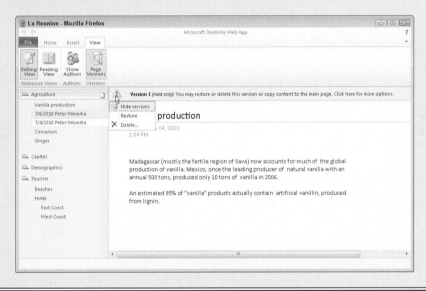

✔ **Styles:** On the Home tab, styles present an easy way to format text. Click in the text you want to format, open the Styles gallery, and choose an option, as shown in Figure 15-5. Choose Heading 1, for example, to make a heading on a note stand out.

✔ **Tables:** On the Insert tab, click the Table button and choose how many columns and rows you want for your table. Then enter the table data. The (Table Tools) Layout tab offers commands for laying out the table. These commands are described in Chapter 10. (They are identical to the commands in Word Web App for formatting tables.)

Chapter 5 explains how to insert pictures and clip-art images in notes.

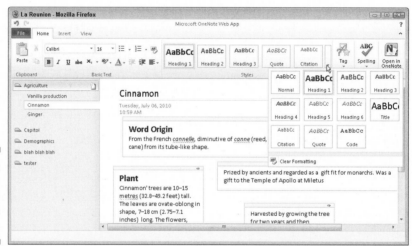

Figure 15-5:
Choose a
style in the
Styles
gallery.

Chapter 16

Organizing Your Notes

*N*otes aren't worth very much unless you can locate them, retrieve them, and copy or move them elsewhere. This chapter explains what you can do with your notes after you write them. It demonstrates how to rearrange sections and view or hide pages in the Navigation bar. You also see how to change views, find out who wrote a note, categorize notes by tagging them, and move and copy notes.

Going from Section to Section and Page to Page

The Navigation bar is your ticket to ride in OneNote Web App. Use it to get from section to section and page to page. It lists the names of sections you created for storing notes, and if pages are displayed, it lists the pages within each section, as shown in Figure 16-1.

Use these techniques in the Navigation bar to get here and there:

✔ **Going to a section:** Click the name of a section to visit it.

✔ **Going to a page or subpage:** Click a page or subpage name to visit a page or subpage. If page names aren't displayed under a section, click the section's name.

Click a section name, if necessary, to see its pages

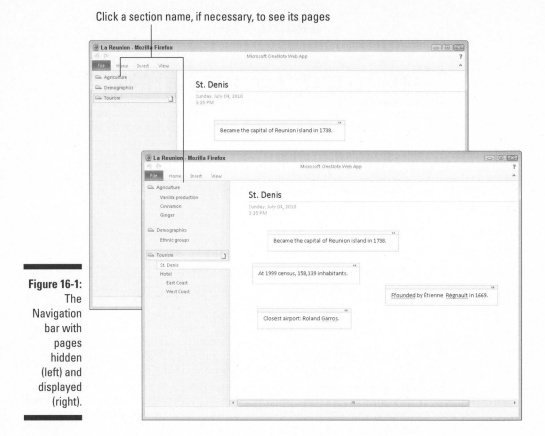

Figure 16-1:
The
Navigation
bar with
pages
hidden
(left) and
displayed
(right).

Making the Navigation Bar Work for You

The Navigation bar is supposed to work for you — not the other way around.
By hiding and displaying pages and by rearranging section names in the
Navigation bar, you can make it do your bidding, as I explain shortly.

Displaying and hiding pages

The Navigation bar can get awfully crowded with pages and subpages if you
aren't careful. To make the Navigation bar less crowded, hide and display
section pages as you need them.

To hide or display a section's pages, click the section's name. As Figure 16-1 (shown earlier in this chapter) demonstrates, clicking a section name hides its pages. Clicking a second time displays them.

Rearranging section names in the Navigation bar

You are hereby invited to change the order of sections in the Navigation bar if changing the order helps you locate and enter notes. Follow these steps to move a section higher or lower in the Navigation bar:

1. **Switch to Editing view if you aren't already there.**

   To switch to Editing view, go to the View tab and click the Editing View button.

2. **Click to select the name of the section you want to move.**

3. **Drag the section name higher or lower in the Navigation bar.**

   As you drag, a black horizontal line shows you where your section will land after you release the mouse button.

Changing Your View in OneNote Web App

As shown in Figure 16-2, OneNote Web App offers two views, Editing view and Reading view. To change views, go to the View tab and click the Editing View or Reading View button:

 ✔ **Editing view:** Write, edit, and organize notes in Editing view. Only in Editing view can you move, copy, delete, and format notes.

 ✔ **Reading view:** Read and study notes in Reading view. To return to Editing view, click the Edit in Browser button.

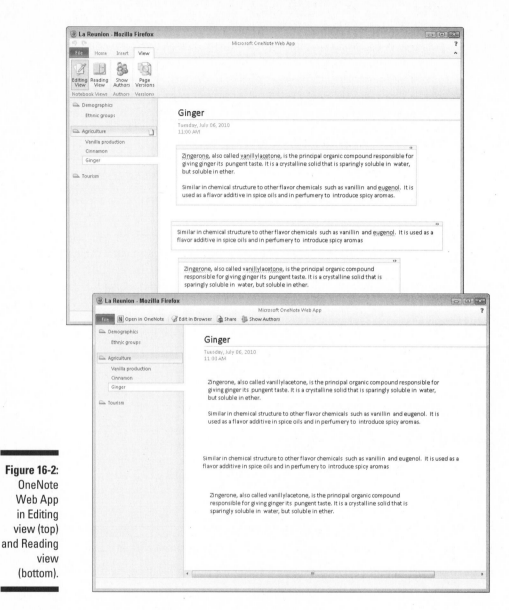

Figure 16-2:
OneNote
Web App
in Editing
view (top)
and Reading
view
(bottom).

Seeing Who Wrote a Note

Especially if you share a notebook with others, you need to know who wrote the notes in your OneNote file. You can find out very easily who wrote a note. Go to the View tab and click the Show Authors button. Names appear beside notes to tell you who wrote them.

To cease seeing the names of authors, click the Show Authors button a second time.

Tagging Notes for Follow-Up

The best way to keep notes from getting lost is to carefully place them in sections, pages, and subpages. Short of that, you can tag notes to make it easier to follow up on them. OneNote offers the Tab drop-down list for that very purpose. Tag a note to highlight its text in a certain color or place an icon beside its name, as shown in Figure 16-3. OneNote offers no fewer than 29 different tags.

Figure 16-3:
Tagging a note with the Tab drop-down list.

Follow these steps to tag a note:

1. **Select the note you want to tag.**

2. **On the Home tab, click the Tag button to open the Tag drop-down list.**

3. **Choose a tag on the menu.**

   Choose More Tags to open a submenu with more tagging choices. Some tags include a check-off box that you can click to mark a note you're finished with.

You can tag a note with more than one tag.

To remove a tag from a note, select the note, click the Tag button, and choose Remove Tag on the Tag drop-down list.

Some Housekeeping Chores

Unless you play loud soul music while you're doing it, housekeeping can be a tedious and irksome activity. Here are methods for handling a few housekeeping chores in OneNote Web App:

- ✔ **Selecting notes:** Click the bar along the top of a note to select it. Sorry, but you can't select more than one note at a time in OneNote Web App.

- ✔ **Moving a note to another page:** Use the tried-and-true cut-and-paste method. Select the note, right-click, choose Cut (or press Ctrl+X), right-click the page where you want to move the note, and choose Paste (or press Ctrl+V).

- ✔ **Copying a note to another page:** Select the note, right-click, choose Copy (or press Ctrl+C), right-click the page where you want to copy the note, and choose Paste (or press Ctrl+V).

- ✔ **Deleting a note:** Select the note you want to delete and press the Delete key.

- ✔ **Deleting a section:** Right-click the section tab and choose Delete on the shortcut menu that appears.

- ✔ **Deleting a page or subpage:** Right-click the page tab and choose Delete.

Coauthoring Notebooks with Others

Too bad the other Office Web Apps aren't as good with the coauthoring feature as OneNote Web App and OneNote 2010 are. "Coauthor" is the term that Microsoft uses to describe two or more people working an Office Web App at the same time. You and a coauthor can open a shared notebook in any combination of OneNote Web App and OneNote 2010 and revise to your hearts' content. For example, one person operating in OneNote 2010 and the other in OneNote Web App can coauthor the same notebook at the same time without a hitch. So can two people working in OneNote Web App or two people working in OneNote 2010. OneNote is very hospitable when it comes to admitting many coauthors to the party.

The remainder of this chapter looks into coauthoring in OneNote Web App and OneNote 2010.

Coauthoring in OneNote Web App

In my experiments, it takes about 20 seconds for a revision made to a notebook in OneNote Web App to appear in other coauthors' notebooks. That means all notebooks are in sync with each other every 20 seconds or so. The only hard part about coauthoring in OneNote Web App is finding out who your coauthors are and handling the rare occasion when notebook pages can't be synchronized.

Seeing who your coauthors are

You can't click the status bar to see a pop-up list with the names of people who are editing a notebook concurrently with you, as you can in the other Office Web Apps. But you can go to the View tab and choose Show Authors to see who authored notes. Beside each note, you see the name of the person who wrote or last edited it. I hope that gives you an idea of who your coconspirators are.

Handling unmerged notes

In the unlikely event that two coauthors make contradicting changes to a note, a message appears on top of the page where the note is stored: "This page has changes that could not be merged during synchronization. Click here to show versions of the page with unmerged changes."

Click the message and you see, on the Navigation bar, a time- and name-stamped version of the page in red. Select this page to open a page that shows you, in red, notes that could not be synchronized, as shown in Figure 16-4. The message at the top of this page reads, "Conflicting changes are highlighted in red. This page cannot be edited, but you can copy changes to the main page. Click here for more options."

To resolve the conflict, you can do one of the following:

✔ **Copy the unsynchronized note:** Copy the red-highlighted note to the page it couldn't be synchronized with (select the text in the note, press Ctrl+C, go to the other page, create a new note, and press Ctrl+V). The page now has two versions of the note, yours and another editor's.

✔ **Abandon the unsynchronized note:** Click the message at the top of the page and choose Delete on the drop-down list (see Figure 16-4).

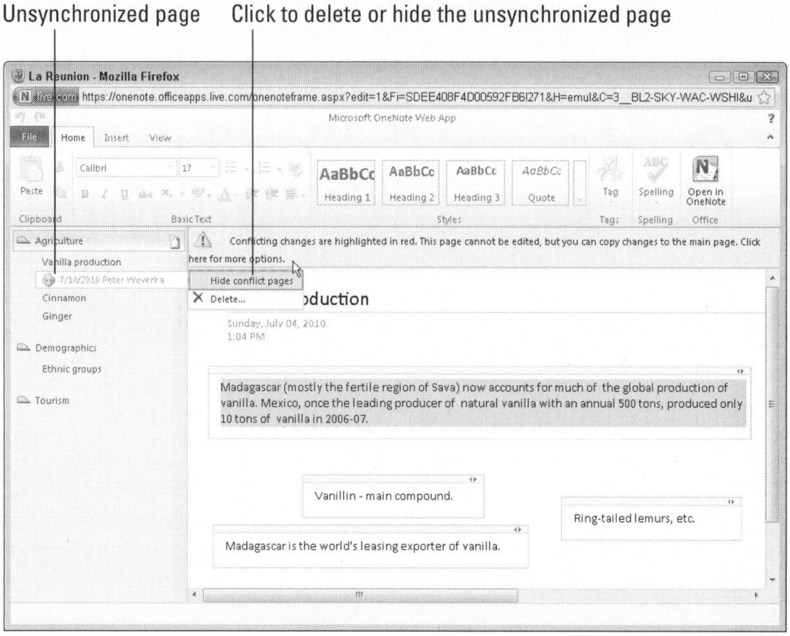

Unsynchronized page   Click to delete or hide the unsynchronized page

Figure 16-4:
Handling
edits that
couldn't be
merged.

Choose Hide Conflict Pages on the drop-down list (see Figure 16-4) to hide
the unsynchronized page on the Navigation bar.

Coauthoring in OneNote 2010

As you probably know, OneNote 2010 is the only Office 2010 program without
a Save button or Save command. Changes made to a OneNote notebook in
OneNote 2010 are saved automatically as soon they are made. Changes are
also synchronized to coauthors' notebooks in a matter of about 20 seconds.

In OneNote 2010, you can tell whether a notebook is synchronized and up-to-
date by glancing at the Sync icon next to its name on the Navigation bar. If
the notebook is up-to-date, a check mark appears on the Sync icon, as shown
in Figure 16-5, and these words appear when you move the pointer over the
icon: "This notebook is connected and syncing changes."

To show you where changes were made to notes when the notebook was most
recently synchronized, notes are highlighted in light green. Look to these
green-highlighted notes to see what your coauthors' latest changes to the
notebook are.

Sync icon   Click to see who wrote notes

Figure 16-5:
OneNote
2010 offers
different
tools for
sharing
notebooks.

Finding out who your coauthors are

Sorry, you can't see who is currently editing a notebook along with you, but you can go to the View tab and click the Show Authors button (see Figure 16-5) to see an author's initials beside each note. (This button is a toggle; click it to see author's initials if they aren't already on display). By moving the pointer over initials, you can read, in a pop-up box, the author's name and when the note was written or last edited.

Synchronizing your notebook with coauthors' notebooks

Unless you change the settings, your notebook is synchronized with your coauthors' notebooks every 20 seconds or so. But you can decide for yourself how and when to synchronize notebooks.

Give the synchronizing command if you aren't sure whether your notebook is properly synchronized:

✔ Right-click the Sync icon on the Navigation bar and choose Sync This Notebook Now on the shortcut menu.

✔ Press Shift+F9.

✔ On the File tab, choose Info, and on the Notebook Information page, click the Settings button next to the name of the notebook you want to synchronize. Then choose Sync on the drop-down list that appears.

Telling OneNote 2010 how to synchronize

Use the Shared Notebook Synchronization dialog box to tell OneNote 2010 how you want to synchronize your notebook. This dialog box is shown in Figure 16-6. Follow these steps to open this dialog box and tell OneNote how to synchronize notebooks:

1. Open the Shared Notebook Synchronization dialog box.

You can open the dialog box with these methods:

- Click the notebook's Sync icon on the Navigation bar (refer to Figure 16-5).

- Right-click the Sync icon and choose Notebook Sync Status on the shortcut menu that appears.

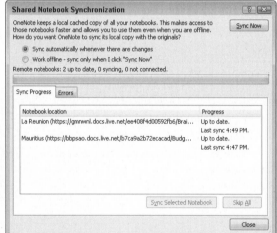

Figure 16-6:
Telling OneNote 2010 how you want to synchronize notebooks.

2. Choose how you want to synchronize the notebook.

Your choices are twofold:

- Choose Sync Automatically Whenever There Are Changes to save changes to the server as soon as they are made.

- Choose Work Offline – Sync Only When I Click "Sync Now" to synchronize the notebook only when you tell OneNote to synchronize. To synchronize, you have to right-click the Sync icon on the Navigation bar and choose Sync This Notebook Now or press Shift+F9.

Part VII
The Part of Tens

"Woo!"

In this part . . .

*E*ach chapter in Part VII offers ten tidbits of rock-solid information you need to know about the Office Web Apps. With three chapters in this part, that makes 30 — count 'em — 30 tidbits in all.

You find out the ten things everybody should know about the Office Web Apps, ten things everybody should know about file sharing, and ten things everybody should know about running a browser with the Office Web Apps.

Chapter 17

Ten Things Everyone Should Know about the Office Web Apps

*T*his chapter describes ten things that everyone should know about the Office Web Apps. Read this brief chapter and you'll get a sense of what the Office Web Apps are all about.

There Are Four Office Web Apps

There are four — count 'em — Office Web Apps:

- ✔ **Word Web App:** For writing letters, reports, and other documents.
- ✔ **Excel Web App:** For crunching numbers in spreadsheets.
- ✔ **PowerPoint Web App:** For creating and showing slides in a slideshow presentation.
- ✔ **OneNote Web App:** For note-taking and organizing notes.

Do the names *Word, Excel, PowerPoint,* and *OneNote* sound familiar? If they do, it's because you're acquainted with the four Microsoft Office programs from which the Office Web Apps take their names. Word Web App, Excel Web App, PowerPoint Web App, and OneNote Web App are online versions of Word, Excel, PowerPoint, and OneNote.

They're Free!

Not many things in this world are free, but signing up to use the Office Web Apps and running the Office Web Apps doesn't cost one red cent.

Next time you have five spare minutes, take the Office Web Apps for a test-drive. You can go to Windows Live, sign up for Windows Live, and run an Office Web App, all in the space of about five minutes (Chapter 2 explains how to sign up with Windows Live and create your first file). Did I mention that using the Office Web Apps is free? How can you resist trying them out?

You Run Office Web Apps through a Browser

The Office Web Apps aren't called "Web apps" for nothing. The difference between the Office Web Apps and conventional computer programs is that you run Office Web Apps through a Web browser. A Web browser is a program for visiting Web sites on the Internet. To run an Office Web App, you start a Web browser, go to the Web site where your files are stored, and open a file with an Office Web App. Commands for running the Office Web App are transmitted through your Web browser. The Office Web App software isn't stored on your computer; it's stored on the Web server where your files are.

In effect, an Office Web App is a program inside another program. Running an Office Web App entails running a Web browser, and, inside the Web browser, running the Office Web App.

Microsoft recommends using these three browsers to run the Office Web Apps: Firefox, Internet Explorer, Safari, and Chrome. Chapter 3 explains all you need to know about operating a browser with the Office Web Apps.

Your Files Are Stored Online

The other major difference between the Office Web Apps and conventional computer programs is that the files you work on aren't kept on your computer;

the files are kept on a Web server on the Internet or a Web server on a company network.

To open a file, you open your browser, use your browser to go to the Web site on the Internet or your company's network where your files are stored, locate the file, and give the command to open it. It opens in an Office Web App.

Keeping files on a Web server instead of your computer's hard drive makes it possible for other people to open the files, too. They can also go to the Web server and open the files. And because more than one person can access the same files, you can share files. You can coauthor files with other people using the Office Web Apps.

The Main Purpose of Office Web Apps Is to Share Files

Because the files you work on with the Office Web Apps are stored online, not on your computer, many people can access and edit them. People scattered hither and yon over the earth can open the same file in an Office Web App and edit it at the same time.

This ability to share files is the primary purpose of the Office Web Apps. In and of themselves, the Office Web Apps don't offer enough features and functions to be worthwhile using. But being able to use the Office Web Apps to share files with others makes the Office Web Apps unique and valuable.

Office Web Apps Are Pale Imitations of Office Programs

If you're a fan of Word, Excel, PowerPoint, or OneNote, you may be disappointed by Word Web App, Excel Web App, PowerPoint Web App, and OneNote Web App. The Office Web Apps are pale imitations of their Office counterparts. One of the first things you notice when you open Word Web App, for example, is how measly it is compared to Word.

Still, if Office 2010 is installed on your computer, all is not lost if a feature you like in Word, Excel, PowerPoint, or OneNote isn't available in Word Web App, Excel Web App, PowerPoint Web App, or OneNote Web App. All is not lost because you can always open your file in an Office 2010 program.

You Can Open Files in Office 2010

Each Office Web App has a command for opening the file you're working on in an Office 2010 program. In PowerPoint Web App, for example, you can click the Open In PowerPoint button to open the PowerPoint presentation you're working on in PowerPoint Web App in PowerPoint 2010. You would click the Open In PowerPoint button when you needed a feature that PowerPoint 2010 has but PowerPoint Web App doesn't have.

Being able to call on an Office 2010 program when an Office Web App falls short is very nice indeed. But to do it, Office 2010 — not Office 2007, Office 2003, or an earlier version of Office — must be installed on your computer.

Office Web Apps Are Companion Programs to Office 2010

The Office Web Apps are designed to be companion programs to Office 2010. Not that you can't use the Office Web Apps on their own without installing Office 2010 on your computer. If your computing needs are modest, you may be able to get by with the Office Web Apps alone.

But realistically, you need Office 2010 if you intend to use, as opposed to just view files in, the Office Web Apps. You need to be able to click the Open In button to take advantage of features in Office 2010 software. As I mention earlier in this chapter, the Office Web Apps fall far short of their Office 2010 namesakes. You probably can't get by without calling on Office 2010 software from time to time to do the tasks you want to do.

You Run Office Web Apps on Windows Live or SharePoint

Everyone can run the Office Web Apps by signing up at Windows Live. Windows Live is a collection of free online services and software products offered by Microsoft. One of these services, called SkyDrive, is for storing files online. After you sign in to Windows Live, you can go to SkyDrive, open an Office Web App, and use it to create and edit Word documents, Excel worksheets, PowerPoint presentations, or OneNote notebooks. Chapter 2 explains how to sign up with Windows Live; Chapter 6 explains how to edit files you store on SkyDrive with the Office Web Apps.

The other way to use the Office Web Apps is to do it by way of a SharePoint 2010 Web site. SharePoint 2010 is a Microsoft software product for storing and sharing files on a company network. To use the Office Web Apps on a SharePoint Web site, an administrator must give you permission to access the site. Chapter 2 describes how to access a SharePoint Web site; Chapter 8 looks into using the Office Web Apps with SharePoint.

You Need to Think about Privacy Issues

Privacy matters more than usual when you run the Office Web Apps because your files are kept on a Web server, not on your computer, and getting at another person's files is easier when the files are on the Internet or a network.

Windows Live offers safeguards for making folders where files are stored private or semiprivate. SharePoint does, too. Make sure you understand these safeguards and that you store files appropriately so that only people who should see your files see them.

Chapter 7 explains how to handle folder permissions on Windows Live. Chapter 8 looks at SharePoint 2010 privacy issues.

Chapter 18

Ten Things to Know about File Sharing

As the saying goes, two heads are better than one, and you can make more of your Word documents, Excel worksheets, PowerPoint presentations, and OneNote notebooks by sharing them online with coworkers and colleagues.

This brief chapter outlines ten things you should know about sharing files, or coauthoring files as Microsoft likes to call it, with the Office Web Apps.

The Office Web Apps Are All about Sharing

Being able to share folders and files with others, and being able to collaborate online with others, is the chief reason to use the Office Web Apps.

In and of themselves, the Office Web Apps aren't much to crow about. Especially if you've used Office 2010 software, the Office Web Apps seem kind of measly and small. They don't offer very many commands compared to their Office 2010 counterparts.

But the Office Web Apps open up the possibility of sharing files with others. You can work on a Word document, Excel worksheet, PowerPoint presentation, or OneNote Web App at the same time as a colleague. Not only that, but if the Office Web Apps don't have a command you want, you can open the file you're working on in an Office 2010 program. Being able to work alongside others on the same file in an Office Web App or Office 2010 program is something special.

You Need a Windows Live Account or SharePoint 2010

To share files with others, you need an account with Windows Live or access to a SharePoint 2010 Web site.

Windows Live is a Microsoft Web site that offers free Web-based applications and services. Anyone can get an account with Windows Live. With SkyDrive, one of the Windows Live services, you can create folders for storing and sharing Word, Excel, PowerPoint, and OneNote files. Chapter 2 explains how to get a Windows Live account. Chapter 7 explains how to share files in folders at SkyDrive.

The other way to share files is to share them on a SharePoint 2010 Web site. To go this route, a network administrator must have set up an account for you. Chapter 8 looks into enrolling at a SharePoint 2010 Web site and sharing files there.

Share Files in Public and Shared Folders

SkyDrive folders come in three basic varieties: private, public, and shared. To share a file, it must be stored in a public or shared folder. Files in private folders are strictly for the use of the folder's owner and are not for anyone else to see.

SkyDrive offers commands for making a folder private, public, or shared. SkyDrive also offers commands for inviting people to edit files in public and shared folders. These commands are described in Chapter 7.

What Sharing Means Is Different in Public and Shared Folders

What file sharing in SkyDrive actually means depends on whether the file being shared is stored in a public folder or a shared folder:

- **Public folder:** You can view (but not edit) and download files kept in a public folder.
- **Shared folder:** You can view, edit, download, and create files in a shared folder. You can also edit files in Office 2010 programs as well as Office Web Apps. And you can create subfolders inside a shared folder.

Chapter 7 explains in gruesome detail all the tasks that you can do to files in public and shared folders.

In an Excel and OneNote Web App, Two People Can Work on the Same File

Two or more people can open the same file at the same time in Excel Web App and OneNote Web App and work simultaneously. For example, coworkers putting together an Excel worksheet, one in Cleveland and the other in Tallahassee, can go to a folder in SkyDrive or a SharePoint 2010 Web site, open the same worksheet in Excel Web App, and work on the worksheet together.

Being able to work together with someone else on an Excel worksheet or OneNote notebook is mighty nice. I just hope all collaborators are doing their share of the work.

You Can Also Share Files in Word, PowerPoint, and OneNote 2010

Besides using the Office Web Apps to work on shared files, you can use Word 2010, Excel 2010, PowerPoint 2010, or OneNote 2010. Each Office Web App offers a button called "Open In." By clicking this button (Open In Word, Open in Excel, Open in PowerPoint, or Open in OneNote), you can open a shared file in Word, Excel, PowerPoint, or OneNote 2010.

The Office 2010 versions of Word, Excel, PowerPoint, and OneNote offer many more commands and features than their Office Web App counterparts. Being able to open a file kept on SkyDrive or a SharePoint Web site with Office 2010 software on your computer is very nice indeed. After you open the file, you can take advantage of the numerous commands in your Office 2010 program that aren't available in an Office Web App.

To share files with Word, Excel, PowerPoint, or OneNote, you must be using Office 2010, not Office 2007, or an earlier version Office.

But there's a hitch, as I explain very shortly. After you or a collaborator opens a shared file in Word 2010, Excel 2010, or PowerPoint 2010 (but not OneNote 2010), others who share the file can't open it.

Except for OneNote, You Can't use Office 2010 Programs with Others

As I explain earlier, you can open a file stored in a shared folder in Word 2010, Excel 2010, or PowerPoint 2010. But after you open it, others can't open it as well in Word Web App, Excel Web App, or PowerPoint Web App. In other words, they can't share it with you. Opening a file in Word 2010, Excel 2010, or PowerPoint 2010 effectively blocks others from opening and editing the file with an Office Web App.

OneNote 2010 is different from Word 2010, Excel 2010, PowerPoint 2010 in that you *can* open a shared OneNote file in OneNote 2010 and still be able to collaborate with others. Opening a shared file in OneNote 2010 does not block others from editing the file as well with OneNote Web App. A dozen people, some running the OneNote Web App and some running OneNote 2010, can open a OneNote file on SkyDrive or a SharePoint Web site and work together in perfect harmony.

You Can See Who Your Collaborators Are

Want to know who besides yourself is working on a file or was invited to coauthor files in a folder?

The lower-right corner of the Office Web App window tells you how many people are currently editing a file. You can click this notice to see a pop-up window that lists your name and the names of other editors.

In Word 2010 and PowerPoint 2010, you can click the Authors icon on the status bar to see who your coauthors are. Clicking the Authors icon brings up a list of coauthors' names. You Can View, Not Edit, Office 97–2003 Files.

To share a Word, Excel, PowerPoint, or OneNote file with others on Windows Live or a SharePoint Web site, the file must be saved in the 07–2010 format. You can view files saved in the 97–2003 format in an Office Web App, but you can't edit the files.

How do you tell whether a Word, Excel, PowerPoint, or OneNote file is in the 07–2010 format or an earlier format? One way is to glance at its file extension. Word, Excel, PowerPoint, and OneNote 07–2010 files have four-letter, not three-letter file extensions. The other way is to glance at the title bar, where the words "Compatibility Mode" in the title bar appear next to the file's name if it is not in the 07–2010 format. (The title bar is located at the top of the screen.)

Follow these steps to convert a 97–2003 file to the 07–2010 format so that you can edit it with an Office Web App:

1. **Go to the File tab and choose Info.**
2. **Click the Convert button.**

Sorry, but You Can't Share Password-Protected Files

As a security measure, Microsoft does not allow you to share files that have been password-protected with an Office Web App. For example, if you try to open a PowerPoint 2010 presentation that has been given a password in the PowerPoint Web App, you get this message: "PowerPoint Web App cannot open this presentation because it is encrypted using a password." You can open the file in PowerPoint 2010, but not the PowerPoint Web App.

Follow these steps to remove a password from an Office 2010 file and be able to share it in an Office Web App:

1. **Open the file that needs its password removed.**

2. **Go to the File tab, and in the Information window, click the Protect button (it's called Protect Document, Protect Workbook, Protect Presentation, or Protect Notebook).**

   A drop-down list appears.

3. **Choose Encrypt with Password on the drop-down list.**

   You see the Encrypt Document dialog box.

4. **Delete the password.**

5. **Click OK.**

   You can now share the file in an Office Web App.

Chapter 19

Ten Things to Know about Browsers and the Office Web Apps

*T*o run an Office Web App, you must run one computer program (the Office Web App) inside another computer program (your Web browser). For that reason, depending on your browser settings, working in an Office Web App can be like building a ship inside a bottle. It can be awfully slow going.

Throughout this book (especially in Chapter 3), I look into what you can do in your browser to make it work hand in hand with the Office Web Apps. This chapter briefly describes what anyone who uses the Office Web Apps should know about browsers.

The Office Web Apps Favor Four Browsers

Microsoft hedges its bets when it comes to recommending which browser to use with the Office Web Apps. Microsoft says that all browsers work just fine but you are better off using one of these browsers: Firefox, Internet Explorer, Safari, or Chrome.

Based on Microsoft's recommendation, I suggest using Firefox, Internet Explorer, Safari, or Chrome. Chapter 3 explains how to download and install these browsers on your computer. It also explains why Firefox is the best browser to use with the Office Web Apps.

JavaScript Must Be Enabled

The Office Web Apps run at the behest of a computer program called JavaScript. Therefore, to run the Office Web Apps, JavaScript must be enabled in your browser.

To spare you a trip to Chapter 3, here is how to enable JavaScript in the four browsers Microsoft recommends for use with the Office Web Apps:

- **Firefox:** Choose Tools⇨Options. The General tab of the Options dialog box opens. Go to the Content tab, select the Enable JavaScript check box, and click OK.

- **Internet Explorer:** Choose Tools⇨Internet Options, and go to the Security tab in the Internet Options dialog box. Then click the Custom Level button to open the Security Settings – Internet Zone dialog box. In the Scripting section, under Active Scripting, select the Enable option button. Finally, click OK twice.

- **Safari:** Choose Safari⇨Preferences (or Edit⇨Preferences on a Windows machine). The General dialog box opens. Go to the Security tab and select the Enable JavaScript check box.

- **Chrome:** Click the Tools button, choose Options on the drop-downlist, and go to the Under the Hood tab in the Google Chrome Options dialog box. Then click the Content Settings button, and in the Content Settings dialog box, go to the JavaScript tab and select the Allow All Sites to Run JavaScript option button.

If the menu bar isn't displayed in your browser and you can't choose menu options, press the Alt key to display the menu bar.

Cookies Must Be Allowed

Cookies, JavaScript — do you get the impression that the people who write software are hyped up on caffeine drinks and sugar snacks?

Anyhow, besides enabling the JavaScript computer language, the browser you use with the Office Web Apps must allow cookies. A cookie is a small text file that Web sites place on your hard disk when you first visit. These files store information about you. Chapter 3 explains what cookies are in detail and why you must allow first-party cookies.

To keep you from having to make the arduous journey to Chapter 3, here are shorthand instructions for allowing cookies in the four favorite browsers Microsoft recommends using:

- ✔ **Firefox:** Choose Tools⇨Options to open the Options dialog box. On the Privacy tab, open the Firefox Will drop-down list and choose Use Custom Settings for History. Then select the Accept Third-Party Cookies check box and click OK.

- ✔ **Internet Explorer:** Choose Tools⇨Internet Options and go to the Privacy tab in the Internet Options dialog box. Then drag the Settings slider downward to Medium High or lower and click OK.

- ✔ **Safari:** Choose Safari⇨Preferences (or Edit⇨Preferences on a Windows machine). The General dialog box opens. Go to the Security tab, and under Accept Cookies, select the Always option button.

- ✔ **Chrome:** Click the Tools button and choose Options on the drop-down list. Then go to the Under the Hood tab in the Google Chrome Options dialog box and click the Content Settings button. In the Content Settings dialog box, make sure no check boxes are selected.

Microsoft Recommends Installing Silverlight

Silverlight is a plug-in program that runs on top of a browser to make playing games, viewing movies, and playing animation possible. Microsoft makes Silverlight, and although Silverlight isn't required to run the Office Web Apps, Microsoft recommends installing it on your computer because it makes the Office Web Apps run more smoothly.

As Chapter 2 explains in painstaking detail, you can download and install Silverlight starting at this address: www.silverlight.net.

Chapter 2 also explains what a plug-in is and how to find out whether Silverlight (and the latest version of Silverlight) is installed on your computer.

Zoom Using Browser Commands

Speaking as one whose eyesight gets worse by the day, I was troubled the first time I opened an Office Web App to discover that the Office Web Apps don't offer Zoom commands. I've grown accustomed to using the Zoom commands in Office 2010 programs. Merely by dragging the Zoom slider in the lower-right corner of an Office 2010 program, you can enlarge or shrink the text. You can read the text on-screen comfortably no matter where you go in an Office 2010 program.

The Office Web Apps don't offer Zoom commands, but you can enlarge and shrink the text by using the Zoom commands in your browser. Not only do these commands enlarge and shrink the text, they enlarge and shrink the Office Web App tabs and buttons.

Use these techniques to zoom in and out in the four browsers that Microsoft recommends for use with the Office Web Apps:

- **Firefox:** Choose View⇨Zoom and choose an option on the submenu (or press Ctrl+plus sign or Ctrl+minus sign).

- **Internet Explorer:** Choose View⇨Zoom and choose an option on the submenu (or press Ctrl+plus sign or Ctrl+minus sign). Zoom options are also available by clicking the Change Zoom Level button on the right side of the status bar and choosing an option on the pop-up menu (choose View⇨Toolbars⇨Status Bar if the status bar isn't displayed).

- **Safari:** Choose View⇨Zoom In or View⇨Zoom Out (or press Ctrl+plus sign or Ctrl+minus sign).

- **Chrome:** Press Ctrl+plus sign to zoom in, or Ctrl+minus sign to zoom out.

If the menu bar isn't displayed in your browser and you can't open the View menu, press the Alt key to display the menu bar.

Open a Second File with the New Window or New Tab Command

One of the luxuries of working in a program installed on your computer is being able to open many files simultaneously. In Word 2010, for example, you can cobble together a new document from several files by opening them, copying text, and pasting the text into the new document.

To open several files simultaneously in the Office Web Apps, you have to rely on your browser's commands for opening new windows and new tabs.

Follow these steps to open a second (or third or fourth) file in an Office Web App:

1. **Right-click the folder with the file you want to open and choose Open Link in New Window or Open Link in New Tab.**

   A new window or tab opens. (In Internet Explorer, the commands are called Open in New Window and Open in New tab.)

2. **In the new window or tab, navigate to the file you want to open and open the file.**

Get More Room on the Screen

All browsers come with menu bars and toolbars of various shapes and sizes. These menu bars and toolbars are meant to help you get from Web page to Web page faster, bookmark your favorite Web sites, and do other things to hasten your adventures on the Internet.

But the menu bars and toolbars can get in the way. They occupy valuable space on-screen that can sometimes be put to better use displaying data in an Office Web App window.

To be more productive with the Office Web Apps, familiarize yourself with the commands in your browser for hiding and displaying menu bars, toolbars, and the status bar. Usually, these commands are found on the View menu. Moreover, you can right-click the menu bar or a toolbar in a browser to see commands for hiding and displaying stuff. Chapter 3 explains in detail how to get more room on-screen in a browser window.

In Firefox, Internet Explorer, and Chrome, you can press F11 (or choose View⇨Full Screen) to strip away all but the Web page you are currently viewing. Press F11 early and often when you're working in an Office Web App. The F11 key is a toggle. Press it a second time to redisplay the menu bars, toolbars, and whatnots that are part of the browser screen.

Bookmark Your Files

Finding a file on SkyDrive or SharePoint so that you can open it can be a cumbersome task, especially if the file you want to open is buried deep in a subfolder where it's hard to get at.

To spare yourself the trouble of clicking around in SkyDrive or SharePoint to find files you want to open, bookmark your files. After a file is bookmarked, all you have to do to open it is open the Bookmarks or Favorites menu in your browser and choose its bookmark's name. Chapter 3 explains the details of bookmarking files in Firefox, Internet Explorer, Safari, and Chrome.

Make Use of the Back, Forward, and History Commands

Your browser has commands for going backward and forward to Web pages you previously visited. It also offers a History menu with commands for revisiting Web sites.

Rather than click hither and yon, you can take advantage of the Back, Forward, and History commands in your browser to get to folders and files that interest you. Click the Back or Forward button (or choose a Web page on their drop-down lists) to leap backward and forward to files and folders you visited. The History menu lists files and folders you visited since you opened your browser. Choose a file or folder on the History menu to retrace your steps.

Your browser's commands for jumping from page to page can save you a lot of time when you're working with the Office Web Apps.

Beware of Right-Clicks and Shortcut Keys

Especially if you work on a laptop, you're probably accustomed to right-clicking and taking advantage of shortcut keys. But right-clicking doesn't get you very far in the Office Web Apps. And except for a handful of shortcut key combinations, pressing the familiar shortcut keys that you know and love doesn't produce any results, either.

Not being able to right-click and press shortcut keys to give all the commands is a drawback of the Office Web Apps. It takes some getting used to.

Index

• Z •

Apple & Macs

iPad For Dummies
978-0-470-58027-1

iPhone For Dummies,
4th Edition
978-0-470-87870-5

MacBook For Dummies, 3rd
Edition
978-0-470-76918-8

Mac OS X Snow Leopard For
Dummies
978-0-470-43543-4

Business

Bookkeeping For Dummies
978-0-7645-9848-7

Job Interviews
For Dummies,
3rd Edition
978-0-470-17748-8

Resumes For Dummies,
5th Edition
978-0-470-08037-5

Starting an
Online Business
For Dummies,
6th Edition
978-0-470-60210-2

Stock Investing
For Dummies,
3rd Edition
978-0-470-40114-9

Successful
Time Management
For Dummies
978-0-470-29034-7

Computer Hardware

BlackBerry
For Dummies,
4th Edition
978-0-470-60700-8

Computers For Seniors
For Dummies,
2nd Edition
978-0-470-53483-0

PCs For Dummies,
Windows
7 Edition
978-0-470-46542-4

Laptops For Dummies,
4th Edition
978-0-470-57829-2

Cooking & Entertaining

Cooking Basics
For Dummies,
3rd Edition
978-0-7645-7206-7

Wine For Dummies,
4th Edition
978-0-470-04579-4

Diet & Nutrition

Dieting For Dummies,
2nd Edition
978-0-7645-4149-0

Nutrition For Dummies,
4th Edition
978-0-471-79868-2

Weight Training
For Dummies,
3rd Edition
978-0-471-76845-6

Digital Photography

Digital SLR Cameras &
Photography For Dummies,
3rd Edition
978-0-470-46606-3

Photoshop Elements 8
For Dummies
978-0-470-52967-6

Gardening

Gardening Basics
For Dummies
978-0-470-03749-2

Organic Gardening
For Dummies,
2nd Edition
978-0-470-43067-5

Green/Sustainable

Raising Chickens
For Dummies
978-0-470-46544-8

Green Cleaning
For Dummies
978-0-470-39106-8

Health

Diabetes For Dummies,
3rd Edition
978-0-470-27086-8

Food Allergies
For Dummies
978-0-470-09584-3

Living Gluten-Free
For Dummies,
2nd Edition
978-0-470-58589-4

Hobbies/General

Chess For Dummies,
2nd Edition
978-0-7645-8404-6

Drawing
Cartoons & Comics
For Dummies
978-0-470-42683-8

Knitting For Dummies,
2nd Edition
978-0-470-28747-7

Organizing
For Dummies
978-0-7645-5300-4

Su Doku For Dummies
978-0-470-01892-7

Home Improvement

Home Maintenance
For Dummies,
2nd Edition
978-0-470-43063-7

Home Theater
For Dummies,
3rd Edition
978-0-470-41189-6

Living the
Country Lifestyle
All-in-One
For Dummies
978-0-470-43061-3

Solar Power Your Home
For Dummies,
2nd Edition
978-0-470-59678-4

Available wherever books are sold. For more information or to order direct: U.S. customers visit www.dummies.com or call 1-877-762-2974.
U.K. customers visit www.wileyeurope.com or call (0) 1243 843291. Canadian customers visit www.wiley.ca or call 1-800-567-4797.

Internet

Blogging For Dummies,
3rd Edition
978-0-470-61996-4

eBay For Dummies,
6th Edition
978-0-470-49741-8

Facebook For Dummies,
3rd Edition
978-0-470-87804-0

Web Marketing
For Dummies,
2nd Edition
978-0-470-37181-7

WordPress
For Dummies,
3rd Edition
978-0-470-59274-8

Language & Foreign Language

French For Dummies
978-0-7645-5193-2

Italian Phrases
For Dummies
978-0-7645-7203-6

Spanish For Dummies,
2nd Edition
978-0-470-87855-2

Spanish
For Dummies,
Audio Set
978-0-470-09585-0

Math & Science

Algebra I
For Dummies,
2nd Edition
978-0-470-55964-2

Biology For Dummies,
2nd Edition
978-0-470-59875-7

Calculus For Dummies
978-0-7645-2498-1

Chemistry For Dummies
978-0-7645-5430-8

Microsoft Office

Excel 2010 For Dummies
978-0-470-48953-6

Office 2010 All-in-One
For Dummies
978-0-470-49748-7

Office 2010 For Dummies,
Book + DVD Bundle
978-0-470-62698-6

Word 2010 For Dummies
978-0-470-48772-3

Music

Guitar For Dummies,
2nd Edition
978-0-7645-9904-0

iPod & iTunes For
Dummies, 8th Edition
978-0-470-87871-2

Piano Exercises
For Dummies
978-0-470-38765-8

Parenting & Education

Parenting For Dummies,
2nd Edition
978-0-7645-5418-6

Type 1 Diabetes
For Dummies
978-0-470-17811-9

Pets

Cats For Dummies,
2nd Edition
978-0-7645-5275-5

Dog Training For Dummies,
3rd Edition
978-0-470-60029-0

Puppies For Dummies,
2nd Edition
978-0-470-03717-1

Religion & Inspiration

The Bible For Dummies
978-0-7645-5296-0

Catholicism For Dummies
978-0-7645-5391-2

Women in the Bible
For Dummies
978-0-7645-8475-6

Self-Help & Relationship

Anger Management
For Dummies
978-0-470-03715-7

Overcoming Anxiety
For Dummies,
2nd Edition
978-0-470-57441-6

Sports

Baseball
For Dummies,
3rd Edition
978-0-7645-7537-2

Basketball
For Dummies,
2nd Edition
978-0-7645-5248-9

Golf For Dummies,
3rd Edition
978-0-471-76871-5

Web Development

Web Design
All-in-One
For Dummies
978-0-470-41796-6

Web Sites
Do-It-Yourself
For Dummies,
2nd Edition
978-0-470-56520-9

Windows 7

Windows 7
For Dummies
978-0-470-49743-2

Windows 7
For Dummies,
Book + DVD Bundle
978-0-470-52398-8

Windows 7 All-in-One
For Dummies
978-0-470-48763-1

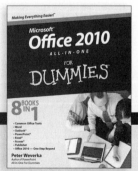

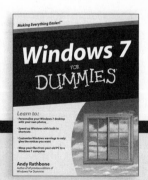

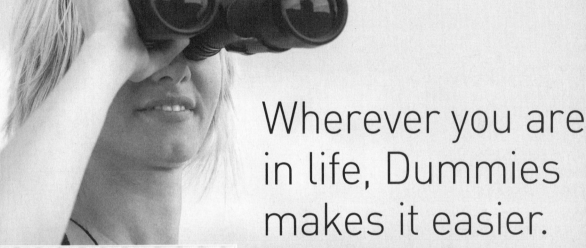

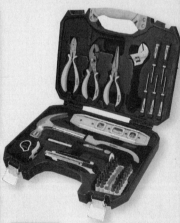